THE GOSPEL AS EPIC
IN LATE ANTIQUITY

SUPPLEMENTS TO

VIGILIAE CHRISTIANAE

Formerly Philosophia Patrum

TEXTS AND STUDIES OF EARLY CHRISTIAN LIFE
AND LANGUAGE

EDITORS

A.F.J. KLIJN – CHRISTINE MOHRMANN – G. QUISPEL
J.H. WASZINK – J.C.M. VAN WINDEN

VOLUME II

THE GOSPEL AS EPIC
IN LATE ANTIQUITY

THE *PASCHALE CARMEN* OF SEDULIUS

BY

CARL P. E. SPRINGER

E.J. BRILL

LEIDEN · NEW YORK · KØBENHAVN · KÖLN

1988

Library of Congress Cataloging-in-Publication Data

Springer, Carl P. E.
    The Gospel as Epic in Late Antiquity: the Paschale carmen of
Sedulius / by Carl P. E. Springer.
        p.   cm.—(Supplements to Vigiliae Christianae, ISSN
0920-623X; v. 2)
    Bibliography: p.
    Includes index.
    ISBN 90-04-08691-9
    1. Sedulius, 5th cent. Paschale carmen. 2. Christian poetry,
Latin—History and criticism. 3. Epic poetry, Latin—History and
criticism. 4. Jesus Christ in literature. 5. Bible in literature.
I. Sedulius, 5th cent. Paschale carmen. English & Latin. 1988.
II. Title. III. Series.
PA6658.S63S6   1988
873'.01—dc19   88-6386
                                                          CIP

ISSN 0920-623X
ISBN 90 04 08691 9

PRINTED IN THE NETHERLANDS BY E. J. BRILL

Uxori et parentibus

CONTENTS

PREFACE

Although nearly forgotten today, Sedulius' *Paschale carmen* was for over a millennium one of Europe's most popular and influential poems. Like other biblical epics of Late Antiquity, the *Paschale carmen* is not to most modern tastes, but Sedulius' attempt to correlate Virgil and the Bible deserves scholarly attention as a valuable witness to the theological and cultural preoccupations of its age. The *Paschale carmen* also played an instrumental role in European literary history, establishing, as it did, the conventions of an enduring Western literary tradition, the biblical epic. Some worthy contributions to Sedulian scholarship have been made in recent years, but there is still no comprehensive, modern study of this important work in any language. The present volume, it is hoped, will help to fill the scholarly void not only for classicists or patrologists but for students of medieval and early modern European literary history as well.

The purpose of this book is to provide a literary analysis of Sedulius' *Paschale carmen* which will situate the poem in its historical, theological, and literary-traditional contexts (Chapters 1-3) and examine closely its content, form, structure, and poetic artistry (Chapters 4-6). A final chapter will consider the reputation and influence of Sedulius' biblical epic from Late Antiquity up to the 17th century. If this study promotes more intelligent criticism of Sedulius' poem and shows the way to more sensitive and sensible readings of other biblical epics of Late Antiquity, it will have served its purpose well.

I owe a scholarly debt to Reinhart Herzog, whose work on the biblical epics of Late Antiquity helped to inspire this study and who encouraged me at an early stage to pursue my interest in Sedulius. My thanks to Michael Roberts for the many stimulating discussions of the biblical poetry of Late Antiquity which we enjoyed—without always finding perfect agreement—and for reading and commenting on the penultimate draft of this book. A stipend from the National Endowment for the Humanities enabled me to do much of the research for the final chapter at the Folger Shakespeare Library in the summer of 1985. I am indebted to the staff of the reading room at the Folger as well as to the inter-library loan staffs of the University of Wisconsin-Madison and Illinois State University for their prompt assistance on innumerable occasions. Many thanks also to Timothy Ryan for his sound advice on questions of word processing.

Much of the credit for whatever is good about this book must go to the unvarying patience and good humor of Fannie LeMoine, my graduate adviser at the University of Wisconsin-Madison. I should like also to express my gratitude to Barry Powell and Paul Plass for reading and criticizing the doctoral dissertation of which this book is a revision as well as to Frank Clover and Christopher Kleinhenz for their comments on the second and last chapters respectively. Needless to say, all such errors as remain are entirely my own. Above all, I am especially grateful to friends and family, too numerous to mention here, without whose support and encouragement this book would surely have been impossible.

ABBREVIATIONS

This list includes abbreviations for reference works and text series. For other abbreviations used, see *The Oxford Classical Dictionary* and *Patrologie*.

AJP	*American Journal of Philology.*
ANRW	*Aufstieg und Niedergang der römischen Welt.*
BMGC	*British Museum General Catalogue of Printed Books.*
BSG	*Berichte über die Verhandlungen der kgl. sächsischen Gesellschaft der Wissenschaften zu Leipzig.*
CC	*Corpus Christianorum. Series latina.*
CF	*Classical Folia.*
CJ	*Classical Journal.*
CP	*Classical Philology.*
CQ	*Classical Quarterly.*
CR	*Classical Review.*
CSEL	*Corpus scriptorum ecclesiasticorum latinorum.*
CW	*Classical Weekly* (or *Classical World*).
EJ	*Encyclopedia Judaica.*
GCS	*Die griechischen christlichen Schriftsteller der ersten drei Jahrhunderte.*
GL	*Grammatici latini.* H. Keil, ed.
HSCP	*Harvard Studies in Classical Philology.*
HTR	*Harvard Theological Review.*
ICS	*Illinois Classical Studies.*
JbAC	*Jahrbuch für Antike und Christentum.*
JTS	*Journal of Theological Studies.*
LG	*Lexicographi graeci.*
MGH AA	*Monumenta Germaniae historica. Auctorum antiquissimorum.*
NCE	*New Catholic Encyclopedia.*
OBMLV	*Oxford Book of Medieval Latin Verse.* 2nd ed. F.J.E. Raby, ed.
OCSL	*Oxford Companion to Spanish Literature.* Philip Ward, ed.
Patrologie	*Patrologie: Leben, Schriften und Lehre der Kirchenväter.* Berthold Altaner, ed. 9th ed.
PG	*Patrologiae cursus completus. Series graeca.* J.P. Migne, ed.
PL	*Patrologiae cursus completus. Series latina.* J.P. Migne, ed.
PLRE	*Prosopography of the Later Roman Empire.*
PVS	*Proceedings of the Virgil Society.*
RAC	*Reallexicon für Antike und Christentum.*
RB	*Revue bénédictine.*
RE	*Real-Encyclopädie der klassischen Altertumswissenschaft.*
REA	*Revue des études augustiniennes.*
RhM	*Rheinisches Museum.*
RPh	*Revue de philologie, de littérature et d'histoire anciennes.*
RSC	*Rivista di studi classici.*
RSR	*Revue des sciences religieuses.*
TAPA	*Transactions of the American Philological Association.*
TLL	*Thesaurus linguae latinae.*
VC	*Vigiliae christianae.*
WA	Martin Luther, *Werke. Kritische Gesamtausgabe.*
WS	*Wiener Studien.*
ZKT	*Zeitschrift für die katholische Theologie.*
ZNTW	*Zeitschrift für die neutestamentliche Wissenschaft.*
ZOG	*Zeitschrift für die österreichischen Gymnasien.*

CHAPTER ONE

PROLEGOMENA

To judge from the lack of attention paid to it by literary historians and critics of the last century, it would be difficult to guess that Sedulius' *Paschale carmen* (traditionally dated to c. AD 425-450) was required reading in schools throughout the Middle Ages and a source of inspiration for Latin and vernacular biblical epics well into the 17th century. In the last hundred years, in fact, this once highly regarded poem has received mostly negative attention from scholars, when it has received any at all. As a result, in part, of the low estimation in general of its literary value, the *Paschale carmen* has not been very well studied as a work of literature. A literary analysis of Sedulius' poem, therefore, which attempts to approach it with as few preconceived judgments as possible, is long overdue and should help us better to understand a work which centuries of European readers found of enduring value. This chapter 1.) reviews Sedulius' critical reputation in the twentieth century, 2.) analyzes "the paraphrase theory" and its application to Sedulius' biblical poem, and 3.) outlines the critical assumptions which underlie my own literary analysis of the *Paschale carmen*.

i. *Sedulius and the Critics*

Sedulius' popularity peaked in the 16th century. Over 30 editions of the *Paschale carmen* appeared between the years 1501 and 1588.[1] The number of editions of the poem fell off sharply in the 17th century, by contrast, and in the 18th and 19th the *Paschale carmen* fared little better. Our own century has produced no new edition of the poem.[2] There has

---

[1] See the list compiled by George Sigerson in *The Easter Song: Being the First Epic of Christendom by Sedulius* (Dublin, 1922), pp. 69-70.

[2] The best text of the *Paschale carmen* (although badly in need of revision) remains that of Johannes Huemer (*CSEL* 10, 14-146). It served as the basis for Francesco Corsaro's Italian translation of the *Paschale carmen* in *Sedulio poeta* (Catania, 1956) and is also the text which I follow throughout this book (with some orthographical variations). Huemer overlooked or was unaware of the existence of a number of important Sedulian MSS. Studies of Sedulian MSS which have appeared since Huemer's edition include C. Caesar, "Die Antwerpener Hs. des Sedulius," *RhM* 56 (1901), 247-71; G. Frank, "*Vossianus* Q 86 and *Reginensis* 333," *AJP* 44 (1923), 67-70; E.K. Rand, "Note on the *Vossianus* Q 86 and *Reginenses* 333 and 1616," *AJP* 44 (1923), 171-2; H. Meritt, "Old English Sedulius Glosses," *AJP* 56 (1936), 140-50; N.R. Ker, "British Museum, Burney 246, 285, 295, 341, 344, 357," *BMQ* 12 (1938), 134-5; G.R. Manton, "The Cambridge Man-

never been an English translation of the *Paschale carmen* in its entirety, and
the poem still awaits a complete modern commentary in any language.[3]
In the years that have passed since the last critical edition of the *Paschale
carmen* (1885), relatively little scholarly interest in the poem has been
demonstrated. Most of the work done on Sedulius has been in the form
of entries in larger literary histories, treatments which are summary
(although not always unoriginal) and have tended simply to repeat the
current "orthodoxy" as to questions of authorship, dating, and provenance, most often parroting the usual derogatory judgments of the
Paschale carmen's literary value.[4]

The major literary studies devoted to the *Paschale carmen* in this century
(such as they are) reveal a disappointing lack of depth or variety. Studies
such as Theodor Mayr's *Studien zu dem Paschale carmen* (1916) and
Giovanna Moretti Pieri's "Sulle fonti evangeliche di Sedulio" (1969) are

uscript of Sedulius' *Carmen paschale*," *JTS* 40 (1939), 365-70; W. Jungandreas, "Die
Runen des *Codex Seminarii Trevirensis* R. III. 61," *Trierer Zeitschrift* 30 (1967), 161-69; and
C. Lewine, "The Miniatures of the Antwerp Sedulius Manuscript. The Early Christian
Models and their Transformations." Diss. Columbia University, 1970. For some
recently suggested emendations in the text of the *Paschale carmen*, see C. Tibiletti, "Note
al testo del *Paschale carmen* di Sedulio," *Forma futuri. Studi in onore di Michele Pellegrino*
(Turin, 1975), pp. 778-85.

[3] George Sigerson produced a flowery English translation of selected passages of
Sedulius' poem in *The Easter Song*. Otto Kuhnmuench included texts and translations of
a few passages of the *Paschale carmen* in *Early Christian Latin Poets* (Chicago, 1929), pp. 258-
68. Nicholas Scheps included a translation and commentary of the preface and the first
two books of the poem in *Sedulius' Paschale carmen Boek I en II: Ingeleid, Vertaald, en Toegelicht*
(Delft, 1938). R.A. Swanson translated the preface and the first book of the *Paschale
carmen* in *CJ* 52 (1957), 289-97. H. Spitzmüller included the text and a French translation
of 1. 17-58 in his *Poésie latine chrétienne du Moyen Age* (Paris, 1971), pp. 117-8.

[4] See, for example, Adolf Ebert, *Allgemeine Geschichte der Literatur des Mittelalters* (Leipzig, 1889), I, pp. 358 ff.; M. Manitius, *Geschichte der christlich-lateinischen Poesie* (Stuttgart,
1891), pp. 303-12; Alexander Baumgartner, *Die lateinische und griechische Literatur der
christlichen Völker* (Freiburg, 1900), pp. 195 ff.; Sisto Colombo, *La poesia cristiana antica*
(Rome, 1910), I, pp. 156-62; H. Jordan, *Geschichte der altchristlichen Literatur* (Leipzig,
1911), pp. 489 ff.; Gustav Krüger, *Die Bibeldichtung zu Ausgang des Altertums* (Giessen,
1919), pp. 9-12; M. Schanz, *Geschichte der römischen Literatur* (Munich, 1920), IV. 2, pp.
368-74; Pierre de Labriolle, *History and Literature of Christianity*, trans. Herbert Wilson
(New York, 1924), pp. 474-6; Otto Bardenhewer, *Geschichte der altkirchlichen Literatur*
(Freiburg, 1924), IV, pp. 642-7; A. Gudeman, *Geschichte der altchristlichen lateinischen
Literatur vom 2-6 Jahrhundert* (Berlin, 1925), pp. 109-111; C. Weyman, *Beiträge zur
Geschichte der christlich-lateinischen Poesie* (Munich, 1926), pp. 121-37; Aurelio Amatucci,
Storia della letteratura latina cristiana, 2nd ed. (Turin, 1927), pp. 335-9; F.J.E. Raby, *A
History of Christian-Latin Poetry* (Oxford, 1927), pp. 108-10; E.S. Duckett, *Latin Writers of
the Fifth Century* (New York, 1930), pp. 77-81; F.A. Wright and T.A. Sinclair, *A History
of Later Latin Literature* (New York, 1931), pp. 73-4; U. Moricca, *Storia della letteratura latina
cristiana* (Turin, 1932), III, pp. 46-58; Filippo Ermini, *Storia della letteratura latina medievale
dalle origini alla fine del secolo VII* (Spoleto, 1960), pp. 237-9; M. Simonetti, *La letteratura
cristiana antica greca e latina* (Milan, 1969), pp. 343-4; and most recently, Jacques Fontaine,
Naissance de la poésie dans l'occident chrétien (Paris, 1981), pp. 248-52.

concerned primarily with source analysis and pay insufficient attention to Sedulius' originality.[5] George Sigerson in *The Easter Song of Sedulius* (1922) waxes enthusiastic in praise of "the first epic of Christendom," as he describes the *Paschale carmen*, but his observations are unfortunately marred by his confusion of the fifth-century poet with the ninth-century Irish poet and scholar, Sedulius Scotus. Between 1945 and 1956, the Italian scholar Francesco Corsaro produced four studies of Sedulius and the *Paschale carmen*, but these are more descriptive than critical and have found only limited circulation.[6] Corsaro's books are useful for the researcher who is interested in lists of figures of speech in Sedulius' poetry, but they contain little in the way of literary analysis and make only a small effort to set the poet and his poem in any larger context.

Despite a small flowering of interest in Sedulius in recent years, the *Paschale carmen* still remains relatively poorly studied. In his *Numen litterarum* (1971) Charles Witke includes only a brief introduction to Sedulius, a sampling of the *Paschale carmen* (1. 17-102 and 5. 261-364), and tantalizingly short analyses of the passages.[7] The first volume of Reinhart Herzog's *Die Bibelepik der lateinischen Spätantike* appeared in 1975, but the author's consideration of the *Paschale carmen* was reserved for a second volume which has not yet appeared as of the time of this writing.[8]

---

[5] Theodor Mayr, *Studien zu dem Paschale carmen des christlichen Dichters Sedulius* (Augsburg, 1916). The five chapters of this study consider the structure of the poem, Sedulius' use of Scripture and commentaries, the poet's borrowings from pagan and Christian authors, and the figures of speech and thought in the *Paschale carmen*. Pieri's study (in *Atti e memorie dell'accad. tosc. di sc. e lett. La Columbaria* 39, n.s. 20 [1969], 125-234) is fairly inaccessible. It was overlooked, for instance, by the editors of *L'année philologique*. For other considerations of Sedulius' sources, see E. Klissenbauer, *Quaestiones de Seduli Paschali carmine* (Vienna, 1939), and E. Bitter, *Die Virgilinterpretation der früh-christlichen Dichter Paulinus von Nola und Sedulius* (Tübingen, 1948). I have not been able to see Hertha Fischer's dissertation, "Sedulius qua ratione auctores antiquos adhibuerit" (Vienna, 1936).

[6] Corsaro's first two studies of Sedulius, *La poesia di Sedulio* (Catania, 1945) and *L'opera poetica di Sedulio* (Catania, 1948), are unavailable in the United States. *La lingua di Sedulio* (Catania, 1949) and *Sedulio poeta* (Catania, 1956) present the reader with a veritable battery of lists. Three pages of *Sedulio poeta*, for instance, are devoted to listing and describing the uses of the participle in Sedulius' poetry. Corsaro includes a list of nearly 300 occurrences of the "appositive participle" in the *Paschale carmen*.

[7] Charles Witke, *Numen litterarum: The Old and the New in Latin Poetry from Constantine to Gregory the Great*, Mittellateinische Studien und Texte 5 (Leiden, 1971). A major contribution of Witke's study is his identification of "Christian Latin poetry as a literary entity separate from the practice of poetry in Latin by men who happened to be Christians" and worthy of close literary study for its own sake. For critical reviews of the work, see the remarks of P.G. Walsh in *CR* 24 (1974), 221-3 and M. Cunningham in *CP* 69 (1974), 296-7.

[8] Reinhart Herzog, *Die Bibelepik der lateinischen Spätantike: Formgeschichte einer erbaulichen Gattung*, Theorie und Geschichte der Literatur und der schönen Künste 37 (Munich, 1975). Published in the same year and by the same press (Fink Verlag), Dieter Kartschoke's *Bibeldichtung: Studien zur Geschichte der epischen Bibelparaphrase von Juvencus bis Otfrid*

Despite the publication in recent years of some specialized studies, such
as a consideration of Sedulius' epic scenery, observations on the
polemical and didactic intentions of the *Paschale carmen*, and an examination of the influence of Virgil on Sedulius,[9] it must be said that this Christian poem is still largely ignored by classicists and medievalists alike.[10]

The former, in particular, have traditionally dismissed Sedulius'
Paschale carmen as an inferior product of an age which witnessed "the
decline and fall" of classical civilization. According to such a view, the
high point of Latin literature was the so-called "Golden Age." One eminent authority on Greek and Latin literature pronounces: "During this
age [the later empire] poetry was at a low ebb. With one exception,
presently to be discussed, Juvenal is the last Latin poet; after him there
are but versifiers."[11] D.P.A. Comparetti observes: "But if among the
orgies and crimes of the imperial palace an echo, as it were, of Vergilian
verse might still sometimes be heard, that was no proof of the existence
of any real poetical feeling."[12] A major criticism of Sedulius and other
poets who lived and wrote in what one scholar has called "the Leaden
Age" of Latin literary history is that they are too imitative of Virgil.[13]
Comparetti had Sedulius (among others) in mind when he spoke of poets
"who had learnt Vergil mechanically and did not know of any better use
to which to put all these verses with which they had loaded their
brains."[14] Speaking of biblical epic poets such as Sedulius, Pierre de
Labriolle remarks rather acidly that their "servile respect for past
masters . . . preserved the art of poetry from a ruin still more complete

---

von Weissenburg devotes some 14 pages to Sedulius but has little original to contribute to
Sedulian studies. For a critique of Kartschoke's "superficial" consideration of the
biblical poetry of Late Antiquity, see Herzog, *Bibelepik*, p. LXI, n. 187.

[9] "Die Szenerie bei Sedulius," *JbAC* 19 (1976), 109-19, by Ilona Opelt, is a com-
panion piece to her study of epic scenery in Juvencus in *VC* 29 (1975), 191-207. M. Donnini, "Alcune osservazioni sul programmo poetico di Sedulio," *RSC* 26 (1978), 426-36,
suggests sensibly that Sedulius' poem must be read in light of the author's "intenzione
di riagganciarsi alla nuova tradizione ed in particolare a Giovenco" (430). A. Grillo, "La
presenza di Virgilio in Sedulio poeta parafrastico," *Présence de Virgile* (Paris, 1978), pp.
185-94, gives Sedulius credit for creative borrowing from Virgil.

[10] Even a quick glance through *L'année philologique* gives a good idea of how poorly
studied the *Paschale carmen* is. For Prudentius, another Christian Latin poet of Late Antiquity, we find over 50 entries between the years 1977 and 1981 alone. For the same years,
by contrast, the editors discovered only four studies which were devoted to the *Paschale
carmen*.

[11] H.J. Rose, *A Handbook of Latin Literature* (London, 1936), p. 524.

[12] D.P.A. Comparetti, *Vergil in the Middle Ages*, trans. E.F.M. Benecke (New York,
1929), p. 53.

[13] A.F. Leach, "Milton as Schoolboy and Schoolmaster," *Proceedings of the British
Academy* 1907-8, 305.

[14] Comparetti, *Vergil in the Middle Ages*, p. 53.

by substituting imitations which are not always without skill, in place of their feeble inspiration.''[15]

Sedulius was only one of a number of Christian poets in the fourth, fifth, and sixth centuries who set about retelling biblical narratives in longer hexameter poems. Christian Latin authors had written in prose during the first centuries of their movement's existence, but after the Edict of Toleration (311) and the so-called Edict of Milan in 313, which marked the end of the persecutions begun during the reign of Diocletian, they began to experiment with verse. The biblical epic was one of the earliest and most popular of the new Christian poetic forms. Other Latin biblical epics which have come down to us besides Sedulius' *Paschale carmen* include: Juvencus' *Evangeliorum libri quattuor* (c. AD 329-330),[16] Proba's *Cento* (usually dated to the 360s),[17] the *Heptateuch* (sometimes ascribed to Cyprianus Gallus and probably to be dated to the first quarter of the fifth century),[18] Claudius Marius Victor's *Alethia* (mid-fifth century),[19] Dracontius' *De laudibus Dei* (end of the fifth century),[20] Avitus' *De spiritalis historiae gestis* (written shortly after AD 500),[21] and Arator's

---

[15] Labriolle, *History and Literature*, p. 314.

[16] Juvencus' poem is in four books of 3190 lines and except for its proem and epilogue draws its subject material from the Gospels. The 1891 edition (*CSEL* 24) of Johannes Huemer is still the most recent text. For an extensive critique and correction of Huemer's edition, see Nils Hannson's *Textkritisches zu Juvencus* (Lund, 1950).

[17] Karl Schenkl's edition of Proba's *Cento* appears in *CSEL* 16 (1887), pp. 569-609. Most recently the cento has been dated between 384 and 388 by Danuta Schanzer, "The Anonymous *Carmen contra paganos* and the Date and Identity of the Centonist Proba," *REA* 32 (1986), 232-48.

[18] The *Heptateuch* originally included treatments of all of the historical books of the Old Testament. Only the Pentateuch, Joshua, and Judges, however, have come down to us. On the authorship and dating of the poem, see Michael Roberts, *Biblical Epic and Rhetorical Paraphrase* (Liverpool, 1985), pp. 93-5. R. Peiper's edition (*CSEL* 23, 1-211) is the most recent.

[19] Gennadius, *De viris illustribus* 61, informs us that Claudius Marius Victor was a rhetor from Marseilles. In three books, following a *precatio* of 126 lines, the author retells the story of the first 19 chapters of Genesis from creation to the destruction of Sodom. P.F. Hovingh's edition of the *Alethia* (*CC* 128, 117 ff.) is the most accessible.

[20] Blossius Aemilius Dracontius' epic is usually dated to the reign of Gunthamund (484-496). The *De laudibus Dei* is in three books of 2326 hexameters. After 117 lines of introduction, the poet tells of the creation of the world in Book 1, relates some stories of divine wonders from the Old Testament, reviews the life of Christ, cites examples of faith and divine rescue in Book 2, and includes a number of biblical *exempla*, such as the story of the rich man and Lazarus (3. 31-98) in the final book. F. Vollmer's 1905 edition of the poem is to be found in *MGH AA* 14, 23-113. P. Langlois supplies a good introduction to the poet in *RAC* 4, 250-69.

[21] Alcimus Ecdicius Avitus was the bishop of Vienne. His biblical epic of 2552 lines treats of the creation, the fall into sin, the expulsion from paradise, the flood, and the exodus of the Hebrews from Egypt. A sixth book is attached to the work on the subject of Christian virginity. R. Peiper edited the poem in 1883 (*MGH AA* 6. 2, 203-94). For a recent discussion of Avitus' biblical epic, see Wilhelm Ehlers, "Bibelszenen in epischer Gestalt: Ein Beitrag zu Alcimus Avitus," *VC* 39 (1985), 353-69.

De actibus apostolorum (AD 544).[22] These (along with Sedulius' *Paschale carmen*) are the Latin works of Late Antiquity which literary historians most often describe as "biblical epics," that is to say, dactylic hexameter poems of some length which owe their "narrative continuity to a biblical sequence of events."[23] Of these authors, Juvencus, Sedulius, Arator, and Avitus were the most popular and influential in the Middle Ages and the Renaissance. Herzog describes their products as the "canonical" biblical epics.[24] Juvencus, Sedulius, and Arator were schoolroom authors, whose biblical epics were often published together in manuscripts and early printed editions. The poems of Claudius Marius Victor and Dracontius, along with Proba's *Cento* and the *Heptateuch*, enjoyed neither the popularity nor the authority of the other four. Herzog describes them as "separated out of the canon" or "deformed."[25] Despite the differences that exist among these eight poems, however, most literary historians agree that they should be studied together and, with a few variations, describe them as "biblical epics." In his chapter on "the biblical epics of the fifth and sixth centuries," for example, Jacques Fontaine considers together Cyprianus Gallus, Sedulius, Dracontius, Avitus, and Arator.[26] (He had already devoted an earlier chapter to Juvencus.) In his study, *Biblical Epic and Rhetorical Paraphrase in Late Antiquity*, Michael Roberts includes a full consideration of all of the Latin authors mentioned above with the exception of Proba and Dracontius, whose poem is described

---

[22] Arator recited the two books of his *De actibus apostolorum* in the church of St. Peter in Chains at Rome in 544. The poem is in 2326 hexameters and retells—with extensive exegesis—the story line of Acts. Arator dedicated his poem to Pope Vigilius, and it was the pope who agreed to a public recitation. A. P. McKinlay's edition of the poem appears in *CSEL* 72. *Historia apostolica* is the title given in the MSS, but since Arntzen's edition (1769), Arator's work has traditionally been called *De actibus apostolorum*. (See Witke, *Numen litterarum*, p. 218, n. 102.) For a fairly recent and sympathetic discussion of Arator, see R.J. Schrader, "Arator: Revaluation," *CF* 31 (1977), 64-77.

[23] For this definition, see Roberts, *Biblical Epic*, p. 4, n. 12. In addition to the Latin biblical epics, we also have a number of Greek biblical verse compositions from Late Antiquity. The Greek poet Nonnos turned the Gospel of John into hexameters, probably in the fifth century. This composition, often referred to as the *Metabole*, has been edited by A. Scheindler (Leipzig, 1881). The *Metaphrasis psalmorum* which has been attributed (probably wrongly) to the heretic Apollinarius of Laodicea is not usually included in the category of biblical epic since it is not narrative. We also know of a number of lost Greek biblical epics. See Roberts, *Biblical Epic*, p. 4, n. 13, for a fuller discussion.

[24] Herzog, *Bibelepik*, p. XIX.

[25] Herzog, *Bibelepik*, p. XXIII. The *Alethia* was not very popular at all in the Middle Ages. Only one manuscript (*Parisin.* 7558, 9th century), which comes from Tours, survives. The *De laudibus Dei* was known only in part before 1791, when Arevalo published the poem in its entirety. In the Middle Ages only a portion of Dracontius' poem, which told of the creation (known as the *Hexaemeron* and supplemented by Eugenius II, Bishop of Toledo), was in circulation.

[26] Fontaine, *Naissance*, pp. 245-64.

as a "non-biblical work" which contains a "secondary" biblical paraphrase.[27]

As a literary form, the biblical epic has come in for special criticism. Along with other poems of its kind, Sedulius' *Paschale carmen* is often faulted for juxtaposing pagan and Christian elements. According to one critic, "phraseology, which had, so to speak, become standardized as epic diction might easily sound ludicrous or even profane if applied to Biblical stories."[28] In a biblical poem, according to this point of view, "the recollection and the reproduction of names and phrases from the pagan epics" is incongruous and out of place.[29] Ernst Robert Curtius dismisses the entire tradition of the biblical epic as "hybrid" and describes it as a "*genre faux.*"[30] According to Curtius, "the Christian story of salvation, as the Bible presents it, admits no transformation into pseudo-antique form." Most students of the Christian poetry of Late Antiquity have found the hymn to be a more authentically Christian literary form and more truly "original" than the biblical epic.[31] A Hudson-Williams observes that "Christianity never found its truest poetical expression as long as its utterances were subject to the influences of old."[32] Another critic remarks: "Latin Christian poetry evolved great statements of its own, but only when writers like Fortunatus and Thomas of Celano celebrated the wonders of their faith in the genuinely heroic Christian tradition of hymnology."[33]

In addition, the biblical epics of Late Antiquity have often been criticized for their lack of originality. The *Paschale carmen* retells the story of the life of Christ according to the Gospels, and critics have suggested that its author was simply interested in turning a prose original into verse. M.L.W. Laistner observes: "The Christian poet would be obliged to reproduce the language of the Bible as faithfully as possible, unless he wished to incur the stigma of impiety. But a prose translation of St. Matthew or of Acts could not easily or satisfactorily be forced into heroic hex-

---

[27] Roberts, *Biblical Epic*, p. 4. Roberts' book is an extensive revision of his 1978 doctoral dissertation, "The Hexameter Paraphrase in Late Antiquity: Origins and Applications to Biblical Texts." Diss. University of Illinois, Urbana.

[28] M.L.W. Laistner, *Thought and Letters in Western Europe, A.D. 500-900*, rev. ed. (Ithaca, 1957), p. 78.

[29] Laistner, *Thought and Letters*, p. 78.

[30] Ernst Robert Curtius, *European Literature and the Latin Middle Ages*, trans. Willard R. Trask (New York, 1953), p. 462.

[31] Labriolle, *History and Literature*, p. 312, for instance, observes that "Christian poetry in Latin was only able to rise to real and true originality in the Church hymn."

[32] A. Hudson-Williams, "Virgil and the Christian Latin Poets," *PVS* 6 (1966-7), 21

[33] Leonard Frey, "The Rhetoric of Latin Christian Epic Poetry," *Annuale mediaeval* 2 (1961), 30.

ameters.''[34] According to this view, the biblical epics of Late Antiquity
are primarily stylistic exercises, "repositories for virtuosity," whose
authors are more interested in rhetorical technique than in their "sacred
matter.''[35] Curtius, for instance, suggests that Sedulius was simply a
"virtuoso" who "had a large measure of literary ambition but . . .
nothing to say.''[36] The *Paschale carmen* demonstrates only that "even a
recent convert could take over the frippery of the pagan school rhetor into
his Christian life, could indeed make it over into Christian clothing and
strut about in it.''[37] Curtius views Sedulius as little more than a "gran-
diloquent" and "vainglorious" wordsmith interested only in the form
and not in the content of his composition.[38]

Given such a critical climate, it is little wonder that the *Paschale carmen*
has suffered neglect. Traditional perspectives of a "decadent" Late Antiquity, of the hybrid qualities of the biblical epics written in the fourth,
fifth, and sixth centuries, and of the *Paschale carmen*'s lack of originality
have in the past made it difficult to justify the literary study of a work
which, the experts agree, reveals no "original talent" and is a "torture
to read.''[39]

In more recent years, it should be said, some of the usual reasons for
ignoring Sedulius' *Paschale carmen* and other biblical epics of Late Antiquity have come to seem less compelling. For one, interest in the cultural
achievement of Late Antiquity has been increasing, especially since
World War II.[40] The idea of decadence is no longer universally held, and
scholars are paying more attention to the artistic and literary products of
the period for their own sakes, rather than for their ability to illustrate
a thesis of "decline and fall." For another, traditional perspectives on the

[34] Laistner, *Thought and Letters*, p. 78.
[35] Frey, "The Rhetoric of Latin Christian Epic Poetry," 30.
[36] Curtius, *European Literature*, p. 462.
[37] Curtius, *European Literature*, p. 460.
[38] Curtius, *European Literature*, p. 148.
[39] Labriolle, *History and Literature*, p. 313, dismisses the authors of the biblical epics of
Late Antiquity as demonstrating no "original talent." Curtius, *European Literature*, p. 36,
declares: "To read them [the biblical epics of Late Antiquity] is torture."
[40] Late Antiquity is beginning to be seen as an epoch of considerable importance for
literary history. See, for example, Manfred Fuhrmann, "Die lateinische Literatur der
Spätantike. Ein literarhistorischer Beitrag zum Kontinuätsproblem," *A&A* 13 (1967), 56
ff. The period (defined by Fuhrmann as extending from the mid-third to the mid-seventh
century) has become a fruitful area of study for classicists interested in questions of
imitatio and *contaminatio* (see, for example, Harald Hagendahl, *Latin Fathers and the Classics:
A Study on the Apologists, Jerome and other Christian Writers*, Studia graeca et latina
gothoburgensia 6 [Göteborg, 1958]) as well as for medievalists engaged in *Toposforschung*.
Archaeologists and art historians have been interested in Late Antiquity even longer than
literary historians (since roughly the turn of the century). For some recent studies of late
antique and early Christian art of the third to the seventh centuries, see *Age of Spirituality*,
Kurt Weitzmann, ed. (Princeton, 1980).

biblical epic are changing, and the need for more scholarship on this literary tradition is widely recognized. In his "*Sacra poesis*: Bibelepik als europäische Tradition," for instance, Max Wehrli points to the importance of the biblical epic for European literary history and observes the need for more careful and sympathetic study. Wehrli argues that the biblical epic must not be dismissed as a "literary curiosity" but rather approached as a "genuine literary tradition" which deserves to be taken seriously.[41] After suffering through several centuries of obscurity, therefore, the time seems ripe to consider Sedulius' *Paschale carmen* as the product of a vital and exciting period in literary history and an early representative of a popular and long-lived European poetic tradition.

ii. *The Paraphrase Theory*

Although some of the hurdles which traditionally faced the prospective student of this and other biblical epics of Late Antiquity have been removed in recent years, one critical problem which has not been solved is that posed by the so-called "paraphrase theory." Some decades ago, in his influential study of medieval Latin literature, E.R. Curtius asserted that "it has heretofore remained almost unnoticed that a large part of early Christian poetry is a continuation of the antique rhetorical practice of paraphrase."[42] The idea was not entirely his own. Joseph Golega had already argued for the connection between *paraphrasis* and the biblical epic in his 1930 study of Nonnos' *Metabole* of the Gospel of John, and the possibility had been tentatively proposed even earlier.[43] In his dissertation on Juvencus' *Evangeliorum libri quattuor* (1910), Hermann Nestler had posited a connection between the works of Juvencus and Nonnos and traditional rhetorical practice and had gone so far as to suggest that these biblical epics belonged to "the genre of *Metaphrasis*."[44] It

---

[41] Wehrli's article appeared in *Festschrift für Friedrich Maurer* (Stuttgart, 1963), pp. 262-83. He observes:

> Wir meinen, es sei damit nicht nur eine literarische Kuriosität, sondern eine echte Tradition gefasst, ein dichterisches Bemühen, das auch grundsätzlich, poetisch, ernst genommen zu werden verdient, und das vielleicht sogar gestattet andere, jüngere Erzählformen und Erzähltechniken besser zu verstehen.

[42] Curtius, *European Literature*, p. 148.

[43] Joseph Golega, *Studien über die Evangeliendichtung des Nonnos von Panopolis. Ein Beitrag zur Geschichte der Bibeldichtung im Altertum*, Breslauer Studien zu historische Theologie 15 (Breslau, 1930), pp. 92 ff.

[44] Hermann Nestler, *Studien über die Messiade des Iuvencus* (Passau, 1910), p. 46, n. 102. The connection had also been suggested by Arthur Ludwich, *Aristarchs homerische Textkritik nach den Fragmenten des Didymos* (Leipzig, 1884-5), II, p. 483, n. 1 and p. 599. (See Roberts, *Biblical Epic*, p. 61, n. 1.) Actually the roots of the idea go back at least as far as Daniel Heinsius, who as early as 1627 had made the connection between Nonnos' biblical poem and *paraphrasis* in his *Aristarchus sacer*, a commentary on Nonnos' *Metabole*:

was Curtius, however, who popularized the idea, and even though he did not offer any evidence for his rather sweeping assertion, the view has become widespread. Reinhart Herzog, who prefers to approach the biblical epic of Late Antiquity as an incipient, independent poetic genre with its own budding tradition, its own set of formal criteria, and its own aesthetic, is one of the few dissenting voices.[45] Most recently the paraphrase theory has found a champion in Michael Roberts, who in his *Biblical Epic and Rhetorical Paraphrase in Late Antiquity* (1985) examines the ancient evidence for the exercise and supports Curtius' thesis.[46]

It is not difficult to see why for Curtius and others this has proved to be such an attractive theory. Sedulius and other biblical poets no doubt had traditional educations, and *paraphrasis*, at least at one time, was a school exercise (*progymnasma*). What could have been more natural for Christians who wanted to recast biblical stories in verse than to return to an exercise they had once practiced in school? The paraphrase theory neatly explains the origin, rationale, and intentions of the biblical epic. The view must have been especially appealing to Curtius insofar as it supported his broader thesis that the biblical epic was a negligible literary category. One suspects that the close connection with a school exercise helped to justify his devaluation of the *Paschale carmen* and other poems of its kind.

Did Sedulius and other biblical epic poets really learn how to write paraphrastic verse from a school exercise? In support of the paraphrase theory, on the one hand, it should be pointed out that *paraphrasis* was a well known exercise in antiquity, practiced in the schools of the *grammatici* (see, e.g., Suetonius, *Gram.* 4. 7), where it served an educative purpose. Students were expected to paraphrase a passage of poetry in order to demonstrate their understanding of it. These "grammatical" paraphrases, as they are often called, are exegetical in purpose, have no stylistic pretensions, and are quite faithful to their originals.[47] Budding rhetors also used the exercise of *paraphrasis*. In the schools of the rhetori-

---

Videtur ergo laxius pro qualibet interpretatione ab iis sumi, et quemadmodum paraphrasis, rhetorices doctoribus in usu inter exercitia scholarum fuit, ita et metabole fortasse. Quod grammatici et alii, in hoc scribendi genere, id agerent, ut verbum verbo commutarent (*PG* 43, 958).

[45] The validity of the paraphrase theory has simply been assumed, for instance, by K. Thraede in his "Untersuchungen zum Ursprung und zur Geschichte der christlichen Poesie," *JbAC* 4 (1961), 113 and by P. van der Nat, *Divinus vere poeta. Enige Beschouwingen over Oustan en Karakter der Christelijke Latijnse Poëzie* (Leiden, 1963), p. 24. For Herzog's critique of the theory, see *Bibelepik*, pp. 65-7.

[46] See Roberts' discussion of the history of the paraphrase theory in *Biblical Epic*, pp. 61 ff.

[47] Roberts, *Biblical Epic*, p. 38. For examples of "grammatical" paraphrases, see pp. 40-4.

cians it was not so much an exercise in understanding, it seems, as in gaining *copia verborum*.[48] The student could use the exercise in order to learn how to express the same idea in many different ways. We hear, for instance, of Sopater, a fourth-century rhetorician, attempting (perhaps as a model exercise) to paraphrase 14 lines of the *Iliad* in 72 different ways.[49] In his *Institutio oratoria* (1. 9. 2; 10. 5. 5), Quintilian suggests that paraphrases could actually rival their originals. The exercise would, therefore, involve more than simply changing the wording of the original: *neque ego paraphrasin esse interpretationem tantum volo, sed circa eosdem sensus certamen atque aemulationem*.[50] From these so-called "rhetorical paraphrases" it is only a short step to what Roberts calls "literary paraphrases," works which are primarily exegetical in nature, such as Themistius' paraphrases of Aristotle, and the biblical epics, which amount to "separate works of literature."[51] Roberts discovers that the authors of the biblical epics used "characteristic paraphrastic techniques," such as *abbreviatio* and *amplificatio*, while retaining the "irreducible narrative core of the text to be paraphrased."[52] His conclusion is that the biblical poets, who must have been educated in the schools of the *grammatici* and *rhetores*, "relied on the paraphrase and its techniques" and "viewed themselves as writing biblical paraphrases."[53]

Under closer scrutiny, however, the paraphrase theory does present a number of problems. In the first place, with regard to the origins of the biblical epics, it should be observed that the exercise of *paraphrasis* was not the only way in which to learn paraphrastic techniques in Late Antiquity. Other school exercises such as *ethopoeia* also involved paraphrase.[54] Indeed, the exercise of *paraphrasis* seems to have "lost its place in the

---

[48] See Fortunatianus, *Ars rhetorica* 3. 3.

[49] See the edition of S. Glöckner in *RhM* 65 (1910), 504-14. 58 of the versions survive.

[50] I use the edition of M. Winterbottom (Oxford, 1970). For an analysis of Quintilian's observations on *paraphrasis*, see Heinrich Lausberg, *Handbuch der literarischen Rhetorik: Eine Grundlegung der Literaturwissenschaft* (Munich, 1960), I, pp. 530-1.

[51] Roberts, *Biblical Epic*, p. 58. None of the poems which have biblical subject matter, not even the most faithful, should really be described as simple or "grammatical paraphrases." In his article on "Epos" in *RAC* 5, 1026 Thraede describes the early Old Testament epics and Juvencus' *Evangeliorum libri quattuor* as "grammatical-historical" paraphrases. Although Juvencus' paraphrase of Gospel stories is closer to the original than Sedulius' it is by no means so "faithful, simple, and unadorned" as F.J.E. Raby, *A History of Christian-Latin Poetry from the Beginnings to the Close of the Middle Ages* (Oxford, 1927), p. 17, and others have suggested.

[52] Roberts, *Biblical Epic*, p. 2 and p. 107.

[53] Roberts, *Biblical Epic*, p. 220 and p. 3.

[54] Augustine is probably referring to this exercise when he speaks of his schoolroom encounter with Virgil in *Conf.* 1. 17. See Reinhard Schlieben, *Christliche Theologie und Philologie in der Spätantike: Die schulwissenschaftlichen Methoden der Psalmenexegese Cassiodors*, Arbeiten zur Kirchengeschichte 46 (Berlin, 1974), pp. 16-24.

canon of *progymnasmata*'' by the time the Latin biblical epic poets began to write their works.[55] In the West, according to Roberts, only Fortuna- tianus refers to the exercise.[56] Nor did the traditional Greek and Roman *progymnasmata* have exclusive rights to such common narrative techniques as abbreviation and amplification. In fact, there was a long tradition of translation and paraphrase of the Scriptures within an ecclesiastical con- text.[57] Some of the Targumim, for example, which came into being when Jews found it necessary to translate the Hebrew Scriptures into Aramaic, include expansive, exegetical paraphrases.[58] The commentary and the homily, both closely linked to the reading aloud of the Bible in synagogues and churches, also involved translation and paraphrase. As early as the end of the second century Christians were actively translating the Septuagint and Greek New Testament into Latin, and a distinctive tradition of Christian preaching and commentary on the Bible had already begun to develop. Christian commentaries often include large sections of paraphrase. Of Theodore of Mopsuestia's commentary on the Psalms, for example, M.F. Wiles observes that much of it ''consists of simple paraphrase, clarifying the meaning of the often obscure phraseology.''[59] Homilies, too, often involved paraphrastic amplification and abbreviation. The metrical homily of Melito of Sardis, for instance, contains a paraphrase of the biblical account of the first Passover (Exodus 12. 21-9). A translation follows:

> Then after Moses had slaughtered the sheep and performed the mystery with the children of Israel by night, he sealed the doors of their houses to guard the people and to confound the angel [of death]. When the sheep was slaughtered and the Paschal lamb eaten, the people rejoiced and Israel was sealed. Then the angel came to smite Egypt, uninitiated into the mystery, without a share in the Passover, unsealed with the blood, unprotected by the Spirit, the enemy, the unbeliever. In one night he smote and killed them.[60]

In this second-century sermon it is possible to discover the same tech- niques of paraphrastic composition that characterize *paraphrasis*. ''In one

[55] Roberts, *Biblical Epic*, p. 27.

[56] Roberts, *Biblical Epic*, p. 28.

[57] Wehrli, ''*Sacra poesis*,'' p. 265, suggests the connection between biblical epics and Targumim without exploring the possibility further.

[58] Of Targumim, B. Grossfeld, ''Bible'' (*EJ* 4, 842), remarks: ''They are often inter- mingled with various paraphrases and aggadic supplements such as one meets in homiletic works like the Talmud and the Midrash.''

[59] M.F. Wiles, ''Theodore of Mopsuestia as Representative of the Antiochene School,'' in the *Cambridge History of the Bible* (Cambridge, 1970), 1, p. 497.

[60] My translation is based on the text of Stuart G. Hall, *Melito of Sardis: On Pascha and Fragments* (Oxford, 1979).

night he smote and killed them,'' for example, is an abbreviation of
Exodus 12. 29:

> At midnight the Lord smote all the first-born in the land of Egypt, from
> the first-born of Pharaoh who sat on his throne to the first-born of the cap-
> tive who was in the dungeon, and all the first-born of the cattle.[61]

On the other hand, Melito's homily considerably amplifies "the land of
Egypt" in the original. The preacher adds 6 epithets to describe the
Egyptian people: "uninitiated into the mystery, without a share in the
Passover, unsealed with the blood, unprotected by the Spirit, the enemy,
the unbeliever."

Rather than looking for the origins of the biblical epic in the school
exercise of *paraphrasis* or, as Herzog suggests, in the practice popular in
the early church of quoting from pagan poets like Virgil to make
apologetic points or to illuminate Scripture passages, it may be more
fruitful to consider the biblical epic as an outgrowth of an ecclesiastical
tradition of biblical paraphrase.[62] The way in which Christian preachers
and commentators retold biblical narratives and interpreted them must
have influenced the biblical poets. We have good reason to believe that
Sedulius was familiar with Christian commentaries; there is no evidence
that he knew Quintilian.[63] It is quite possible that Christian poets like
Juvencus fancied their role to be akin to that of Jerome and other
translators of the Bible. Jerome describes Juvencus (*De viris illustribus* 84)
as *transferens* the four Gospels into hexameters.[64] Instead of rendering the
Greek text into Latin, Juvencus may have thought of himself as engaged
in turning a stylistically unattractive original into polished hexameters,
which would appeal to the classically inclined reader. If so, the tradition
to which he belongs is as closely connected with the church as it is with
the rhetorical schools. Certainly in the case of Sedulius' *Paschale carmen*,
which includes a great deal of sophisticated exegesis, and Arator's *De*

---

[61] Here (as elsewhere) I use the Revised Standard Version of The Holy Bible, 2nd ed.
(Cleveland, 1971).

[62] See Roberts, *Biblical Epic*, p. 61, n. 3.

[63] Mayr discusses Sedulius' debt to patristic exegesis, such as Ambrose's commentary
on Luke and Augustine's exposition of the Lord's Prayer (*Serm.* 56 and 57) in Chapter
3 of *Studien zu dem Paschale carmen* ("Sedulius und die alten Kommentare"), pp. 54-68.

[64] Since Juvencus evidently had the Greek New Testament before him (see A.R.
Gebser, *De Caii Vettii Aquilini Iuvenci presbyteri hispani vita et scriptis* [Jena, 1827], p. 35) and
did not restrict himself to the versions of the so-called *Itala* which he ordinarily followed
(see K. Marold, "Über das Evangelienbuch des Iuvencus in seiner Verhältniss zum
Bibeltext," *Zeitschrift für die wissenschaftliche Theologie* 33 [1890], 341), he should then properly be described as engaged in the exercise of translation, not paraphrase. It is, after
all, only the fact that the latter involves different languages that distinguishes the two (see
Roberts, *Biblical Epic*, p. 9).

actibus apostolorum, which is practically a commentary in verse, the connection with the literary practice of the church is obvious.[65]

It is one thing to suggest that Juvencus and other authors of biblical epics were acquainted with school exercises which involved paraphrasing and were influenced by them in the composition of their biblical epics. It is quite another, however, to suggest that all of the biblical epics of Late Antiquity can be *fully* described and analyzed as "paraphrases."[66] If the essence of *paraphrasis* is "to recast a given subject in different language: that is, to retain the content of an original while varying its form,"[67] then Sedulius' *Paschale carmen* resists analysis as a typical example of the exercise. The question of the "original" is especially problematic. Sedulius does not follow any one Gospel, for instance, in retelling the miracles of Christ, nor, for that matter, does he confine himself to material taken from the four Gospels. In Book 2, for instance, Sedulius draws the story of the Magi from the Gospel according to Matthew but follows it with Luke's account of the 12-year-old Jesus in the temple. The story of Jesus' baptism which follows (2. 139-65) includes a flashback to the story of John the Baptist's birth (Luke 1. 57 ff.), a paraphrase of John 1. 5, and a reference to Psalm 114. 5. The author of the *Paschale carmen* ranges freely through the Scriptures. In his reaction to the crucifixion of Jesus, for instance, we find Sedulius paraphrasing 1 Corinthians 15. 55:

> Dic ubi nunc tristis victoria, dic ubi nunc sit
> mors stimulus horrenda tuus, quae semper opimis
> insaturata malis cunctas invadere gentes
> poenali dicione soles? (5. 276-9)

In his description of the trial of Jesus before Caiphas, Sedulius inserts a rewording of Psalm 1:

> . . . namque hoc resident cathedra
> pestifera falsis agitatum testibus ardet
> concilium, iam iamque volant mendacia mille

---

[65] Judith McClure makes the point in "The Biblical Epic and its Audience in Late Antiquity," *Papers of the Liverpool Latin Seminar* 3 (Liverpool, 1981), p. 307 that "fifth and sixth-century paraphrases all include interpretative expansions and are clearly related to contemporary exegesis." Unfortunately she does not explore the connections further. See Chapter 4, below, for a discussion of Sedulius' exegetical methods.

[66] Some of the Greek biblical poems of Late Antiquity present fewer problems to analysis as simple paraphrases. In Nonnos' *Metabole*, for example, we find no introduction, no prayer for inspiration, no epilogue, and no division into books. Nonnos follows only one original, the Gospel. He does expand at some length upon a word or group of words in John's Gospel, but this could be accurately described as amplification. To conclude, however, from this isolated example that all biblical epics, Latin as well as Greek, are examples of *paraphrasis* is to ignore other biblical poets' clear intentions to write in independent poetic genres.

[67] Roberts, *Biblical Epic*, p. 21.

in Dominum, vanis hominum conflata favillis,
et pereunt levitate sui, velut ignis oberrans
arentes stipulas, vires cui summa cremandi
materies infirma rapit, victoque furore
labitur invalidae deformis gloriae flammae. (5. 85-92)

Sedulius also incorporates into the *Paschale carmen* non-Scriptural material, which he must have drawn from commentaries and from other sources such as sermons, Christian Latin poetry, and undoubtedly from his own imagination. No Gospel writer, for example, indicates the presence of an ass at Jesus' birth, but Sedulius describes the donkey which carried Christ into Jerusalem as *non illius inpar, / qui patulo Christum licet in praesepe iacentem / agnovit tamen esse Deum* (4. 300-2). The *Paschale carmen* cannot be said to follow any one "original" text, and yet the fact of a single original seems to be assumed in most ancient definitions of the exercise of *paraphrasis* (see, for example, Quintilian's discussion in *Inst.* 1. 9. 2).[68]

The first book of the *Paschale carmen*, in particular, presents special difficulties to analysis as a paraphrase, since most of it is of the poet's own invention. Sedulius begins the poem with a preface of 16 lines and over 80 lines of introductory material before he retells the first biblical story. These initial lines cannot be described as amplification because they do not expand upon any original. It should also be noted that the last 125 lines of the book are not paraphrastic either. The *Paschale carmen* contains substantial sections of original material which cannot be analyzed as examples of *amplificatio*, that is to say, "stylistic embellishments of an original text."[69] This is true, incidentally, of other biblical epics as well (cf., e.g., the extensive introductory *precatio* of Claudius Marius Victor's *Alethia*). In the first book of his poem Sedulius does retell 18 biblical stories drawn from the Old Testament, ranging from Genesis to Daniel. Sedulius says (in 1. 291-2) that it is the miracles of the Old Testament which he has presented in condensed form: *per digesta prius veteris miracula legis / retullimus*. If there is an original text which Sedulius has in mind, it is the entire Old Testament or, at least, all of the miracles of the Old Testament. *Paschale carmen* 1. 103-241 could, therefore, be considered an example of drastic abbreviation. Quintilian says (*Inst.* 10. 5. 4) that it is proper in a paraphase "to cut away the excessive" (*effusa substringere*), and Roberts suggests that the biblical poets' practice of trimming or

---

[68] It may, indeed, be a mistake to suggest that Sedulius had any written text at all before him as he wrote the *Paschale carmen*. Many Christians in antiquity knew the Bible virtually by heart. St. Anthony was said to have memorized the Scriptures simply by hearing them read aloud.
[69] Roberts, *Biblical Epic*, p. 162.

eliminating subject material should be traced to the practice of *abbreviatio*
which they learned in the school exercise of *paraphrasis*. In fact, however,
it is just as likely that Sedulius learned how to condense a long story into
a few words from other poets. It is possible, for instance, to see Ovid's
Metamorphoses 15. 771-3 as an example of such extreme abbreviation:

> natum [i.e. Aenean] longis erroribus actum
> iactarique freto sedesque intrare silentum
> bellaque cum Turno gerere. . . .[70]

In just three lines Ovid has come close to summarizing the content of the
Aeneid. No one has suggested, however, that Ovid was consciously hark-
ing back to his school days or consulting rhetorical handbooks for
guidance at this point in the composition of the *Metamorphoses*. Nor do we
analyze Ovid's epic poem, which is also to some degree paraphrastic,
solely (or even primarily) in terms of its *amplificatio* and *abbreviatio* of
sources.

iii. *Presuppositions and Procedures*

No one would argue that the *Paschale carmen* is not a paraphrastic work
in general. Obviously Sedulius did not invent the story of the life of
Christ. The *Paschale carmen* follows (for the most part) the narrative
sequence of the life of Christ as given in the four canonical Gospels, and
its author is clearly reluctant to make substantive changes of fact in the
biblical account. Not surprisingly, considering the emphasis which he
lays on the veracity of his subject matter, Sedulius does not create many
new details in the life of Christ which are not to be found in Matthew,
Mark, Luke, or John. The truth of their new poetic content (as opposed
to the *mendacia* which constituted the usual theme of pagan poetry)[71] is
a fundamental point to which Juvencus (*Praefatio* 19-20), Sedulius
(*Paschale carmen* 1. 22), and other biblical poets of Late Antiquity
emphatically appeal in defense of their Christian poetry.

It should be noted, however, that a great deal of Latin poetry has
unoriginal subject matter. The earliest Latin authors (e.g., Livius
Andronicus, Plautus, and Terence) drew heavily from Greek sources.

---

[70] I use the edition of W.S. Anderson (Leipzig, 1977).

[71] The lying poet is practically a commonplace in the Christian literature of Late Antiquity. The *locus classicus* is, no doubt, Augustine's reference to the *figmentorum poeticorum
vestigia* in *Conf.* 1. 17. See also *Serm.* 105. 7. 10 on Virgil as *mendax vates*. Even Claudian
joins the chorus of protests against the lies of the poets in his *De bello getico*, vv. 14-15,
27: *licet omnia vates / in maius celebrata ferant* and *nil veris aequale dabunt*. (I use the edition
of J.B. Hall [Leipzig, 1985].)

Catullus translated Sappho into Latin, and Virgil's *Eclogues* are deeply indebted to Theocritus. In the "Silver Age" Valerius Flaccus drew the subject matter for his *Argonautica* from the Hellenistic epic of Apollonius of Rhodes and its scholia. It is well known that Latin poets traditionally assigned less importance to the originality of their subject material than to the quality of its treatment. Horace sums up the sentiment well in *Ars poetica* 131-5:

> publica materies privati iuris erit, si
> non circa vilem patulumque moraberis orbem
> nec verbo verbum curabis reddere fidus
> interpres, nec desilies imitator in artum,
> unde pedem proferre pudor vetet aut operis lex.[72]

It should also be noted that although scholars have assumed or even posited the existence of a genre of "paraphrase" or "metaphrase" in antiquity, the designation as applied to verse composition is conspicuous by its absence in such important discussions of poetic genre as Horace's *Ars poetica* and Diomedes' *Ars grammatica*. Latin literary theorists did not make a rigorous distinction between verse with original and verse with unoriginal subject matter. Quintilian, for example, includes Aratus, the Hellenistic author of a verse paraphrase of the *Phaenomena* of Eudoxus of Cnidus, in the same category as Homer and Hesiod, describing his work not as a "rhetorical paraphrase" but as an "epic" (*Inst.* 10. 1. 46-57). For Quintilian and others, poetic genre was a question to be determined by means of formal categories such as meter; little or no attention was paid to the originality of the poetic subject matter.

Even though paraphrasing was an important literary technique in antiquity, it was not very common at all to describe a verse composition as a "*paraphrasis*."[73] *Paraphrasis* was a term ordinarily applied to attempts to turn poetry into prose and only rarely the reverse. When Porphyry, for example, describes a verse rendition of Plato's *Critias* by Zotikos (a contemporary of Plotinus), it is not as a *paraphrasis* but as a *poiesis*.[74] The modern reader might well be tempted to refer to this kind of literary product as a "paraphrase," but it is important to recognize that the term was not commonly employed by ancient poets or their readers to describe verse with unoriginal subject matter.[75] When Sedulius himself refers to

---

[72] I use the edition of S. Borzsák (Leipzig, 1984).

[73] We do not even know for certain that verse composition was taught as a school exercise in antiquity. A Latin verse paraphrase of *Aeneid* 1. 477-93 from the third or fourth century survives on papyrus, but there is no agreement as to whether it was a school exercise or not (see the discussion in Roberts, *Biblical Epic*, p. 71, n. 39).

[74] Roberts, *Biblical Epic*, p. 58.

[75] Roberts, *Biblical Epic*, p. 71, argues that the fact that the biblical epics are in verse does not prevent them from being considered "paraphrases." He points out that "the

his paraphrastic work in his prefatory epistle to Macedonius, he calls it
a *carmen*, a word used by Quintilian to refer to the products of authors
such as Virgil, Horace, Lucretius, and Simonides (*Inst.* 8. 6. 26-27; 3.
1. 4; 11. 2. 11) and also to describe verse as opposed to prose (1. 8. 2).
The distinction between "the developed rhetorical paraphrase"
(Roberts' category for the biblical epics) and an original and independent
literary composition is somewhat less than precise,[76] and there is no
reason to believe that in Late Antiquity or the Middle Ages biblical epics
like Sedulius' were considered under the former head rather than the
latter.

Neither the authors of the biblical epics of late antiquity nor those contemporaries who referred to their works used the words *paraphrasis* or
metaphrasis to describe them.[77] Sedulius claims that his composition will
rival the works not of "paraphrasts" but of *gentiles poetae* (1. 17).
Juvencus, too, has high poetic aspirations and chooses to group himself
in a class with such eminent poets as Homer and Virgil. It is significant
that he should mention the authors of epic poems in the proem to
Evangeliorum libri quattuor. If Juvencus had really conceived of himself as
writing in the *paraphrasis* tradition, we might have expected him to cite
for his literary precedent an author like Gregory Thaumatourgos, who
wrote a prose paraphrase of Ecclesiastes in the third century.[78] If, in fact,
the authors of the longer hexameter biblical poems of Late Antiquity
thought of their works as belonging to any traditional literary genre, it
was no doubt (as we shall see in a subsequent chapter) the epic.

Perhaps the greatest deficiency in the paraphrase theory is that while
it attempts to trace whatever continuity there might be between the
biblical epic and any long established literary practice of antiquity, it fails
to recognize and account for discontinuity. In many ways the biblical
epic is a completely new literary tradition which begins in the fourth century.[79] Regardless of where Sedulius' paraphrastic tradition derives its

---

objection that the verse paraphrase finds no sanction in paraphrastic theory depends on
a qualitative distinction between prose and verse which owes more to modern preconcep-
tions than to ancient literary theory.'' While Roberts is correct to caution against projec-
ting all of our modern distinctions between prose and poetry back into ancient literature,
it would also be a mistake to blur the differences between them entirely. Quintilian recognized the need to distinguish the two. In *Inst.* 1. 8. 2, he observes that poetry is *non quidem
prosae similis, quia et carmen est et se poetae canere testantur.*

[76] Roberts himself makes this point in *Biblical Epic*, p. 35 and p. 219.

[77] Although the terms *paraphrasis* and *metaphrasis* were sometimes distinguished in antiquity, as, for example, by the sixth-century rhetorician, Georgius Choeroboscus, it seems
that they were more often used interchangeably. For a fuller discussion, see Golega, *Studien über die Evangeliendichtung Nonnos*, p. 92, n. 2.

[78] For an edition of Gregory's *Metaphrasis*, see *PG* 10, 987-1018.

[79] Note should be taken of the fragmentary Jewish-Hellenistic epics of Philo and
Theodotus, written most probably in the second century BC. Only two dozen lines of

ultimate origin (whether a product of the church, or the school, or
neither), Sedulius himself surely did not get the idea of retelling the life
of Christ in verse from exercises which he practiced in the schools of the
grammatici or *rhetores* but from reading Juvencus. There can be no doubt
that Sedulius was intimately familiar with the fourth-century poet.[80]
Whether or not, therefore, Juvencus was inspired by schoolroom
recollections, the literary tradition to which Sedulius and other biblical
epic poets of Late Antiquity belong begins with the *Evangeliorum libri quattuor*, not the exercise of *paraphrasis*. Even if Juvencus himself did conceive
of his work as an example of the exercise, it does not necessarily follow
that Sedulius and other later poets went back to any model other than
Juvencus' pioneering work.[81]

The boundaries between original literary composition and paraphrase
in antiquity were not altogether indistinct. Sedulius, for one, recognized
and preserved a difference. Sometime after he completed the *Paschale
carmen*, he wrote a paraphrase of it in prose, a work which he called the
Paschale opus.[82] Although Sedulius does not himself use the word
"paraphrase" of it, the *Paschale opus* could well be analyzed as an example of an exercise which has been described as "primarily stylistic."[83] In
the prefatory letter to Macedonius which he wrote introducing the
Paschale opus, Sedulius himself observes of the two compositions: *nec
impares argumento vel ordine, sed stilo videntur et oratione dissimiles*. The *Paschale*

Philo's hexameter poem on Jerusalem and 47 lines of Theodotus' epic on the Jews have
come down to us. J.J. Collins has discussed problems concerning the provenance and
historical context of Theodotus' epic in "The Epic of Theodotus and the Hellenism of
the Hasmoneans," *HTR* 73 (1980), 91-104. See also R.J. Bull, "A Note on Theodotus'
Description of Shechem," *HTR* 60 (1967), 221-7. Y. Gutman has made a study of the
religious and philosophical content of Philo's poem in *Scripta hierosolymitana* 1 (1954), 36-
63. Texts for both poems may now be found in *Supplementum hellenisticum*, H. Lloyd-
Jones, J. Parsons, eds. (Berlin, 1983), pp. 328-31; 360-5. Although these biblical epics
were known in the fourth century (Eusebius quotes from them) there is no reason to think
that any of the biblical epic poets of Late Antiquity were influenced by them.
    [80] On Sedulius' debt to Juvencus, see Salvatore Costanza, "Da Giovenco a Sedulio:
I proemi degli *Evangeliorum libri* e del *Carmen paschale*," *Civiltà classica e cristiana* 6 (1985),
253-86.
    [81] Like other biblical epic poets, Sedulius worked with a number of poetic models—
besides Juvencus, he was also influenced by Paulinus of Nola and Prudentius, among the
Christian poets, and Virgil and Ovid, among the pagans. In this regard, it is more
accurate to compare Sedulius with other Latin poets involved in *aemulatio* and *imitatio*
within a lively literary tradition than to portray him as an isolated paraphrast working
on some sort of an academic exercise.
    [82] Although the manuscripts and early printed editions often refer to Sedulius' biblical
epic and its prose paraphrase as *Carmen paschale* and *Opus paschale* respectively, I prefer
to use the poet's own designations for both works. In the first prefatory letter to
Macedonius, Sedulius refers to his verse composition as *Paschale carmen*; in the second letter to Macedonius, he describes the prose work as *Paschale opus*.
    [83] Roberts, *Biblical Epic*, p. 47.

opus has no historical context of its own. It addresses no issues, for
instance, which have arisen in the years since the original was composed.
Nor does the paraphrast make significant decisions as to what he will
include or exclude. He has no independent thematic criterion by which
he selects material. Indeed, Sedulius follows his original here with little
sense of discrimination. The work does not claim to belong to a traditional literary genre, such as the epic. It is simply called (by its author)
an *opus*. Nor does it have an independent structure. Like the poem which
it paraphrases, it is also in five books and follows the sequence of its
original with little variation.[84] It has no new preface, or introduction, or
epilogue. Nor does Sedulius introduce new exclamations, hymns,
prayers, outbursts of rage, and rhetorical questions into the *Paschale opus*.
The author's main purpose, as he indicates in the letter to Macedonius,
is to change the style of the *Paschale carmen*, to turn material originally
written in verse into prose (*stilo . . . liberiore*).[85]

The originality and independence of the *Paschale carmen*'s composition
becomes clearer when viewed against the background of the *Paschale opus*.
The *carmen* dresses its first-century subject matter in fifth-century garb.
Sedulius has independent didactic and polemical interests and is concerned not only with "how" he should say something but also with
"what" he should say. The *Paschale carmen* includes biblical material
which helps to support the author's vision of Christ and eliminates what
will not. Sedulius' poem also has an independent theme. Although its
general subject is, of course, a traditional one, the *Paschale carmen* does not
simply follow the narrative sequence of any one biblical "original."
Sedulius uses the thematic criterion of "the miraculous" to design the
shape of his composition. Furthermore, the author of the *Paschale carmen*
challenges "pagan poets" and places his poem squarely within the
prestigious epic tradition. Sedulius' poem draws heavily upon the formal
aspects of traditional Latin epics, especially the *Aeneid*. In addition, the
structure of the *Paschale carmen* is independent to some extent of the narrative structures of Sedulius' biblical material. The *Paschale carmen* has an
architectonic design which counteracts the temporality of the Gospel narrative and suggests another, loftier realm of meaning. The style of the
Paschale carmen is, of course, far different from that of the Gospels—
Sedulius reshapes and artistically transforms his subject material—but
there are many other changes, too, which cannot be described as
"primarily stylistic."

---

[84] This, at least, is its format in the earliest extant manuscripts (e.g., *Parisin.* 12279).
[85] For a discussion of *stilo . . . liberiore* as a periphrase for "in prose," see Roberts,
Biblical Epic, p. 81. In the *Paschale opus* Sedulius does add material which is not to be
found in the *Paschale carmen*, but it is confined largely to Scriptural quotations.

In the following chapters we shall approach the *Paschale carmen* as an independent and original literary composition. Sedulius has not usually been studied in this way. Most studies of the *Paschale carmen* have concentrated on the biblical texts which Sedulius followed and from which he deviated, while larger aspects of the poem's composition, such as its structure, imagery, meaning, unity, and artistry, have very often gone unobserved. While it is important to acknowledge the presence of paraphrastic elements in the *Paschale carmen* and to discover how Sedulius abbreviates and amplifies his original, this kind of source analysis is not the only way in which to approach paraphrastic verse. It would be absurd, for instance, in the case of Milton's *Paradise Lost* (which could be described as an amplificatory paraphrase of the first chapters of Genesis), not to examine the poem in relation to other sources and literary traditions, nor to consider aspects of the poem's composition other than its amplification of Genesis 1-3.

Modern readers must be careful not to let Sedulius' dependence upon biblical narratives prevent their appreciation of what is new about the artistic product which he has created. To a great extent attitudes such as Curtius' towards the biblical epics of Late Antiquity are an outgrowth of the romantic insistence on "originality" in poetry. But, of course, to dismiss a piece of verse which does not have original subject matter as a "paraphrase," that is to say, a stylistic exercise which does not deserve careful reading, is to dismiss much of Latin literature. While it used to be popular to accuse some Latin poets (e.g., Valerius Flaccus and Statius) of "servile imitation," most students of Latin literature now agree that however much a Latin poet "may have owed in style, characterization and episode to his various models, this does not exclude originality and inventiveness."[86] Sedulius, like any other Latin poet using traditional subject material, transforms his sources and models. "Elements are thrown into the crucible and fused in a new compound, and it is hardly possible to find or to use a catalyst that can separate them again."[87] The result is a completely new and organic composition, which must be approached as such if it is to be read aright.

This book, then, could well be described as an experiment in reading a work which has often been dismissed as practically unreadable. The chapters that follow present a series of different literary approaches to the *Paschale carmen*. Chapter 2 locates Sedulius' biblical epic within a

---

[86] David Vessey, *Statius and the Thebaid* (Cambridge, 1973), p. 69. For other discussions, see *Creative Imitation and Latin Literature*, David West, Tony Woodman, eds. (Cambridge, 1979) and M. Schumacher, "*Imitatio*—A Creative or an Annihilating Force?" *CF* 20 (1966), 47-56.

[87] Vessey, *Statius and the Thebaid*, p. 68.

historical and theological context; Chapter 3 examines the *Paschale carmen*'s place within a ''Life of Christ'' tradition in the Christian poetry of Late Antiquity; Chapter 4 studies the dynamic of the relationship between the epic form of the poem and its biblical content; Chapter 5 explores the narrative and architectonic structures of the *Paschale carmen*; Chapter 6 offers a close reading of *Paschale carmen* 3. 1-11 against the background of its original Gospel source and other (more or less contemporary) Christian poetic treatments of the same subject; Chapter 7 traces the history of Sedulius' *Paschale carmen* as a popular and influential text which continued to be read through the Middle Ages and the early modern period. It is hoped that such a literary analysis will shed new light on the meaning and artistry of an important, but much neglected and often misread text.

CHAPTER TWO

TEXT AND CONTEXT

Although we do not know as much as we should like about the author,
audience, and intentions of the *Paschale carmen*, it is possible by using the
evidence of subscriptions, prefatory letters, and the poem itself to place
Sedulius' work within a general historical and theological context. As we
shall see, Sedulius was more than a literary "virtuoso" who retold
biblical stories simply to amuse himself or others. Despite Curtius' suggestion that Sedulius was an author who had "nothing to say,"[1] a close
examination of his biblical epic reveals him to be a discriminating poet
who rarely fails to interpret the traditional stories which he retells. The
Paschale carmen is, in fact, didactic and polemical in tone and more concerned than is often supposed to address issues which would have seemed
both contemporary and important to its audience.

i. *The Date and Provenance of the Paschale carmen*

When and where was the *Paschale carmen* written? According to a
subscription preserved in a number of Sedulian manuscripts (the earliest
dated to the ninth century), the author of the *Paschale carmen* is supposed
to have written his works during the reign of the emperors Theodosius
II and Valentinian III, that is, between AD 425 and 450:

> Sedulius versificus primo laicus in Italia philosophiam didicit; postea cum
> aliis metrorum generibus heroicum metrum Macedonio consulente docuit.
> In Achaia libros suos scripsit tempore imperatorum Theodosii et Valen-
> tiniani.[2]

Although it is prudent to read subscriptions like this one with a healthy
degree of scepticism, it is difficult to discount such a source altogether,
given the paucity of biographical information about Sedulius provided by

---

[1] Curtius, *European Literature*, p. 462.
[2] The subscription is preserved in *Cod. Par.* 14143, *Cod. Par.* 9347, and *Cod. Par.*
13377, among others. For the text of the subscription and a discussion of the same, see
Johannes Huemer, *De Sedulii poetae vita et scriptis commentatio* (Vienna, 1878), pp. 21-2. The
reigns of Valentinian II and Theodosius I also overlapped (AD 379-392), but the
reference is most likely to the fifth-century emperors. At least one later version of the
subscription (*Cod. Vind.* 85) specifies "the younger Theodosius, son of Arcadius, and
Valentinian, son of Constantius." Huemer discusses the problem of dating in "Zur
Bestimmung der Abfassungszeit und Herausgabe des *Carmen paschale* des Sedulius," *ZÖG*
27 (1876), 500-5.

other sources. So far as it is possible to tell, the subscription appears to be reliable, in as much as the details which it provides do not appear simply to have been extrapolated from Sedulius' own works and do not contradict any other surviving evidence either. Nothing, for example, in the most reliable source for Sedulius' life, the first dedicatory epistle which he addressed to a certain Macedonius, conflicts with the biographical information provided by the subscription.[3]

Unfortunately, Sedulius tells us very little about himself in the letter to Macedonius. The author of the *Paschale carmen* does mention the names of a number of friends of Macedonius in the letter, but it is difficult to identify any of them precisely. Macedonius himself was a priest—Sedulius addresses him as *presbyter* and *venerabilis pater*—and apparently the head of one of the spiritual communities so popular in Late Antiquity. Like Hilary of Arles, Sidonius Apollinaris, and Fulgentius of Ruspe, Sedulius' patron seems to have gathered a group of like-minded religious literati and ascetics about himself. Sedulius mentions the names of seven of Macedonius' friends: a bishop named Ursinus; three priests named respectively: Laurentius, Gallianus, and Ursinus; an ascetic named Felix (*cui crucifixus est mundus*); and two sisters named Syncletica and Perpetua.[4] The only name in this circle of Macedonius which may help us to date the poem is that of Syncletica. It is just possible that she is the same Syncletica to whom Eustathius dedicated his Latin translation of the *Hexaemeron* of St. Basil.[5] If so, this suggests a *terminus post quem* of c. AD 400 for the *Paschale carmen*'s composition. A much more secure *terminus post quem* is the passing reference which Sedulius makes to Jerome in this same prefatory letter to Macedonius. The famous controversialist is mentioned in the letter as providing a well-known precedent for dedicating literary works *ad generosas feminas*:

---

[3] We know nothing else about this Macedonius. There are eight Macedonii listed in *PLRE* II, pp. 697-8, but none are priests.

[4] Sedulius describes each of the seven associates of Macedonius. I excerpt the following:
i. habes antistem plenum reverentiae sacerdotalis Ursinum. ii. habes Laurentium difficili comparatione presbyterum. iii. habes quoque meum Gallianum aeque presbyterum. iv. quid Ursini dicam quoque presbyteri annosam patientiam? v. quidve Felicem referam vere felicem, saeculi huius inimicum, cui crucifixus est mundus? vi. quis non optet et ambiat eximio Syncletices, sacrae virginis ac ministrae?... vii. habet germanam nomine meritoque Perpetuam.

[5] This is the suggestion offered by B. Altaner, "Eustathius, der lateinische Übersetzer der Hexaëmeron-Homilien Basilius des Grossen," *ZNTW* 39 (1940), 168. Altaner shows that Augustine made use of Eustathius' translation in his *De Genesi ad litteram* (begun in 401) and concludes that Eustathius' work must have been completed before this time. Hence 400 as a *terminus post quem* for the *Paschale carmen*.

Nec Hieronymi, divinae legis interpretis et caelestis bibliotechae cultoris, exemplar pudeat imitari atque ad generosas quoque feminas et praeclarae indolis fama subnixas, in quarum mentibus sacrae lectionis instantia sobrium sapientiae domicilium conlocavit, propriae disputationis documenta transmittere.

It cannot be determined from context whether the solitary of Bethlehem was still alive at the time Sedulius was writing, but the reference to Jerome does prove that the *Paschale carmen* must have been written sometime after the 380s or 390s, when Jerome was busy dedicating a number of works to his female friends, in particular, Paula and Eustochium.[6]

As far as a *terminus ante quem* is concerned, we know from external evidence that the *Paschale carmen* must have been written before the end of the fifth century. According to another subscription preserved in the oldest extant Sedulian manuscript (*Taurinensis* E. IV. 42), Turcius Rufius Apronianus Asterius, a consul of Rome in 494 who produced a famous "edition" of Virgil's poetry in that year, also published the *Paschale carmen* as an ex-consul, that is, in 495 or later:

Incipit sacrum opus, id est ex vetere testamento liber primus, et ex novo quattuor, quod Sedulius inter cartulas suas sparsas reliquit, et recollecti adunatique sunt a Turcio Rufio Asterio v. c. et exconsule ordinario atque patricio, supra scriptorum editore librorum.[7]

The subscription's claim that Asterius had to collect and organize the *Paschale carmen* because he found the work in disarray (*inter cartulas suas sparsas*) doubtless exaggerates the extent of the consul's "editorial"

---

[6] Jerome does not mention Sedulius in the *De viris illustribus* (written in 392), although he includes an entry for another popular biblical epic, Juvencus' *Evangeliorum libri quattuor*. Sedulius' poem would probably have merited a comment from Jerome if it had been in circulation before that date.

[7] This is Huemer's (*De Sedulii poetae vita*, pp. 32-3) edition of the subscription found in *Taurinensis* E. IV. 42. The identification of the consul in the Sedulian subscription with the editor of Virgil described in the subscription to the Medicean MS (for a reproduction of the latter, see L.D. Reynolds and N.G. Wilson, *Scribes and Scholars: A Guide to the Transmission of Greek and Latin Literature*, 2nd ed. [Oxford, 1974], plate 9) is not without problems. The different versions of the Sedulian subscription, for example, hopelessly garble the name of the consul. He is referred to variously as: Ruffus Asterius, Turtius Ruffus Asterius, Turcius Rufus Asterius Quintus, Tertius Rufius Austerius, and Turcius Russius Asterius Quintus. The only other possibility is that the original Sedulian subscription referred to Flavius Astyrius, consul in 449 (see *PLRE* II, 174-5), but his name is even harder than Turcius Rufius Apronianus Asterius' to reconcile with the names offered in the versions of the Sedulian subscription. In lieu of a better solution, I follow most students of the subscriptions, including Otto Jahn, "Über die Subscriptionen in den Handschriften römischer Classiker," *BSG* 3 (1851), 335 ff., and the editors of *PLRE*, in simply assuming that the consul of 494 produced both editions.

work.[8] One version of the subscription (*Vindobonensis* 85) even suggests that Asterius had to complete Sedulius' work because the poet died before he could finish the *Paschale carmen* (*moriens ergo indigestum dereliquit hoc opus in cartulis scriptum*). The very existence of Sedulius' own paraphrase of the poem (the *Paschale opus*), however, implies that there was an organized and finished original work to paraphrase. If Sedulius had not completed the *Paschale carmen* before he died, he would obviously have been unable to write the *Paschale opus*. We can, in fact, be fairly certain that Sedulius' biblical epic was in circulation in completed form before c. 495. The so-called Gelasian Decree, which most scholars date to the first part of the sixth century, gives the *Paschale carmen* a very favorable review, suggesting that the poem was in circulation for at least some time before the decree was composed: *Item venerabilis Sedulii paschale opus, quod heroicis descripsit versibus, insigni laude praeferimus.*[9] There are also clear Sedulian echoes in other Christian poetry of the second half of the fifth century. Paulinus of Pella's *Eucharisticos*, for example, contains many Sedulian parallels, including half of a line (102 a: *omnipotens aeterne Deus*) which is identical with *Paschale carmen* 1. 60.[10] Paulinus of Périgueux's *De vita sancti Martini* (written c. AD 470) also contains a number of striking resemblances to Sedulian passages. Compare, for example, Paulinus' *Dei cui prona facultas* (2. 288) with Sedulius' *Deo cui prona facultas* (4. 6).[11] If Asterius' edition of the *Paschale carmen* was analogous to his edition of Virgil, his motive in editing the work was probably not to restore a neglected or lost work to light (the *Aeneid* was extraordinarily popular in Late Antiquity) but to issue a new edition of a well established and frequently quoted author.[12]

---

[8] See J.E.G. Zetzel, "The Subscriptions in the Manuscripts of Livy and Fronto and the Meaning of *Emendatio*," *CP* 75 (1980), 56-7, on the differences between ancient "editions" and "recensions" and "modern critical technique." Even if Asterius' edition was not "scientific," it is not impossible that the text of the *Paschale carmen* had already undergone some corruption by the 490s, and the consul may have actually done some rudimentary editing. See Roberts, *Biblical Epic*, p. 78, n. 67.

[9] *PL* 59, 161. See also E. von Dobschütz, "Das Decretum Gelasianum," *Texte und Untersuchungen* 38. 4 (1912), and E. Schwarz, "Zum Decretum Gelasianum," *ZNTW* 29 (1930), 161-8. Surprisingly, Sedulius is not mentioned in the *De viris illustribus* of Gennadius, which appeared in the 470s. Huemer (*De Sedulii poetae vita*, pp. 18 ff.) argues that our present text of Gennadius is defective and that the original did include an entry for Sedulius and the *Paschale carmen*.

[10] See *PLRE* I, p. 677 for the dating of the *Eucharisticos*. W. Brandes lists this and other examples of borrowing in *CSEL* 16, 315. As Roberts, *Biblical Epic*, p. 78, n. 66, observes, "not all of these passages need be explained as imitations of Sedulius, but the residue of probable imitations is sufficient to suggest both poets [Paulinus of Pella and Paulinus of Périgueux] knew the *Carmen Paschale*."

[11] For Dracontius' knowledge of the *Paschale carmen*, see M. Manitius, *RhM* 46 (1891), 494.

[12] On this point, see Roberts, *Biblical Epic*, pp. 77-8.

The question of the provenance of the *Paschale carmen* is equally vexed. The first subscription mentioned above informs us that Sedulius taught philosophy and later poetry (probably as a *grammaticus*) in Italy but wrote his works in Greece. There is little in the prefatory letter or the *Paschale carmen* itself to confirm or reject this biographical information as erroneous. A.D. McDonald's suggestion that Sedulius came from southern France, northern Spain, or nothern Italy because the poet's description of the slaughter of the innocents shows similarities to an iconographic tradition popular in this area is rather tenuous.[13] McDonald observes that, according to Sedulius, Herod's soldiers killed the infants of Bethlehem by dashing them to their deaths on the ground (rather than using their swords or lances to kill them):

> . . . Herodes Christo stimulatus adempto
> sternere *conlisas* parvorum strage catervas
> inmerito non cessat atrox. . . . (2. 115-7)

Since this is also the way in which artistic representations in northern Italy and Spain, or southern France, depicted the slaugher of the innocents, McDonald identifies this general vicinity as Sedulius' locale. It is just as likely, however, that Sedulius was simply following Prudentius' gruesome description of the slaughter in *Cathemerinon* 12. 117-20. Prudentius also represents the infants of Bethlehem as being dashed to their deaths:

> O barbarum spectaculum!
> *Inlisa* cervix cautibus
> spargit cerebrum lacteum
> oculosque per vulnos vomit.

Since we are fairly confident that Sedulius read and was influenced by the poetry of Prudentius, the argument based on iconographic influence loses some of its cogency.

Worth mentioning here is a stubborn tradition that Sedulius was a Roman. An eighth-century poem, sometimes ascribed to Aldhelm but actually written by Aethilwald, confidently asserts that Sedulius was a native of Rome (*Romae urbis indigena*).[14] Paschasius Radbertus also claims that Sedulius was *rhetor Romanae ecclesiae*[15] and the idea has been repeated

---

[13] A.D. McDonald, "The Iconographic Tradition of Sedulius," *Speculum* 8 (1933), 150-6. The author also considers iconographic parallels to Sedulius' description of the women's visit to Christ's tomb on Easter morning.

[14] *Carmina rhythmica* 2. 8 (*MGH AA* 15, 529). On the ascription to Aethilwald, see Michael Lapidge and Michael Herren, *Aldhelm: The Prose Works* (Ipswich and Totowa, 1979), pp. 147-8.

[15] In *De partu virg.* 2 (*PL* 120, 1385).

many times since. This locale may have been extrapolated from the
Asterian subscription—it is a consul in Rome, after all, who supposedly
finds and edits the *Paschale carmen*—but it may also reflect a reliable early
tradition. It is not impossible that Sedulius was born in Italy, spent part
of his life teaching in Rome, and retired to Greece to write his *libros*.[16]

There is much, then, that remains tantalizingly uncertain about the
date and provenance of the *Paschale carmen*. At the very least, however,
we can establish that Sedulius' poem was a product of the fifth century
(roughly speaking), with a *terminus post quem* of c. 390 and a *terminus ante
quem* of c. 495. If the subscriptional testimony is trustworthy—and there
is no overwhelming reason to doubt it—Sedulius lived in Italy and
Greece and wrote his Christian epic sometime during the years 425-450.

ii. *The Author and his Audience*

We know very little about Sedulius' development as a Christian
author. Quite obviously he was a devout and well educated believer, but
there is conflicting evidence about his precise relationship to the church.
According to Isidore of Seville (*De viris illustribus* 20), the author of the
Paschale carmen was a priest:

> Sedulius, presbyter, edidit tres libros, dactylico heroico metro compositos,
> quorum primus signa et virtutes Veteris Testamenti potentissime resonat;
> reliqui vero gestorum Christi sacramenta vel miracula intonant.[17]

In the subscriptions, however, Sedulius is described as *laicus*, at least at
the beginning of his career. In the letter to Macedonius Sedulius claims
to have been devoted at one time to secular studies and only later in life
attracted to the idea of writing Christian literature:

> Cum saecularibus igitur studiis occupatus vim inpatientis ingenii, quod
> divinitatis in me providentia generavit, non utilitati animae sed inani vitae
> dependerem, et litterariae sollertia disciplinae lusibus infructuosi operis,

---

[16] There is a patently false tradition that Sedulius was Irish. It seems to have first
arisen in the fifteenth century when Johannes Trithemius confused Sedulius with his
namesake, the ninth-century poet and biblical commentator, Sedulius Scotus (see
Huemer, *De Sedulii poetae vita*, p. 11). Trithemius was only the first in a long line of
scholars to confuse the two. In the 1920s, the Irish patriot-scholar, George Sigerson,
simply assumed that Sedulius was a fellow countryman, making this the basis of his somewhat extravagant claims for the genius of the *Paschale carmen*. The confusion still persists.
See, for instance, H. Lülfing, "Ein Brief Siegmund Hellmans an Emil Jacobs zur
Seduliusüberlieferung," *Philologus* 115 (1971), 179-82. Schafer Williams, *Codices Pseudo-
Isidoriani: A Paleographico-historical Study*, Monumenta iuris canonici, Series C: Subsidia,
v. 3 (New York 1971), p. 4, demonstrates that it is still possible to confuse the two
Sedulii.

[17] *PL* 83, 1094.

non auctori serviret: tandem misericors Deus, rerum conditor, clementius fabricam sui iuris aspexit et stultos in me mundanae sapientiae diutius haberi sensus indoluit ac fatuum prudentiae mortalis ingenium caelesti sale condivit.

The rejection of an earlier preoccupation with things pagan is virtually a commonplace in early Christian literature, but the convention must have reflected reality in some instances, as it perhaps does here. Sedulius may indeed have been a convert to Christianity. *Codex Vat. Pal.* 242 contains a suggestion that Sedulius was a pagan who was converted to Christianity and baptized by Macedonius.[18]

There is also a tradition that Sedulius eventually became a bishop. The *Carmina* of Belisarius and Liberatus, which are appended to Sedulius' work in some manuscripts, describe him as *antistes*.[19] Alcuin refers to Sedulius as *beatus episcopus*,[20] and several of the later manuscripts also describe Sedulius as *episcopus*.[21] Since the matter of Sedulius' exact status in the world or the church is not of great importance here, let us suspend our judgment. Suffice it to say that Sedulius considered himself attached in some way to a religious circle, perhaps an ascetic community with literary interests, which was centered around a priest and included a bishop, three priests, and other dedicated Christians.[22]

This circle of Macedonius, the group of Christians described in the prefatory letter, is clearly the immediate audience for the poem. These select readers, however, are not the only group to whom Sedulius addresses himself either in the prefatory letter to Macedonius or in the poem itself. In the letter to Macedonius Sedulius envisions himself as setting forth the good, sound nourishment of the Gospel to those altogether unacquainted with it:

> Inter diversas tamen anxiae trepidationis ambages ad iaciendum huius operis fundamentum ob hoc maxime provocatus accessi, ut alios exhortationibus veritatis ad frugem bonae messis invitans. . . .

---

[18] *PL* 19, 436. This latter testimony is somewhat suspect because it could easily have been extrapolated from Sedulius' own remarks in the prefatory letter to Macedonius.

[19] The initial and final letters of the 16 lines of both of these poems spell out *Sedulius antistes* (for their texts, see *CSEL* 10, 307-10). For the meaning of *antistes* in Christian usage, see *TLL* 2. 1, 185.

[20] In his *Officia per ferias* (*PL* 101, 609).

[21] E.g., *Cod. Ambr.* R. 46. (See Huemer, *De Sedulii poetae vita*, p. 29.)

[22] One additional biographical item: concerning the poet's name there is good reason to disbelieve the testimony of later MSS which assign Sedulius the *praenomen* of Caelius or Coelius (or, less frequently, Cellius, Caecilius, C. Caecilius, and Circilius). The poet is called only Sedulius in the oldest MSS, *Ambrosianus* R. 57 and *Taurinensis* E. IV. 42. As Huemer has suggested (*De Sedulii poetae vita*, p. 11), the whole tradition of a *praenomen* for Sedulius may very well rest upon a scribal error. Some copyist probably mistook for a proper name the epithet *caelius*, which an adulatory monk originally used to describe (but not to name) the "heavenly" poet.

And in 1. 38-44 Sedulius assumes the stance of the Apostle to the Gentiles
as he imagines himself, like a latter-day Paul, addressing the Athenians
(cf. Acts 17. 16-34):

> Hanc constanter opem laesis adhibite medullis,
> quos letale malum, quos vanis dedita curis
> Attica Cecropii serpit doctrina veneni,
> sectantesque magis vitam spirantis odorem
> legis Athenaei paedorem linquite pagi.
> Quid labyrintheo, Thesidae, erratis in antro
> caecaque Daedalei lustratis limina tecti?

He calls on the Athenians, who are no doubt meant to stand for pagans
in general, to forsake the ''filth of the Athenian field'' and the ''barren
wasteland'' of their philosophy and religion:

> Parcite pulverei squalentia iugera campi
> et steriles habitare plagas, ubi gignere fructum
> arida nescit humus, nec de tellure cruenta
> livida mortiferis vellatis toxica sucis,
> Tartareo damnata cibo. . . . (1. 49-53)[23]

The Christian poet offers instead the pleasant green fields of paradise:

> . . . sed amoena virecta
> florentum semper nemorum sedesque beatas
> per latices intrate pios, ubi semina vitae
> divinis animantur aquis et fonte superno
> laetificata seges spinis mundatur ademptis,
> ut messis queat esse Dei mercisque futurae
> maxima centenum cumulare per horrea fructum. (1. 53-9)[24]

It would be a mistake, to be sure, to press Sedulius' statements in the letter to Macedonius or in the opening lines of the poem. Most pagan
readers, uninitiated into the Christian religion and not thoroughly
acquainted with the Bible, would have failed fully to understand the
Paschale carmen. The complex of Scriptural images, references, and
allegory in a passage like 1. 70-8 assumes considerable Christian
background on the part of its readers:

> Qui pereuntem hominem vetiti dulcedine pomi
> instauras meliore cibo potuque sacrati

---

[23] For another, more famous, application of wasteland imagery to a spiritual condi-
tion, see Augustine, *Conf.* 2. 10 (*CC* 27, 26):
> Defluxi abs te ego et erravi, deus meus, nimis devius ab stabilitate tua in adulescen-
> tia et factus sum mihi regio egestatis.

[24] Sedulius was neither the first nor the last Christian poet to apply the language of
Virgil's description of the Elysian fields to the Christian paradise. Cf. Prudentius, *Cath.*
3. 101, and Dracontius, *De laudibus Dei* 3. 752. Curtius, *European Literature*, p. 200, n. 31,
has a general discussion of the *locus amoenus* in Christian poetry.

sanguinis infusum depellis ab angue venenum,
qui genus humanum praeter quos clauserat arca
diluvii rapida spumantis mole sepultum
una iterum de stirpe creas, ut mystica virtus,
quod carnis delicta necant, hoc praesule ligno
monstraret liquidas renovari posse per undas,
totum namque lavans uno baptismate mundum.[25]

Sedulius takes it for granted that at least some in his audience possess a
thoroughgoing knowledge of Scripture. Without ever mentioning the
names of either Eve or Noah, he alludes to the temptation in the garden
of Eden (Gen. 3. 1-7) and the story of the flood (Gen. 7-8). He also
makes reference to the church ritual of baptism. It is hard to imagine
anyone unfamiliar with Christian doctrine and practice fully
appreciating the story of the flood as an allegory of baptism.[25]

In speaking of the pagan world as his audience Sedulius is no doubt
posturing to some extent. Addressing the pagans was a time-honored
Christian literary *topos*, and Sedulius still preserves the traditional appeal
to a pagan audience even though he pitches his poem at a level which
only a well informed Christian could appreciate.[26] Juvencus (to pick an
earlier poet with whom we know Sedulius to have been familiar) wrote
his verse rendition of the story of the Gospels shortly after the end of the
great persecutions begun by Diocletian and probably felt that pagan
readers could really make use of his Virgilian version of the Gospels.
There must have been many educated unbelievers who were attracted to
the truths of Christianity, but who, like the youthful Augustine, were put

---

[25] For early Christian interpretations of the flood, see J.P. Lewis, *A Study of the Interpretation of Noah and the Flood in Jewish and Christian Literature* (Leiden, 1968), pp. 101-20.

[26] Sedulius shows familiarity with a number of standard literary *topoi* especially in the
epistolary defense of his literary project. In his remarks to Macedonius, for instance,
Sedulius likens his subject to an ocean. He himself is an inexperienced sailor who feels
daunted by the prospect of crossing it in his little boat:

> Priusquam me, venerabilis pater, operis nostri decurso volumine censeas et rite for-
> san severitatis obiurges, utpote qui nulla veteris scientiae praerogativa suffultus tam
> inmensum paschalis pelagus maiestatis et viris quoque peritissimis formidandum
> parva tiro lintre cucurrerim: huius apud te facti causas expurgem, ut cum me non
> audacem fuisse probaveris sed devotum, in pectoris tui portum blanda tranquillitate
> recipias, quem gubernante Deo laetaberis nulla pertulisse naufragia.

On the conventionality of descriptions of literary composition in nautical terms, see Curtius, *European Literature*, pp. 128-130. See also Godo Lieberg, "Seefahrt und Werk:
Untersuchungen zu einer Metapher der antiken, besonders der lateinischen Literatur,
von Pindar bis Horaz," *Giornale italiano di filologia* 21 (1969), 209-40. We should also be
aware that Sedulius' self-depreciation, as for example, in his description of himself as a
tiro is a typical sentiment found in many literary prefaces of antiquity. For other conven-
tional protestations of literary incompetence, see Tore Janson, *Latin Prose Prefaces: Studies
in Literary Conventions*, Studia latina stockholmiensia 13 (Stockholm, 1964), pp. 124-41.

off by the unclassical style of the Christian Scriptures.[27] But when Sedulius wrote his biblical epic a century or so later the situation had changed dramatically. Christianity was now not only tolerated but had been made the state religion.

This is not to say, however, that the *topos* should be dismissed as having nothing at all to do with reality. The problem of audience is rarely a simple one for any writer. The imagined readership can change even as the author creates his work. He looks behind him at audiences of the past and ahead to a faceless posterity. Even when he has a definite popular audience in mind, he may still look over his shoulder to observe how the critical few, whose approval he ultimately seeks, are reacting to his efforts. Sedulius may very well have hoped that his poem would be as popular as Juvencus' and help to finish the conversion of pagans to Christianity. After all, there were still pagans left in the first half of the fifth century, and the Christian poet may have cherished some hope that unbelievers presented with his life of Christ and its redemptive significance would embrace the Christian Gospel, even though they might be able to catch on to only a little of the complicated allegorical exegesis of the *Paschale carmen*. Like the evangelists themselves and like Juvencus too, Sedulius believes in the universality of the Gospel's appeal and thus at one level conceives of his audience as the entire human race. In 1. 137, for example, the poet orders "all people" to pay attention to what he has to say: *mentes huc vertite cuncti*. It should be added that it is also quite possible that the author of the *Paschale carmen* was directing his address to the pagans not only to outright unbelievers but also to "nominal Christians," who were dedicated to the learning and culture of the Greek and Roman past, like, for instance, Ausonius, Jovius (the correspondent of Paulinus of Nola), and Licentius (the poet and friend of Augustine).[28] But at another, more intimate level, it is clear that Sedulius has an initiated audience in mind. The poet's immediate intended readers are the circle of Macedonius, fifth-century orthodox Christians, devoted and knowledgable believers, concerned not only with the general problem of paganism but also with Christian heresy. This is the audience of the *Paschale carmen* with which we will be concerned in the following pages.

---

[27] Augustine complains of this in *Conf.* 3. 5:
   Non enim sicut modo loquor, ita sensi, cum attendi ad illam scripturam, sed visa est mihi indigna, quam Tullianae dignitati comparem.
[28] For this last point I am indebted to the observations of Professor Roberts.

iii. *The Poet as Teacher and Polemicist*

Despite Curtius' suggestion that the main purpose of Sedulius' *Paschale carmen* was to enable its author to show off his "grandiloquence" or "strut about in the frippery of the pagan school rhetor,"[29] there is every reason to believe that Sedulius did not write his work in academic isolation, removed from the problems of contemporary life and thought. In fact, Sedulius presents himself in the *Paschale carmen* as engaged not only with a text but with people, like himself, who are occupied with the interpretation of that text. The proper understanding of various biblical passages was critical for a number of doctrinal positions taken by fifth-century Christians, and Sedulius' interpretation of Scripture in the *Paschale carmen* often reflects these larger hermeneutical issues.

Like other Latin poets before him, Sedulius was concerned to make his poetry not only sweet (*dulce*) but useful (*utile*). When the Christian poet describes his work to Macedonius, he stresses its didactic and edifying intentions. Indeed, he practically apologizes to Macedonius for his use of verse. Sedulius explains that the metrical form will make what he has to say more attractive:

> Cur autem metrica voluerim haec ratione conponere, non differam breviter expedire. Raro, pater optime, sicut vestra quoque peritia lectionis adsiduitate cognoscit, divinae munera potestatis stilo quisquam huius modulationis aptavit, et multi sunt quos studiorum saecularium disciplina per poeticas magis delicias et carminum voluptates oblectat. Hi quicquid rhetoricae facundiae perlegunt, neglegentius adsequuntur, quoniam illud haud diligunt: quod autem versuum viderint blandimento mellitum, tanta cordis aviditate suscipiunt, ut in alta memoria saepius haec iterando constituant et reponant. Horum itaque mores non repudiandos aestimo sed pro insita consuetudine vel natura tractandos, ut quisque suo magis ingenio voluntarius adquiratur Deo.

To judge from his remarks to Macedonius, Sedulius has intentions which go beyond stylistic concerns, even though he also hopes to satisfy to some degree his audience's taste for *poeticas delicias* and *carminum voluptates*. Like Lucretius, Sedulius describes his verse composition as medicine made sweet with honey,[30] and, like the *De rerum natura*, which inculcates the teaching of Epicurus and attacks other views, the *Paschale carmen* also has a didactic and polemical purpose.[31]

---

[29] Curtius, *European Literature*, p. 148 and p. 460.

[30] *De rerum natura* 1. 936-50 and 4. 11-25. For the same metaphor, see also Lactantius, *Inst.* 1. 1. 14, and Jerome, *Ep.* 133. 3. 7. K. Thraede investigates this *topos* more fully in "Untersuchungen zum Ursprung und zur Geschichte der christlichen Poesie," *JbAC* 5 (1962), 149-50. For the *voluptas* of poetry, see Quintilian, *Inst.* 10. 1. 28.

[31] See *De rerum natura* 1. 635-704, for example, for an attack on Heraclitus and the Stoics.

The didactic intentions of the *Paschale carmen* are clear. In fact, literary
historians have often assumed that the *Paschale carmen* (along with other
biblical epics of Late Antiquity) was written for use in Christian education.[32] It is tempting to read Sedulius' allusion to memorization in the
letter to Macedonius (*ut in alta memoria saepius haec iterando constituant et
reponant*) as a reference to the poem's intended use in school. The
reference could just as easily, of course, be applied to adult readers. We
do know, however, that at least one other biblical epic of Late Antiquity
was intended for Christian children. In the preface to his *Alethia* (vv. 104-
107), Sedulius' contemporary, Claudius Marius Victor, writes:

> dum teneros formare animos et corda paramus
> ad verum virtutis iter puerilibus annis
> inclita legiferi quod pandunt scrinia Moysis
> quae sit origo poli vel quae primordia mundi. . . .

Sedulius himself was a "curriculum author" who enjoyed considerable
popularity in the schools already in the early Middle Ages,[33] and it is not
at all impossible that, like Claudius Marius Victor, he intended his
biblical poem to be a "school epic."[34]

In this connection it is often pointed out that when Julian the Apostate
passed a decree in June of 362 banning Christians from teaching in the
schools, a Christian father and son of Laodicaea (both named
Apollinarius) set parts of the Bible to verse in order to replace authors
like Homer, whose works were traditionally taught in the schools.[35]
Although it has often been assumed that the origins of the biblical epic
are to be sought in this event, it should be remembered that Juvencus
composed his Virgilian version of the Gospels long before 362. We have
no hard evidence, either, to prove definitely that Sedulius intended his
poem to be read by school children as a replacement for Virgil or that

[32] Labriolle, *History and Literature*, p. 313, for instance, makes the following observation:
> It was a question with them [the biblical poets], in the first place, of being helpful
> to young minds by instilling into them sacred teaching transposed in an attractive
> form, expurgated of those difficult details with which certain episodes in the Bible
> might oppress their youthful imaginations.

[33] On Sedulius and other biblical epic poets of late antiquity as "curriculum authors"
in the Middle Ages, see Curtius, *European Literature*, pp. 49 ff.

[34] K. Thraede uses this descriptive term in his article on "Epos" in *RAC* 5, 991.

[35] Julian, *Ep.* 42 (36). For a translatation, see J. Stevenson, *Creeds, Councils, and Controversies* (New York, 1966), pp. 71-3. See also G. Downey, "The Emperor Julian and
the Schools," *CJ* 53 (1957), 97-103. Gustave Bardy, "L'église et l'enseignement au IVᵉ
siècle," *RSR* 14 (1934), 542-9, casts some doubt on the connection between Julian's
decree and the poetic activity of the Apollinarii. For a general discussion of Christian
teachers in pagan schools in Late Antiquity, see M.L.W. Laistner, "Pagan Schools and
Christian Teachers," *Liber floridus: Mittellateinische Studien* (St. Ottilien, 1950), pp. 47-61.

he wrote it with the needs of catechetical instruction in mind. But
whether the poet meant the *Paschale carmen* to be read by children, or
adults, or both, his general instructive intentions are clear. The purpose
of the work, as Sedulius himself explains it in the prefatory letter to
Macedonius, is: *ut quisque suo magis ingenio voluntarius adquiratur Deo.*
Sedulius is clearly interested not only in entertaining but also in edifying
his audience.[36]

Let us consider, by way of illustration, the poet's treatment of the Old
Testament episodes which he retells in the first book of his poem. Far
from being mindless literary exercises, Sedulius' retellings of these
biblical stories are very pointed indeed, designed to instruct the faithful,
not only to dazzle them with virtuosity. Sedulius concentrates on events
from the Old Testament which "teach" of the coming Messiah. The ram
caught in the bush, for example, which Abraham sacrifices in place of his
son Isaac, is a type of Christ:

> O iusti mens sancta viri! Pietate remota
> plus pietatis habens contempsit vulnera nati
> amplexus praecepta Dei, typicique cruoris
> auxilio ventura docet, quod sanguine Christi
> humana pro gente pius occumberet agnus. (1. 116-20)

The story of Abraham and Isaac teaches (*docet*) us what Christ will do as
the lamb of God. The Genesis account of the near-sacrifice of Isaac does
not explicitly mention Christ or his coming sacrifice, but for Sedulius, as
for his Christian contemporaries, the Hebrew Scriptures are filled with
shadows, types, and references, all of them pointing to Christ and the
events of his life, passion, and death.[37] Joshua is another Old Testament
character whose name and life prefigure Jesus, according to Sedulius:

> Sol stetit ad Gabaon mediique cacumine caeli
> fixit anhelantem dilato vespere lucem,
> insolitus frenare diem, nec luna cucurrit
> ordine pigra suo, donec populantibus armis
> fervidus ingentem gladius consumeret hostem
> coniurante polo: iam tunc famulata videbant
> sidera venturum praemisso nomine Iesum. (1. 163-9)

---

[36] On the interrelationship between exegesis, edification, and entertainment in the
Christian poetry of Late Antiquity, see Reinhart Herzog, "Exegese-Erbauung-*Delectatio*:
Beiträge zu einer christlichen Poetik der Spätantike," in Walter Haug, ed., *Formen und
Funktionen der Allegorie: Symposion Wolfenbüttel 1978*, Germanistische Symposien-
Berichtsbände 3 (Stuttgart, 1979), pp. 52-69.

[37] The Christological interpretation of the Old Testament, of course, goes back to the
first century. See, for example, Krister Stendahl, *The School of St. Matthew and its Use of
the Old Testament* (Philadelphia, 1968).

Christ was also himself present, Sedulius tells his readers, at the crossing
of the Red Sea as the *vox Domini* (1. 143-4) and as the rock from which
water sprang in the wilderness, when Moses struck it with his rod (1. 158-
9). Clearly Sedulius' intentions here go beyond simply improving the
style of his original. The Christian poet is also a Christian teacher. As
Sedulius relates Old Testament narratives, they are told from a distinctively Christian perspective and given a distinctively Christian point.

    Didactic intentions are frequently connected with polemical. The poet-
teacher is able to make his own doctrine clearer by stating his objections
to ideas which he does not consider correct. Sedulius identifies viewpoints
with which he does not agree and takes issue with them, as, for instance,
he does with Judaism. The Jews have not recognized Christ in their
Scriptures, nor did they acknowledge him as Messiah when he was in
their midst. When the poet tells of the Father's response to Jesus' request
to glorify his name (cf. John 12. 28), he attacks Jesus' contemporaries for
confusing the voice of God with thunder:

> Ac nec sic agnoscere Christum
> gens voluit Iudaea Deum; pars esse ferebat
> hoc tonitruum, pars angelicam crepuisse loquellam.
> O gens caeca oculis, o gens durissima corde! (5. 11-14)

Sedulius holds the leaders of the Jews responsible for the crucifixion. The
people to whom Jesus came as a king have done away with him:

> Plange sacerdotes perituros, plange ministros
> et populum, Iudaea, tuum pro talibus ausis.
> Non tuba, non unctus, non iam tua victima grata est.
> Quaenam bella tibi clanget tuba, rege perempto? (5. 351-4)

    If Sedulius is a harsh critic of the Jews, he is even more polemical when
he must deal with Christian heretics. Unlike his predecessor Juvencus,
who criticizes the Jews but does not mention heresies, the fifth-century
poet saves his most vehement attacks for Christian heretics.[38] The two
aberrations from orthodoxy which Sedulius singles out for explicit mention in the *Paschale carmen* are Sabellianism and Arianism.

    The heretic Sabellius is a somewhat shadowy figure in church history,
who seems (like Praxeas before him) to have blurred the distinction
between Father and Son. Praxeas, a Patripassionist, as adherents of this
doctrine were also sometimes called, taught the complete identity of the
Father and the Son. It was actually the Father, according to this view,

---

[38] For an exhaustive study of Juvencus on the Jews, see J.M. Poinsotte, *Juvencus et
Israël. La représentation des Juifs dans le premier poème latin chrétien* (Paris, 1979). On Sedulius
and the Jews, see H. Schreckenberg, "Juden und Judentum in der altkirchlichen
lateinischen Poesie," *Theokratia* 3 (1973-5), 81-124.

who suffered, died, and rose from the dead. Sabellius seems to have systematized modalist doctrine, attributing to God three modes of operation: as Father, creator; as Son, redeemer; as Spirit, sanctifier. The Father was the primary essence, which could also express itself as Son and Spirit. Sabellius was excommunicated under Pope Callistus (AD 217-222).[39] Sedulius mentions him only in passing in Book 1:

> Rursus: ego atque Pater unum sumus. Arrius unum
> debet scire sumusque Sabellius esse fatendum.
> Iste fidem ternam, hic non amplectitur unam. (1. 322-4)

The heresy of Arius seems to distress the poet even more than Sabellianism. Sedulius devotes 24 lines (1. 299-322) to a blistering critique of *Arrius infelix* and his ideas. Arius was an Alexandrian priest (d. 336) who began to expound in 318-19 his doctrine of the Son of God who could not have existed from eternity.[40] According to his will, Arius declared, Christ was capable of evil as well as of virtue and was creature and created. This heresy was rejected by a local synod in Alexandria around 320 and then condemned at the famous council gathered at Nicaea in 325 by the emperor Constantine. In his attack on Arius, Sedulius even reproduces some of the terminology of the Nicene Creed, which was drafted at the council:

> At Dominus, verbum, virtus, sapientia, Christus,
> et totum commune Patris, de lumine lumen,
> de solo solus, cui nec minus est Patre quicquam,
> nec quo crescat habet, genitus, non quippe creatus:
> ipse est principium. Nam sicut clarus habetur
> in genitore manens, genitor quoque clarus in ipso
> permanet, et rerum caput est Deus unus ubique. (1. 312-18)

The Arian idea that Christ did not exist from eternity because there must have been a time when he was begotten as the Son and, therefore, a time when he did not exist is steadfastly denied by our poet. Father and Son are different persons of the Godhead, but, as Sedulius explains in 1. 319-20, they share in the same substance:

> Non quia qui summus Pater est, et Filius hic est,
> sed quia quod summus Pater est, et Filius hoc est.

Arianism was probably of greater interest to Sedulius than Sabellianism because it was a more contemporary heresy. Sabellianism was something of a dead issue by the fifth century, but the heresy to

---

[39] See *NCE* 12, 783 for a concise discussion of Sabellianism.
[40] See Sozomen, *Historia ecclesiastica* 1. 15 ff. (*PG* 67, 903 ff.). For my overview of the Arian controversy, I am indebted to J.N.D. Kelly, *Early Christian Doctrines*, 2nd ed. (New York, 1960), pp. 223-309.

which Arius gave his name was still very much on the minds of orthodox Christians contemporary with Sedulius. Although by the end of the fourth century the Nicaean faith had been made the official religion of the Roman empire by the emperors Gratian, Valentinian II, and Theodosius I,[41] Arianism was still very popular among the Germans, thanks largely to the efforts of Ulfilas. After his consecration as bishop by Eusebius of Nicomedia in 341, Ulfilas had returned as an Arian apostle to his own people. He invented a Gothic alphabet, translated the Bible, and gave the Goths the Arian creed of the council of Constantinople.[42] Thus, as the brand of Christianity to which the barbarians were converted, the Arian heresy continued to trouble orthodox Christianity long after the death of Arius. In the first half of the fifth century the Arians were still a political, social, and military threat. Alaric and his barbarian troops entered the walls of the city of Rome in 410. By the time of Augustine's death in 430, the Vandals had advanced in Africa as far east as Hippo. By 439 they had taken Carthage, and in 455 under the leadership of Gaiseric they had captured Rome itself.

Not only in his explicit attack of Arius and Sabellius but throughout the *Paschale carmen*, Sedulius' orthodoxy is evident. When he retells the story of the gifts of the Magi, for example, Sedulius explains to an imagined interlocutor that the number of the gifts brought to Christ is an indication of the Trinity (a doctrine which the Gospels themselves do not explicitly set forth in detail):

> Cur tria dona tamen? Quoniam spes maxima vitae est
> hunc numerum confessa fides, et tempora summus
> cernens cuncta Deus, praesentia, prisca, futura,
> semper adest semperque fuit semperque manebit
> in triplici virtute sui. (2. 97-101)

Here and elsewhere in the *Paschale carmen* Sedulius is at pains to make it clear that his Son is not the same as the Father. There are three persons in the Godhead, as Sedulius informs Sabellius in the first book of the poem. When Jesus weeps, for instance, at the tomb of Lazarus (*Paschale carmen* 4. 276), Sedulius describes him as crying not as God but as a man: *Flebat et omnipotens, sed corpore non deitate*. But Sedulius also insists *contra* Arius that the Son is no less divine than the Father. Sedulius' Christ is *omnipotens*, true God as well as true man, existing along with the Father before the creation of the world. In the *Paschale carmen* Christ is described as *rerum creator* (2. 38), *genitor rerum* (4. 13), *conditor* (4. 254), *auctor* (5. 104),

---

[41] See *Cod. Theod.* 16. 1-2. For a translation, see Stevenson, *Creeds, Councils, and Controversies*, p. 160.

[42] On Ulfilas, see Theodoret, *Historia ecclesiastica* 4. 37 (*PG* 82, 1196-7).

and *mundi pater* (4. 181; 5. 49). Sedulius' Son and Father share the same substance; they are one (*ego atque Pater unum sumus*) even though they are different persons in the Godhead.

It would be a mistake to dismiss Sedulius' heated theological polemics against heretics like Sabellius and Arius as so much "sound and fury." Even Edward Gibbon, who had little patience himself with theology, admits the importance that such issues assumed for Christians of Late Antiquity. "These speculations," he writes in *Decline and Fall of the Roman Empire*, "instead of being treated as the amusement of a vacant hour, became the most serious business of the present, and the most useful preparation for a future life."[43] Sedulius and his fifth-century contemporaries took theological questions, such as the problem of Christ's relationship to the other members of the Trinity, as seriously as other people at other times have taken the pressing political, economic, or social issues of their day. To conclude, despite Sedulius' own declaration of his intentions in the prefatory letter to Macedonius and the general didactic and polemical tone of the *Paschale carmen*, that the piece was meant to be no more than a stylistic exercise is simply perverse. To be sure, Sedulius is interested in paraphrasing biblical stories in altered language and style, but clearly he has other, less detached, intentions as well. This Christian poet is engaged not only with a text but also with contemporary or near contemporary religious ideas, hermeneutical issues, and ecclesiastical personalities, all of them of considerable interest and relevance to late antique readers like Macedonius and his friends who shared Sedulius' particular vision of the Christian faith.

iv. *Sedulius and the Nestorian Controversy*

Unlike the third and fourth centuries which witnessed the emergence of Trinitarian disputes centering around the question of the Son's connection with the Father, the fifth century saw a growing interest in the question of Christ's nature as God-man. Was Christ perfectly God, perfectly man, or both? Around these issues a number of notorious theological battles were waged during the first half of the century. Even though Sedulius does not explicitly enter into any of these controversies in the *Paschale carmen*, several passages in the poem and indeed the overall thrust of the work would appear to have special relevance in the light of fifth-century Christological issues. Sedulius' portrait of Christ, while drawn from Gospel sources, is not exactly the same as the Gospels'.

---

[43] As quoted by Gerhart Ladner, "The Impact of Christianity" in *The Transformation of the Roman World*, ed. Lynn White (Berkeley, 1966), p. 66, n. 22.

Christ is presented in the *Paschale carmen* as perfectly divine, as God even
in the manger, as the miraculous, powerful Savior, with the emphasis on
his status as Son of God rather than Son of Man. Sedulius attacks the
familiar Trinitarian heresies of Sabellius and Arius by name in the
Paschale carmen, but his representation of Christ may be directed at a more
contemporary (and relevant) Christological heresy which burst onto the
theological scene in the second quarter of the fifth century—
Nestorianism.

Let us briefly review the controversy here. Nestorius himself was a
gifted preacher brought from Antioch to Constantinople in 428 to fill the
vacant bishopric there, who shortly after his arrival began to reject the
term *theotokos* as it was commonly used to describe Mary.[44] Nestorius did
not feel that the infant Jesus could be properly described as God. This
position caused great offence among clergy and laity who were used to
acknowledging Christ's divinity without qualification. Nestorius sent
Pope Celestine in Rome an explanation (Nestorius preferred *Christotokos*
as a Marian epithet), but the reaction to this teaching in the West and
especially in Alexandria was violently antipathetical.[45] Cyril, bishop of
Alexandria, sent letters (*Ep*. 2 and *Ep*. 4) to Nestorius warning him of
the possibility of heresy. A synod which met in Rome in August of 430
condemned Nestorius' Christological views as did a synod in Alexandria
in November of the same year. Cyril wrote another letter (*Ep*. 17) to
Nestorius containing twelve anathemas and Nestorius, in turn, asked
Theodosius II to convoke a council.

Nestorius was perceived by his opponents as asserting that "the Word
was a mere man."[46] In particular, his separation of the divine and
human natures in Christ seemed to open up the possibility of viewing
Christ as a God-bearing man only or as a man actuated by God the
Word. When seen in such a light, Nestorius' reluctance to use *theotokos*
and his emphasis on the distinction between the two natures of Christ
must have seemed to many to place him in the same camp as Arius and
other earlier heresiarchs who had undermined the divinity of Christ.[47] In

---

[44] For this and other details of Nestorius' ecclesiastical career, see Socrates, *Historia
ecclesiastica* 7. 29 ff. (*PG* 67, 801 ff.).

[45] News of Nestorius' heresy spread as far west as Gaul. At the invitation of Leo, the
archdeacon of Rome (later to become pope), John Cassian wrote a work (*De incarnatione*)
devoted to refuting the bishop of Constantinople. For a discussion, see Owen Chadwick,
John Cassian, 2nd ed. (Cambridge, 1968), p. 141.

[46] Nestorius himself later claimed that he shared the same Christology as Pope Leo I
and that his views had been misrepresented. See his self-defense in *The Bazaar of
Heracleides*, G.R. Driver and L. Hodgson, eds. (Oxford, 1925).

[47] Cyril actually quotes the Nicene creed against Nestorius in his third letter to him
in *Ep*. 17 (*PG* 77, 109).

fact, the tradition of Antiochene Christology to which Nestorius' doctrine belonged had long been known for its emphasis on the full humanity of Christ. Antiochenes like Theodore, bishop of Mopsuestia from 392 to 429, were well known for concentrating on Jesus' manhood rather than his godhead.[48] Western theologians like Hilary of Poitiers, on the other hand, could maintain that Christ ate and drank not because his body needed nourishment but only in conformity with custom (see *De trinitate* 10. 24). Alexandrians especially felt that the Antiochene emphasis endangered the divinity of Christ and was heretical.

If Nestorius did not believe that the divine and human natures of Christ could be completely united and preferred to speak of a connection or close participation of natures while thinking of unity only at the level of personality, Cyril, his adversary, insisted on the unity of natures. The Council of Ephesus met to decide the question in June of 431 with Cyril presiding. Nestorius refused to appear before it and was condemned, deposed, and excommunicated. But his supporters held a rival council a few days later at which they deposed Cyril. The emperor Theodosius, despairing of a solution, decided to treat both as deposed and dissolved the council in September of 431. Cyril eventually returned to Alexandria, while Nestorius was sent to a monastery at Antioch.[49]

The Council of Ephesus was hardly a decisive one, and the Nestorian controversy continued to be troublesome through the 430s and 440s. Theodoret of Cyrrhus took Nestorius' side and published an extensive attack in 431 on Cyril and the decision of the Council. He also became involved in a controversy over the monophysite views of Eutyches, who maintained a position directly opposite to Nestorius, insisting that there was only one nature in the Son of God—the view of Christ popular especially in Egypt at this time. At the "Robber Synod" of Ephesus in 449, which was charged with putting an end to Nestorianism, Theodoret was deposed, but he was reinstated at the Council of Chalcedon (451) after he pronounced an anathema upon Nestorius.[50] At this same council both the heresies of Nestorius and Eutyches were condemned and there was formulated once and for all the orthodox definition of the Lord Jesus Christ, born of the Virgin Mary *theotokos*, with only one person, perfectly God and perfectly man, "to be acknowledged in two natures, without

---

[48] See, for example, fragments of *De incarnatione* in H. B. Swete's edition of Theodore's commentaries on the Pauline epistles (Cambridge, 1882), II, pp. 290-312.

[49] Evagrius, *Historia ecclesiastica* 1. 7 (*PG* 86. 2, 2433 ff.). For my survey of the events of 428-431 as well as for my discussion of the Council of Chalcedon, I am indebted to R.V. Sellars, *The Council of Chalcedon* (London, 1953), pp. 3-29 and pp. 103-31.

[50] J.D. Mansi, *Sacrorum conciliorum nova et amplissima collectio* (Paris and Leipzig, 1901-1927), VII, p. 189.

confusion, without change, without division, without separation; the
distinction of natures in no way abolished because of the union. . . .''[51]
Chalcedon represented a decisive defeat for the Nestorians, but the
heresy continued to be popular in the East—the Syrian church of Persia
adopted Nestorianism at the Synod of Seleucia in 486—and eventually
even reached as far east as China.[52]

A close reading of several passages in the *Paschale carmen* suggests that
Sedulius was not unaware of the major Christological points of view
which clashed so dramatically in the first part of the fifth century. For
instance, in the second book of the *Paschale carmen*, Sedulius treats of the
incarnation of Christ in the following way:

> Haec ventura senes posquam dixere prophetae,
> angelus intactae cecinit properata Mariae:
> et dictum comitata fides, uterumque puellae
> sidereum mox implet onus, rerumque creator
> nascendi sub lege fuit. Stupet innuba tensos
> virgo sinus gaudetque suum paritura parentem. (2. 35-40)

The poet is clearly interested in the divine nature of Mary's son. He
repeats the idea of the infant Jesus' divinity three times: "A starry
burden fills Mary's womb; the creator of the world is obliged to be born;
a virgin is about to give birth to her own father." In the last line, as he
highlights the paradoxical nature of Christ's birth, Sedulius uses an
oxymoron, *paritura parentem*, a phrase closely resembling *Deipara*, the
usual Latin translation of *theotokos*. In 2. 62, Sedulius also quite explicitly
calls the helpless baby in the manger God (*et angusto Deus in praesepe
quievit*). Given the importance of the idea of *theotokos* in contemporary
Christology, the poet's stress on Christ's divinity even as an infant is
most likely more than a coincidence.[53]

Sedulius' failure to mention important figures in the Nestorian controversy by name in the *Paschale carmen* has been seen as proof for a date
of composition before 431. Karl Leimbach argues that this Christological
controversy was so well known that Sedulius' poem about the life and
deeds of Christ would have explicitly referred to Nestorius or Cyril if it
had been written after 431.[54] Leimbach's argument is *ex silentio*, however,

---

[51] The translation is from Stevenson, *Creeds, Councils, and Controversies*, p. 337.
[52] For a fuller discussion of the fortunes of the Nestorians after Chalcedon, see Aubrey
R. Vine, *The Nestorian Churches* (London, 1937), pp. 37 ff.
[53] The expression *theotokos* had been applied to Mary long before the Nestorian controversy broke, but its use only became controversial in the second quarter of the fifth
century (see Kelly, *Early Christian Doctrines*, p. 311).
[54] Karl Leimbach, *Über den christlichen Dichter Caelius Sedulius and dessen Carmen paschale*
(Goslar, 1879), pp. 59-60, as quoted in Nicholas Scheps, *Paschale carmen, Boek I en II*, p.
17, n. 5:

and therefore questionable. For one thing, Nestorius' teaching was known in Rome and elsewhere already in 429. Why should 431 be chosen as the *terminus ante quem?* Furthermore, and more important, the lack of explicit mention in the *Paschale carmen* does not necessarily prove that Sedulius was unfamiliar with Nestorius. It was not all that uncommon in the fifth century to leave one's theological opponents unmentioned by name. Cyril defends *theotokos* and attacks Nestorius' Christological dualism in 430 in a critical examination of a collection of Nestorius' sermons, which although clearly aimed at Nestorius does not once refer to him by name.[55] If he were living in the eastern half of the empire, Sedulius may have felt it unwise to attack this popular heresy openly. If the Macedonian circle was an intimate one, it may simply have seemed unnecessary.[56]

Whether Sedulius intended to attack Nestorius himself in the *Paschale carmen* is largely a moot point. The Christological point of view which Nestorius represented was larger than Nestorius himself. The bishop of Constantinople's Christology was already in existence long before its most famous popularizer appeared on the scene and continued to thrive long after his death. But even if Sedulius had never heard of Nestorius, we can be sure (if the *Paschale carmen* appeared between AD 425-450) that at least some of its first readers would have read this Christocentric poem

---

> Nun aber ist das fünfte Jahrhundert die Zeit, in welcher das Morgenland die Fragen nach der Person Christi zu lösen suchte und den Streit über die eine oder die beiden Naturen in Christo mit grossem Eifer . . . geführt hat. Da auch das Abendland . . . an der richtigen Entscheidung deiser Streitfragen lebhaftes Interesse hatte . . . so lässt sich von Sedulius, falls er nach 431 geschrieben hatte, ein Eingehen auf diese Fragen um so mehr erwarten, da sich sein ganzes Gedicht mit dem Leben und den Taten Christi beschäftigte. . . . Die Namen des Cyrill oder des Nestorius erwähnt er mit keiner Silbe. . . . Aus diesen Gründen setze ich die Abfassung des *Carmen paschale* vor das Jahr 431 p. Chr., vor das Ephesinum.

Despite the rather tenuous basis for Leimbach's dating of the *Paschale carmen*, it has been picked up and repeated by some of the literary handbooks (e.g., Altaner, *Patrologie*, p. 411).

[55] *Adversus Nestorii blasphemias* (*PG* 76, 9-248). See the discussion in Johannes Quasten, *Patrology* III (Utrecht and Antwerp, 1966), p. 126.

[56] Other Christian Latin poems of Late Antiquity besides Sedulius' may also contain such oblique references to contemporary heresies or schisms. Critics have suggested, for example, that Prudentius' *Apotheosis* was really intended to attack Priscillianism, a contemporary heresy, even though the author does not mention it by name. Prudentius only inveighs explicitly against Jews, Ebionites, and Manichaeans, but Ronald Rank has argued in "The *Apotheosis* of Prudentius: A Structural Analysis," *CF* 20 (1966), 28 that even though "the names he used are those of men long dead, and the heresies he denounces had been long ago condemned . . . Prudentius' concern was real, directed squarely at a doctrinal problem in this own native Spain. This error, called Priscillianism, began in Spain in 370. . . ." For a similar contextual approach applied to Avitus, see Daniel Nodes, "Avitus of Vienne's *Spiritual History* and the Semi-Pelagian Controversy. The Doctrinal Implications of Books I-III," *VC* 38 (1984), 185-95.

against the Christological background with which they were most familiar, a background dominated by the Nestorian controversy. We find at least one reader of the *Paschale carmen* still quoting it, even a century later, against those "who are boiling over with the pestilential breath of Nestorius and Eutyches" (*qui Nestorii et Eutychis pestifero vapore fervetis*).[57] In his *Expositio Psalmorum* (*ps.* 81 *conclusio*), Cassiodorus (c. AD 490-c. 583) cites *Paschale carmen* 1. 325 (Sedulius' attack on Arius and Sabellius: *ambo errore pares, quamquam diversa sequantur*) to refute the Nestorians, who, he declares, erroneously believe that there are two natures and two persons in Christ the Lord, and the Eutychians, who claim that Christ has only one nature. It is more than likely that other readers of Sedulius' Christocentric poem in Late Antiquity besides Cassiodorus read the *Paschale carmen* not as a curious literary exercise but as a work which lent support to their own view of Christ and contradicted others.

v. *The Christ of the Paschale carmen*

Whether or not Sedulius intended it to be so, the *Paschale carmen* turned out to be a work which could speak to the most burning questions of the fifth century. Any poem which featured Christ as its hero was bound to be of the greatest interest to the majority of Sedulius' contemporaries and the *Paschale carmen* is centered around the person and work of Christ. Even when Sedulius retells stories from the Old Testament in Book 1 which do not directly involve Christ, his approach is still Christocentric. The Christian poet includes Old Testament episodes in his epic only because he considers them good prefatory material to what will occupy him for the rest of the poem: the miracles which Christ did with the assistance of the Father's power:

> Per digesta rudis necnon miracula legis
> dicemus, sancti coniuncto Spiritus actu
> quae Natus socia Patris virtute peregit. (1. 294-6)

Unlike Claudius Marius Victor, Avitus, and other biblical poets of Late Antiquity who retold the story of creation and the origins of mankind, Sedulius expresses little interest in such intriguing Old Testament subjects as the creation of the world, the history of the Northern and Southern Kingdoms, the Psalms, or the prophets. The *Paschale carmen*'s concerns are primarily soteriological rather than cosmological or historical.

Whether Sedulius takes his stories from the Old or the New Testament, Christ is at the center of his attention. Incidents which do not

---

[57] I use the translation of James J. O'Donnell in *Cassiodorus* (Berkeley, 1979), p. 152.

center around Christ are excluded from Books 2-5 of the *Paschale carmen*.
So, for instance, Sedulius says not a word about the death of John the
Baptist, even though this event receives quite a bit of attention in Matthew. The *Paschale carmen*'s cast of Gospel characters is drastically
reduced, and the poet tells us much less about them than we learn from
the Gospels. Sedulius has time only for his central character. Everyone
else moves in his shadow. We hear nothing, for instance, of Nicodemus,
Caiphas, or Jesus' brothers. Joseph, his earthly father, is never mentioned, not even in Sedulius' recounting of the nativity. Mary is an
exception, but even in his adulatory address of her in 2. 63-72 Sedulius
makes it clear that his regard for her is based upon her intimate connection with Christ. The mother's perpetual virginity probably reflects more
on her son than herself. The disciples are introduced on occasion, but
only a few are mentioned by name, and frequently their presence is
ignored altogether, as in Sedulius' version of the wedding of Cana (3.
1-11).

Sedulius' selectivity with regard to his Gospel sources goes even further. His particular focus is on Christ the great miracle worker. The subject of the *Paschale carmen*, as Sedulius announces in the first lines of his
poem, is *clara miracula Christi*. In his treatment of the life of Christ, therefore, Sedulius proceeds to eliminate a lot of the non-miraculous events
recorded in the Gospels. The *Paschale carmen* never even mentions the sermon on the mount, the parables, or Jesus' great controversies with the
Pharisees. Moreover, in episodes included in the *Paschale carmen* which
are not obviously miracles, such as the baptism of Jesus, Sedulius will
often insert a miraculous element. So, for instance, when Jesus steps into
the Jordan, the poet tells us:

> Senserunt elementa Deum, mare fugit, et ipse
> Iordanis refluas cursum convertit in undas. (2. 162-3)

The Gospel writers make no allusion to the Jordan's flowing backward
at Jesus' baptism. Sedulius borrows the image from Psalm 114. 5 and
applies it here in order to make the event even more supernatural than
its description in the Gospel suggests.

Sedulius will also often highlight a miraculous feature in a Gospel narrative and give it a prominence which it did not enjoy in the original.
When he discusses the darkness which occurred during the crucifixion,
for instance, the poet devotes far more time to wondering at this remark-
able phenomenon than he does to describing Christ's suffering:

> Interea horrendae subito venere tenebrae
> et totum tenuere polum maestisque nigrantem
> exequiis texere diem; sol nube coruscos

abscondens radios, tetro velatus amictu,
delituit tristemque infecit luctibus orbem.
Hunc elementa sibi meruerunt cernere vultum,
auxiliis orbata patris, laetata per ortum,
maesta per occasum. (5. 232-9)

Sedulius chooses to emphasize the miracle of the darkness at noon instead
of Jesus' inability to carry his cross, for instance, or his cry of anguish:
"My God, my God, why have you forsaken me?"[58] Like the serene
figure depicted by a contemporary artist on the doors of the church of
Santa Sabina in Rome (c. 422-432), Sedulius' Christ, even when
crucified, is relatively unperturbed. The *Paschale carmen* represents the
crucifixion as a moment of triumph rather than defeat: *et cruce conplexum
Christus regit undique mundum* (5. 195). At the moment of his most obvious
helplessness, even on Golgotha, Jesus is still God, still superior to nature.
At the hour of his crucifixion nature mourns to bid Christ farewell, just
as the elements rejoiced to greet their Lord in 3. 46-69 (the tempest on
Galilee):

Non erat illa feri pugnax audacia ponti,
in Dominum tumidas quae surgere cogeret undas,
nec metuenda truces agitabant flamina vires:
sed laetum exiliens Christo mare conpulit imum
obsequio fervere fretum, rapidoque volatu
moverunt avidas ventorum gaudia pinnas. (3. 64-9)

The picture of Christ with which one emerges from a reading of the
Paschale carmen is not of a "suffering servant," or of a profound teacher
who called himself "the son of man," but rather of a powerful miracle
worker. Sedulius' Christ actually does very little suffering at all. The
hero of the *Paschale carmen* is a fiercely independent and self-sufficient
character, quite remote from the mortals who surround him, who proceeds from the cradle to the cross in unruffled and majestic dignity. This
is a Christ who resembles the popular "holy men" of Late Antiquity, like
Simeon Stylites, St. Martin of Tours, and others, who effortlessly held
demons at bay, endured physical suffering with little regard, and
betrayed none of the usual signs of human frailty.[59]

---

[58] Sedulius does show Christ suffering on occasion, as when he is mocked by the
soldiers of Pilate (5. 93-103). But this is exceptional, and Sedulius does not dwell on the
episode for its own sake. Christ's abuse at the hand of the soldiers had a redemptive
purpose:

Namque per hos colaphos caput est sanabile nostrum,
haec sputa per Dominum nostram lavere figuram.
His alapis nobis libertas maxima plausit. (5. 101-3)

[59] On "holy men" in Late Antiquity, see Peter Brown, *The World of Late Antiquity*
(London, 1971), pp. 96-109. Sedulius' choice of *miracula Christi* as his thematic principle
as well as his structuring of Books 2-5 (see Chapter 5, below) suggest the influence of

Throughout the *Paschale carmen* Sedulius underscores Christ's full divinity. The poet, to be sure, assures his readers that Christ does have two natures, one of them divine, one human (cf. 1. 353 and 4. 97), but Sedulius does not pay equal attention to both natures. Christ is far more often referred to as *Deus* (see 2. 62, 96, 162, 216; 3. 275, 322, 338; 4. 110, 292, and 302) than as *vir* or *homo*. The hero of the *Paschale carmen* is described as *tonans* (an epithet which Virgil often uses of Jupiter) and *pater*. Sedulius also makes sure that we do not read in his poem any episode which fails to support the idea of the omnipotence and full divinity of Christ. Readers of the *Paschale carmen* never learn, for instance, about Christ losing his temper (see Mark 3. 5) or angrily driving the money changers out of the temple (see John 2. 13-22). Sedulius' Christ does not admit his ignorance of when the last day will be, nor does he ask the rich young ruler: "Why do you call me good?"

The general emphasis on the miraculous throughout the *Paschale carmen* helps Sedulius to emphasize the fulness of Christ's divinity, a timely fifth-century point. Jesus is never more clearly God than when he is doing something which ordinary mortals cannot do. Sedulius accentuates the "otherness" of the divine Christ and stresses the difference between the Redeemer and man who needs to be redeemed. Sedulius' Christ represents an intrusion of the divine into the world of humans, savoring more of the beyond than of the here and now. He is *salutifer*, as Sedulius describes him (1. 26), bringing divine healing and eternal salvation to his creation.

It should be clear by now that the *Paschale carmen* is not simply an anti-heretical tract but a positive expression as well of the author's view of Christ. In fact, Sedulius' Christology coincides essentially with that of western theologians like Leo I (440-461), which eventually won wide recognition at the Council of Chalcedon.[60] On the other hand, it is also clear—and this is the point which needs to be made here—that Sedulius is not a neutral (or unthinking) paraphrast of the Gospels. The author of the *Paschale carmen* obviously does not share the Christological beliefs popular at the time in Antioch and elsewhere in the East. Sedulius has his own distinctively fifth-century vision of Christ, the product of a Christology shared with some of his contemporaries and emphatically rejected by others, and it is revealed by the way in which he selects cer-

---

hagiography. The sequence of early life, followed by miracles and death, is standard in the genre. One of Sedulius' earliest imitators, Paulinus of Périgueux (as Professor Roberts has kindly pointed out to me), follows this same pattern in his life of Martin of Tours, as does Venantius Fortunatus.

[60] See, for instance, the conclusions of B. Gladysz, *Dogmatyczne Teksty w Poetyckich Utworach Seduliusa* (Posnan, 1930).

tain Scriptural elements for his poem and excludes others and by the way
in which he shapes and interprets Gospel narratives.

To do it justice, in sum, it makes better sense to view the *Paschale
carmen* as arising from within a specific set of historical and theological circumstances (or necessities) rather than as the product of an "inflated,
vain, soulless, and unintelligent rhetor's" need to show off.[61] There is little reason to think that Sedulius was merely "playing with forms" when
he wrote this Christocentric epic.[62] Christ was a very controversial subject in Late Antiquity and in the fifth century Christology could be (quite
literally) a matter of life and death. One thinks, for instance, of Proterius,
the bishop of Alexandria, who was killed by a mob of Monophysites
during Holy Week 457 for accepting the creed of Chalcedon.[63] In Late
Antiquity believers took their Christologies seriously. The usual percep-
tion of Sedulius as a "virtuoso" writing his *Paschale carmen* in isolation
from contemporary life and thought needs revision. Reading this text
against a specific historical and theological background suggests that the
author selected his subject material and interpreted it with a view to
addressing the concerns which most challenged Christian men and
women of the fifth century.

---

[61] Curtius, *European Literature*, p. 460.
[62] Curtius, *European Literature*, p. 462.
[63] See Jean Maspero, *Histoire des patriarches d'Alexandrie* (Paris, 1923), pp. 44-5.

CHAPTER THREE

TRADITION AND DESIGN

In the opening lines of the *Paschale carmen*, Sedulius complains that pagan poets have made falsehoods (*mendacia*) the subject of their "overblown" works and asks rhetorically why he should be silent about the truth, the famous miracles of the saving Christ: *cur . . . clara salutiferi taceam miracula Christi*? If Sedulius had really needed to justify his decision to treat the life of Christ in verse, his strongest appeal might have been to precedence. Christians had been making biblical narratives the subject of their poetry since the first half of the fourth century, and one of their favorite topics was the life of Christ—not a surprising choice in view of this story's fundamental importance for Christian kerygma and creed. Among the subjects adopted by Christian poets of Late Antiquity only the stories of Genesis could compete with the Gospels in popularity.[1] As we have seen, Juvencus, the first Latin biblical poet and perhaps the first Christian poet to write in Latin, chose to draw his subject matter from the four Gospels.[2] Juvencus' conception of the *vitalia gesta* of Christ as a fit subject for a poem was something of a literary master stroke. The Gospel has an easily identifiable literary structure. It is a powerful narrative with a clear beginning, middle, and end. In the fourth century, in addition, it was rapidly becoming the most important of all stories for a growing number of people. A few decades after Juvencus wrote his pioneering work, Proba retold the life of Christ in the second half of her Virgilian *Cento*, and around the turn of the fifth century, Prudentius wrote a hymn (*Cathemerinon* 9) in which he also related the life of Christ.[3] Thus, by the second quarter of the fifth century, there were actually a number of possible models before Sedulius as he set out in his "little

---

[1] The most thorough study of the poetic treatments of Genesis in Late Antiquity still remains S. Gamber's *Le livre de 'Genèse' dans la poésie latine au V*[e] *siècle* (Paris, 1899).

[2] Commodian, a Christian Latin poet whose homeland is assigned variously to Syria, Gaul, and Africa, may have anticipated Juvencus, but his dates are still debated. For the most recent (1961) edition of Commodian's poetry, see *Commodiani carmina*, ed. J. Martin, *CC* 128, 1-113. See also the discussion in Roberts, *Biblical Epic*, p. 74, n. 50.

[3] Christian poets also, of course, retold individual episodes from the Gospels. Prudentius, for example, concentrated on the story of Peter walking on the water (Mt. 14. 22-33) in the preface to his *Contra Symmachum* 2. Among Paulinus of Nola's biblical paraphrases, the longest (330 hexameter lines), *Carmen* 6, deals only with the birth and abbreviated ministry of John the Baptist.

boat'' over what he describes to Macedonius as ''the boundless sea of the Paschal majesty, which terrifies even the most learned of men.''[4]

The author of the *Paschale carmen* is clearly indebted to Christian poets who preceded him, but it should be recognized that the fifth-century poet also brings something new to his Christian literary tradition. Sedulius adheres to the Juvencan model—he, too, chooses to write an ambitious life of Christ in hexameters—but applies to it his own thematic emphasis. Without disturbing the general biblical chronology and without resorting to purely topical treatment, Sedulius uses *miracula Christi* as a criterion for omission and inclusion of narrative material. The effect of this thematic strategy is to unify the subject and broaden the scope of the poem.

i. *The Narrative Subject of the Paschale carmen*

It is important, at the outset, to be precise in describing the narrative subject of the *Paschale carmen*. Literary historians have often used subject categories very loosely to describe the *Paschale carmen* and other biblical poems of Late Antiquity. Kartschoke, for instance, groups together the poems of Juvencus, Sedulius, and Arator under the category of ''New Testament epic paraphrase.''[5] This is somewhat misleading. Christian poets of Late Antiquity did not attempt to paraphrase the entire New Testament. With the exception of Prudentius' *Dittochaeon*, which retells events from the life of Christ but also devotes four quatrains to stories from Acts and one to Revelation, Christian poets confined their attention to single books or sections of the New Testament. Sedulius himself is also sometimes described as a ''paraphrast of the Gospel,''[6] as though the *Paschale carmen* were a paraphrase of a single Gospel. But neither a Gospel nor the Gospels can really be said to constitute the subject of Sedulius' poem. Nestler's description of the *Paschale carmen* as a ''Messiad'' is more accurate.[7] As we have seen, Sedulius eliminates a large number of episodes and details from the Gospel stories (especially those which do not center around Christ) and concentrates on the Savior. The *Paschale carmen* does much more, to be sure, than simply retell the life of Christ. The poet introduces his story with great ceremony and at some length in Book 1. He exegizes freely throughout the poem, drawing explanatory

---

[4] *CSEL* 10, 1-2.

[5] Kartschoke, *Bibeldichtung*, p. 93.

[6] Colombo, *La poesia cristiana antica*, p. 156.

[7] See Nestler, *Studien über die Messiade des Iuvencus*, p. 43. Neither ''Messiad'' nor ''Christiad'' were titles used by the poets of Late Antiquity, but even though somewhat anachronistic, they are the most accurate descriptive titles which can be applied to Sedulius' poem.

material from the Psalms, Pauline epistles, and elsewhere. He apostrophizes biblical characters and objects (such as the cross) and interrupts the narrative to ask rhetorical questions. Still, it is the story of the life of Christ which must be said to give the poem its major narrative thrust.

The *Paschale carmen* begins with a preface of eight elegiac distichs in which Sedulius invites the reader to the humble repast of his poetry. The entire first book which follows can also be described as prefatory. Almost two-thirds of the material here is of Sedulius' own invention. The poet first defends his right to sing of the *miracula Christi* after attacking the lying content of pagan poetry (1. 17-59). Then he thanks God (1. 60-102) for giving mankind better sustenance (the blood of Christ) than "the old serpent's poison" and asks for guidance on the path to paradise. Sedulius introduces Old Testament examples of divine miracles in 1. 103-219. After confronting nature with the evidence of its dominant Lord (1. 220-41), Sedulius blasts the pagans, who worship the creature rather than the creator (1. 242-90). Then, after a reiteration of his theme (the miraculous), Sedulius launches an anti-heretical attack (1. 299-333). The book closes with a continuation of the prayer for inspiration (1. 351-4), followed by the representation of the four evangelists (1. 355-68), who will serve as Sedulius' sources. With these preliminaries out of the way, the poet is now ready to plunge into his story line.

In Book 2 the actual narrative of the life of Christ begins, but only after the poet considers first the fall of man and the necessity for divine redemption (2. 1-34). The story of the incarnation then follows. The second book carries the reader from Jesus' birth (2. 35-72) to the calling of his twelve disciples (2. 220-30). Sedulius concentrates on just a few episodes from Jesus' early career in this book. He retells the stories of Herod and the Magi (2. 73-133), the twelve-year-old Jesus in the temple (2. 134-8), Jesus' baptism (2. 139-74), and the temptation in the wilderness (2. 175-219). Sedulius' own exegesis of the Lord's Prayer (2. 231-300) concludes the book.

The third and fourth books of the *Paschale carmen* tell of the miracles of Christ in a roughly chronological sequence. Sedulius draws miracles from all four of the Gospels and attempts to put them into some sort of order.[8] The third book retells some 25 miracles beginning with the wed-

---

[8] In 3. 182-98, for instance, Sedulius follows Matthew 12. 9-14 and 22-32 as he tells of two miracles (the healing of the man with the withered hand and the healing of the blind and dumb man) the first of which, according to the evangelist, Jesus performed in a synagogue. But before continuing with the sequence of miracles as found in Matthew, Sedulius inserts a miracle recorded only in Luke (13. 10-19), the healing of the crippled woman on the Sabbath. Sedulius continues with accounts of the feeding of the 5000,

ding at Cana. Sedulius includes the calming of the storm, the healing of the Gadarene demoniac, the raising of Jairus' daughter, the feedings of the 5000 and the 4000, and the transfiguration. The central episode in the book (3. 158-75) is the commissioning of the twelve disciples, who will themselves perform miracles of exorcism, healing, and resurrection:

daemoniis auferte locum, depellite lepram
functaque subductae revocate cadavera vitae. (3. 163-4)

The last episode in the book (3. 320-39) presents Jesus in one of his rare appearances in the *Paschale carmen* as a "marvelous teacher" (*doctor mirabilis*) instructing his disciples about the importance of humility.

Book 4 includes 16 miracles. The book begins with a discourse of 30 lines on God's ability to do the impossible. Sedulius then proceeds to tell of such miracles as the withering of the fig tree, the raising of the young man at Nain, the healing of the ten lepers, and the resurrection of Lazarus. Again a commissioning, this time of the 70, is centrally located in the book (4. 150-71). Sedulius includes some stories which are not strictly miraculous, such as Jesus and the woman of Samaria whom he meets at a well (4. 222-32), the adulterous woman whom Jesus refuses to condemn (4. 233-50), and the triumphal entry into Jerusalem (4. 291-308). Even though they include nearly every miracle of Christ recorded in the four Gospels, Books 3 and 4 are not simply catalogues of miracles.[9] They also must be described as narrative in character insofar as they carry the reader from what John calls "the beginning" of Christ's miracles (3. 1-11) to the raising of Lazarus, the last miracle (according to John) which Jesus performed before entering into Jerusalem.

The fifth book tells the story of the passion, the resurrection, and the ascension. It begins with a description of Jesus' request that the Father glorify his name (5. 1-19). There follows the story of the last supper (5. 20-31), an account of Judas' plans for betrayal (5. 32-58), and a long imprecation against the disciple who betrayed his master (5. 59-68). The events surrounding the capture and trial of Jesus are told next (5. 69-181). The shape of the cross moves the poet to a fine ecphrastic frenzy (5. 188-95), and the thought of paradise in connection with Jesus' words to the repentant criminal crucified with him occasions another (5. 202-31), but the narrative thrust predominates. Christ's death and its

---

Jesus' walk on the water, and the general healing in Genesar. The poet probably inserted Luke's miracle at this point because, like the healing of the man with the withered hand, it too was supposed to take place in a synagogue. Sedulius very neatly has Jesus perform both miracles on the same Sabbath in the same synagogue.

[9] The one miracle which, inexplicably, Sedulius does not include in the *Paschale carmen* is the healing of the man at the pool of Bethesda (John 5. 1-18).

significance occupy the poet's attention in 5. 232-94, and the deposition from the cross and burial of the body are considered in 5. 295-314. The story of the resurrection is outlined in 5. 315-50, and the poet upbraids the Jews for their unbelief in 5. 351-64. Sedulius tells of Jesus' appearance to Thomas in 5. 365-91 and to Peter in 5. 392-415. An account of Jesus' farewell to his disciples (5. 416-21) and his ascension into heaven (5. 422-35) concludes the book. The final lines of the poem are:

> Nam si cuncta sacris voluissent tradere chartis
> facta redemptoris, nec totus cingere mundus
> sufficeret densos per tanta volumina libros. (5. 436-8)

It is significant that Sedulius should choose to end his poem on this note, a simple paraphrase of the ending of the Gospel of John (21. 25). The conclusion suggests that the fifth-century poet conceived of himself as a latter-day evangelist, like Matthew, Mark, Luke, or John, the canonical biographers of the Savior. Sedulius does not add an epilogue of his own composition but rather adopts the conclusion of John's Gospel as his own.

ii. The "Life of Christ" Tradition in the Christian Poetry of Late Antiquity

When Sedulius decided on the life of Christ as the subject of a poem whose narrative parameters would be the beginning and end of the Savior's life on earth, he was not the first and certainly not the last Christian poet to do so. An acquaintance, at least, with other poems of Late Antiquity which retell the story of the life of Christ will prove helpful in locating the *Paschale carmen* within a specific Christian poetic tradition. The fifth-century poet was influenced by poetic predecessors like Juvencus and Prudentius and became himself, in turn, a source and model for poets who followed him in Late Antiquity. In the following pages, we shall trace the outlines of the tradition and attempt to determine Sedulius' place within it.

According to the entry on Juvencus in Jerome's *De viris illustribus* (84), the first Christian poet to tell of the life of Christ in verse was a Spanish aristocrat and priest who flourished during the reign of Constantine:

> Iuvencus, nobilissimi generis Hispanus, presbyter, quattuor Evangelia hexametris versibus paene ad verbum transferens, quattuor libros conposuit et nonnulla, eodem metro, ad sacramentorum ordinem pertinentia. Floruit sub Constantino principe.[10]

---

[10] I use the text of E.C. Richardson in *Texte und Untersuchungen zur Geschichte der altchristlichen Literatur* 14. 1 (Leipzig, 1896). For a discussion of the entry, see H. Marti,

As Jerome indicates, the Spanish poet divided his hexameter poem into four books, no doubt in imitation of the number of the canonical Gospels. The books average between 750 and 850 lines each. The entire work is over 3200 lines long and includes a much studied proem of 27 lines in which Juvencus states his reasons for writing the poem.[11] This Christian poet intends to vie with the greatest pagan writers of epic in the past in his presentation of the *vitalia gesta* of Christ in song and hopes to earn salvation in the process. The proem ends with an invocation of the Holy Spirit.

Throughout the body of the work Juvencus follows the Gospel of Matthew for the most part. He almost entirely ignores Mark but does excerpt some material from Luke and John.[12] In 1. 1-180, for instance, the poet follows the Lucan account of the birth of John the Baptist and the nativity of Christ. Parts of Book 2 are drawn from John's Gospel, but in Book 3 Juvencus follows only Matthew. In Book 4 Juvencus borrows details of the passion story from Matthew, Luke, and John.

Although Juvencus has far fewer digressions than Sedulius, his paraphrase is not nearly so *paene ad verbum* as Jerome suggested. In his description of the storm on the Sea of Galilee (2. 25-32), for instance, Juvencus elaborates at some length upon the Gospel's quite simple description (Mt. 8. 23-7):

> Conscendunt navem ventoque inflata tumescunt
> vela suo, fluctuque volat stridente carina.
> Postquam altum tenuit puppis, consurgere in iras
> pontus et inmissis hinc inde tumescere ventis
> instat et ad caelum rabidos sustollere montes;
> et nunc mole ferit puppim nunc turbine proram,
> inlisosque super laterum tabulata receptant
> fluctus disiectoque aperitur terra profundo.

Since Juvencus is interested in retelling and ornamenting the deeds or accomplishments (*gesta*) of Christ, he often streamlines the discourses of

---

Übersetzer der Augustin-Zeit: Interpretation von Selbstzeugnissen, Studia et testimonia antiqua 14 (Munich, 1974), pp. 73-6. Elsewhere (*Chron. ad ann.* 329), Jerome dates Juvencus' work more precisely. On Eliberri in Baetica as Juvencus' birthplace, see Fontaine, *Naissance*, pp. 71-2.

[11] On the proem, see (among others) P.G. van der Nat, "Die *Praefatio* der Evangelien-paraphrase des Juvencus," in *Romanitas et Christianitas* (Amsterdam, 1973), 249-57, F. Quadlbauer, "Zur *Invocatio* des Iuvencus," *Grazer Beiträge* 2 (1974), 185-212, and F. Murru, "Analisi semiologica e strutturale della *Praefatio* agli *Evangeliorum libri* di Giovenco," *WS* 14 (1980), 133-51.

[12] Hannson, *Textkritisches zu Juvencus*, p. 8, provides a convenient list of Juvencus' borrowings from the different Gospels.

Jesus. He also omits most repetitions and Hebraisms.[13] But Juvencus does include in his poem all of the pertinent details of Christ's life as recorded in the four Gospels. The poem concludes with an expression of gratitude. Juvencus appreciates the tranquility provided by Constantine's reign of peace, which has permitted him the leisure to write his poetry:

Haec mihi pax Christi tribuit, pax haec mihi saecli,
quam fovet indulgens terrae regnator apertae
Constantinus, adest cui gratia digna merenti,
qui solus regnum sacri sibi nominis horret
inponi pondus, quo iustis dignior actis
aeternam capiat divina in saecula vitam
per dominum lucis Christum, qui in saecula regnat. (4. 806-12)

Evangeliorum libri quattuor must have been widely read and admired soon after its composition. Jerome referred to it on two other occasions, once commending the poet for the boldness of his undertaking (*nec pertimuit evangelii maiestatem sub metri leges mittere*) and again, in a citation of a Juvencan line, passing a favorable judgment (*pulcherrime*) on the Christian poet's abilities.[14] The authors of the so-called Gelasian Decree also expressed their admiration for Juvencus' poem (*Item Iuvenci nihilominus laboriosum opus non spernimus, sed miramur*).[15] Almost every Christian Latin poet of Late Antiquity seems to have been influenced by Juvencus' poem. Juvencan borrowings and reminiscences have been detected in the works of Ausonius, Prosper Tiro, Orientius, Claudius Marius Victor, Paulinus of Pella, Paulinus of Périgueux, Ennodius, Avitus, Rusticius Helpidius, Corippus, Paulinus of Nola, Prudentius, and Sedulius.[16]

After Juvencus, the next Christian poet to turn to the life of Christ was an aristocratic lady named Proba, who was already an experienced versifier. According to Proba's own admission (vv. 1-8) she had already written an epic along more traditional lines, on the uprising of Magnen-

---

[13] Roberts, *Biblical Epic*, p. 109, makes these observations. For a list of Juvencus' more significant omissions, see H. Widmann, *De Gaio Vettio Aquilino Iuvenco carminis evangelici poeta et Vergilii imitatore* (Breslau, 1905), pp. 24-32.

[14] *Ep.* 70. 5 and *In Mattheum* 1. 14. For a discussion of Jerome's references to Juvencus, see Poinsotte, *Juvencus et Israël*, p. 27, n. 78.

[15] See Chapter 2, n. 9, above.

[16] For all of the poets mentioned above with the exception of the last three, see Huemer's list in the introduction to his edition of Juvencus (*CSEL* 24, pp. viii-ix). Charles Witke (*Numen litterarum*, p. 206) follows Klaus Thraede in asserting that Sedulius was the first poet to display a knowledge of Juvencus, but even a quick glance at Hartel's index will suffice to show the debt which Paulinus owed to Juvencus (see P.G. Walsh's observations in his review of *Numen litterarum* in *CR* 24 [1974], 223). For Prudentius' knowledge of Juvencus, see M. Manitius, "Zu Juvencus und Prudentius," *RhM* 45 (1890), 485 ff., and A.C. Vega, "Juvenco y Prudencio," *La ciudad de Dios* 157 (1945), 209 ff.

tius against Constantius II. In the 360s or perhaps the 380s, Proba wrote
a Virgilian cento (made up of lines and half-lines taken from Virgil's
Eclogues, *Georgics*, and the *Aeneid*) on the creation of the world and the life
of Jesus.[17] The poem is 694 lines long and has two easily distinguishable
parts. Proba begins with the Genesis story of creation and other early
events in biblical history but leaves the rest of the Old Testament for
other poets to finish when she reaches the story of the Hebrews' exodus
from Egypt:

> cetera facta patrum pugnataque in ordine bella
> praetereo atque aliis post me memoranda relinquo. (331-2)

The second half of her poem is introduced by a proem (333-45) in which
Proba announces the beginning of a greater work (*maius opus moveo*). She
will sing of the fulfillment of ancient prophecies (*vatum praedicat priorum
adgredior*), namely, the incarnation of Christ (*virum populis terrisque super-
bum / semine ab aetherio, qui viribus occupet orbem*).

Although the cento technique makes close paraphrase difficult, if not
impossible, we can sometimes determine which evangelist Proba is
following. She seems to prefer Matthew and Mark but ranges freely
through all four Gospels. Proba follows the Gospel of Luke, for instance,
in her retelling of the nativity story, borrowing her flowery description
of the manger scene from Virgil's fourth *Eclogue*:

> Hic natum angusti subter fastigia tecti
> nutribat teneris inmulgens ubera labris.
> Hic tibi prima, puer, fundent cunabula flores,
> mixtaque ridenti passim cum baccare tellus
> molli paulatim colocasia fundet acantho. (375-9)

After dealing briefly with the subject of Jesus' youth, Proba relates just
a few episodes from Jesus' ministry, such as the temptation in the
wilderness, the sermon on the mount, the encounter with the rich young
ruler, and the stilling of the storm, before she tells of Jesus' entry into
Jerusalem, his passion, death, resurrection, and ascension (561-688). In
a conclusion of six lines Proba urges her husband to remain true to his
faith in Christ.

Proba's poem was considerably shorter than Juvencus' and most
Christian poets who wrote on the life of Christ thereafter produced even
more summary paraphrases, sometimes passing over the major events of

---

[17] For a discussion of Proba's dates, see Chapter 1, n. 17, above. The most recent
literary study of Proba's cento is Elizabeth Clark and Diane Hatch, *The Golden Bough,
the Oaken Cross: The Vergilian Cento of Faltonia Betitia Proba* (Chico, Calif., 1981). Still
invaluable for a complete study of the *Cento* is Filippo Ermini, *Il centone di Proba e la poesia
centonaria latina* (Rome, 1909).

the Gospels with great speed. One of the best known of these is *Hymnum dicat turba fratrum*, a poem of 74 lines in trochaic tetrameters, which begins by praising Christ, follows by tracing the life of Jesus from the annunciation to Mary up to his final appearances before his disciples, and ends with a nine-line invitation to sing Christ's praises. If we can trust the attribution of the *Antiphonary of Bangor*, the author was Hilary of Poitiers (d. 367), one of the earliest Christian hymn writers.[18]

Another well known hymn which retells the life of Christ is Prudentius' *Cathemerinon* 9. The Spanish-born poet reviews the *gesta Christi insignia* in 114 trochaic tetrameter lines, including many of the miracles, such as the changing of water into wine, the stilling of the storm, and the raising of Lazarus. The narrative part of the poem begins, after a prefatory address to Christ as creator, with his birth and ends with his ascension. The hymn concludes with an epilogue.

Prudentius also composed 49 quatrains—the last 25 on New Testament subjects—commonly known as the *Dittochaeon*. These tetrastichs were probably *tituli*, intended to describe biblical scenes depicted on the walls of a basilica.[19] Of the 49 quatrains, 25-44 retell episodes from the life of Christ in chronological order. The poet draws episodes from all four of the Gospels and shows special interest in visual details. In the 44th quatrain, for instance, Prudentius is more concerned to describe the olive tree which grows on the very top of the Mount of Olives and the stone which bears the imprint of Christ's foot than he is in telling of the ascension itself.

Sedulius himself wrote an alphabetical hymn in iambic dimeter quatrains on the life of Christ, usually called after its first line, *A solis ortus cardine*. This 23-stanza composition consists of an opening verse of praise, followed by a chronological account of the life of Christ, which begins with the stories surrounding his birth (stanzas 2-7) and concludes with a stanza on the ascension.[20] A less well known hymn also attributed to Sedulius is an epanaleptic composition of 110 lines, *Cantemus, socii, Domino*. The second half of the hymn presents the life of Christ in outline

---

[18] See F.J.E. Raby's comments in *OBMLV*, p. 450.

[19] The most recent and complete study is that of R. Pillinger, *Die Tituli historiarum oder das sogenannte Dittochaeon des Prudentius* (Vienna, 1980). On the *Dittochaeon* as *tituli*, see also Jean-Louis Charlet, "Prudence lecteur de Paulin de Nole: A propos du 23e quatrain du *Dittochaeon*," *REA* 21 (1975), 61-2. (For the latter reference I am indebted to Professor Roberts.)

[20] For a brief discussion of the hymn, see Joseph Szövérffy, *Die Annalen der lateinischen Hymnendichtung* (Berlin, 1964), I, pp. 98-101. For a fuller consideration, see my "Sedulius' *A solis ortus cardine*: The Hymn and its Tradition," *Ephemerides liturgicae* 101 (1987), 69-75.

form.[21] Unfortunately for an accurate study of the tradition, the dating
of the hymns of Sedulius and some of the other shorter poems tends to
be exceedingly problematical. We can only speculate as to whether they
preceded or followed the composition of the *Paschale carmen*.

Other shorter poems on the life of Christ of some interest for a study
of this tradition include a summary life of Christ, 137 hexameters long,
which has come down to us under the title of *De Iesu Christo Deo et
homine*.[22] After an introduction to the subject of the incarnation (1-32),
the author leads his readers through the life of Jesus, beginning with the
wedding at Cana and continuing with brief accounts of the feeding of the
5000, the raising of Lazarus, and the woman with the issue of blood (32-
64). After summing up Jesus' success as a miracle worker, the poet continues by telling of the bestowal of the keys of the church upon Peter, the
preparation for Jesus' last supper with his disciples, and Judas' betrayal.
Lines 76-106 describe the trial and passion of Jesus, and in 107-22 the
stories of the resurrection and of Jesus' final appearances to his disciples
are related. Jesus ascends to heaven in the last lines of the poem (123-
137), where he is enthroned and receives the praises of animate and
inanimate creation alike. *De Iesu Christo Deo et homine* has been attributed
to the fourth-century rhetorician and theologian, Marius Victorinus, but
it contains many obvious similarities to Sedulian passages. For instance,
the author of *De Iesu Christo Deo et homine*, like Sedulius (*Paschale carmen*
4. 290), describes Lazarus as his own *haeres* after he is raised from the
dead by Jesus. It is just possible that it was Sedulius who made use of
De Iesu Christo Deo et homine, but more likely, given the relative obscurity
of the shorter poem, that its author was indebted to the *Paschale carmen*.

Another shorter poem (114 hexameters), given the title *De evangelio* by
its Renaissance editor, begins with an address to Christ and a free description of the incarnation, the nativity, and the visit of the Magi.[23]
There follows an apostrophe of 18 lines in which the poet marvels over
the virginity of Mary and adorns her divine child with epithets. Lines 43-
59 describe the prophecies of the Christ in the Old Testament and feature
the four *animantia* which surround the throne of God with faces of a man,
a lion, an eagle, and an ox (the symbols of the four evangelists). In lines
71-80 we are shown the heavenly choir singing praises to God. The poem
ends with two miracles of healing: the lame man of Matthew 9. 6 ff. and

---

[21] For editions of both of Sedulius' hymns, see Huemer, *CSEL* 10, 155-68.

[22] There is no modern critical edition of the poem. I have followed the text given in
Georg Fabricius, *Poetarum veterum ecclesiasticorum opera christiana* (Basel, 1562), pp. 761-4.

[23] For the text of *De evangelio*, see *CSEL* 23, 270-4. M. Manitius, *Geschichte der christlich-
lateinischen Poesie bis zur Mitte des 8. Jahrhunderts* (Stuttgart, 1891), p. 104, discusses the
poem briefly.

the man born blind (John 9. 1 ff.). There can be little doubt that as we possess it *De evangelio* is fragmentary. The ending is too abrupt to conclude a poem which starts out on such a grand note. *De evangelio* begins impressively with the story of the nativity and continues with several miracles of Christ. Perhaps it is the first half of a *Carmen de Christo* which was supposed to end with an account of Christ's passion, resurrection, and ascension. Again the questions of date and authorship are vexed. The poem has been attributed to Hilary, but the language of the short piece shows some affinities to that of the *Paschale carmen*. Lines 108-9, for instance, are very close to *Paschale carmen* 3. 98 and 102. Again it is quite likely that the author of this fragmentary and not very widely known poem was influenced by Sedulius.

A set of 24 stanzas—probably *tituli*—known as the *Tristicha* and attributed to Rusticius Helpidius (usually dated to the second half of the fifth century) have come down to us.[24] The first 16 tristichs set up events from the Old and the New Testament in contrasting sets of two. The first pair of stanzas, for instance, tell of Eve's beguilement by the serpent and the annunciation to Mary. Just as Eve is responsible for mankind's woes, Mary is the source of human salvation:

> 1. Evae viperea vetitum decerpere pomum
> invidus arte parat, tantae quae nescia fraudis,
> credidit infelix, socio peritura marito.
> 2. Angelus illaesum Mariae per somnia Ioseph
> connubium servare monet: hic dote repleta
> Spiritus, hac quod fit flagrans, salvatur honore.

The poet must have lost interest after eight such sets. The last tristichs are all taken from the Gospels and show no particular chronological or thematic organization. It is quite possible, as Corsaro has argued, that the author of the *Tristicha* knew of Sedulius' work. The *Paschale carmen* makes some of the same typological connections. For instance, Eve and Mary are also compared and contrasted in *Paschale carmen* 2. 30-5. Sedulius was not the first, however, to connect these two famous biblical mothers, and it is impossible to determine with certainty whether Rusticius Helpidius borrowed this (or other examples of typological interpretation) from Sedulius.

Miracula Christi (of uncertain authorship) may also be a collection of

---

[24] The most accessible edition of the poem is still *PL* 62, 543 ff. Francesco Corsaro includes an edition of the *Tristicha* in his *Elpidio Rustico* (Catania, 1955), pp. 126-33. In the third chapter of his study Corsaro argues that the *Paschale carmen* was a literary source for the author of the *Tristicha*. See also W. Brandes, "Studien zur christlich-lateinischen Poesie," *WS* 12 (1890), 303. For more biographical details, see *PLRE* II, p. 537.

tituli.[25] Without much respect for the order of the miracles as they are to be found in the Gospels, the poet begins with the annunciation and proceeds to retell the story of the visit of the Magi, the wedding at Cana, the feeding of the 5000, the healing of the man born blind, the resurrection of Lazarus, Peter walking on the water, the woman with a bloody flux, and the healing of the paralytic. Again there are striking similarities with the *Paschale carmen.* Line 12, for example (*et durae mortis lex resoluta perit*) is very close to *Paschale carmen* 4. 286-7: *mortisque profundae / lex perit.*

Space does not permit us even to mention here all of the shorter passages reviewing the life of Christ which are embedded within longer poems.[26] *De passione sua* is a good example of how a brief life of Christ can be fit into a larger narrative. This short poem is mostly concerned with the story of Christ's passion, as the title indicates, but also includes a passage wherein the crucified Jesus himself narrates the story of his life to a passerby.[27] A short *Carmen de Christo*, which may have been written by a contemporary of Sedulius named Merobaudes, contains a central passage summarizing Christ's earthly career.[28] The second book of Dracontius' *De laudibus Dei* includes an outline of Christ's life (2. 77-153). The African poet most probably knew the *Paschale carmen.*[29] *De laudibus Dei* 1. 648 and 2. 1 bear resemblances, for example, to *Paschale carmen* 3. 89 and 1. 60. A Virgilian cento once commonly attributed to Sedulius himself, *De verbi incarnatione*, concentrates on the birth of Christ but also sketches out his life and concludes with his ascension into heaven.[30] In addition to his *Tristicha*, Rusticius Helpidius also wrote a short poem, *De beneficiis Christi*, which includes a brief survey of Christ's miracles.[31]

So far in our review of poetic treatments of the life of Christ in Late Antiquity we have considered only Latin poets, who were more likely to have influenced or been influenced by Sedulius than Greek poets. It is not impossible, however, that Sedulius knew Greek. According to the subscriptional testimony, he wrote his books in Greece. In the second letter to Macedonius (prefatory to the *Paschale opus*), Sedulius refers to the works of Origen, the famous Greek theologian, and in *Paschale carmen* 1.

---

[25] See Birt's edition in *MGH AA* 10, 412-3.

[26] These "secondary paraphrases," as they are sometimes called, are usually ignored in studies of verse biblical paraphrases in Late Antiquity. Kartschoke does include a brief consideration of some examples of biblical paraphrase within hymns in *Bibeldichtung*, pp. 114-21.

[27] For a text of *De passione sua*, see *CSEL* 27, 148-51. On the problem of dating the poem, see the comments of A. Roncoroni, "Sul *De passione Domini* Pseudolattanzio," *VC* 29 (1975), 208-21.

[28] See the discussion in *PLRE* II, 757.

[29] On Dracontius' knowledge of Sedulius, see Chapter 2, n. 11, above.

[30] See Schenkl's edition in *CSEL* 16, 615-20.

[31] Corsaro includes the text of this poem in his *Elpidio Rustico*. See n. 24, above.

185-7 Sedulius plays on the similarities between the name of the prophet Elijah (*Helias*) and the Greek word for the sun (*helios*). If Sedulius did know Greek—and the question must remain open—he might have read the works of Greek biblical poets who were contemporaries of his or who antedated him.

Although his poetic talents are often ignored, Gregory of Nazianzus, the Cappadocian theologian (AD 320-389), was a prolific poet who composed hundreds of pieces of Greek verse towards the end of his life during his retirement at Arianzum.[32] Of these, there are eleven poems written in hexameters or elegiac distichs which have Gospel episodes as their subjects. The poems range from five to 106 lines in length. Gregory's regular practice is to isolate and concentrate on one episode or a group of connected episodes from the Gospels. Unlike the quatrains which make up Prudentius' *Dittochaeon*, however, these poems do not have any kind of narrative continuity when they are read together. In all but the final composition, Gregory seems to be interested in setting to verse parts of the Gospels which are difficult to remember, such as a list of the 12 disciples or the genealogy of Christ. Four of the poems are devoted to listing the miracles of Christ as recorded in each of the four Gospels.

The Greek poet Nonnos, who is most famous for his lengthy epic, the *Dionysiaca*, also turned the Gospel of John into hexameters. The dating of the *Metabole*, as Nonnos' paraphrase is known, is somewhat problematic.[33] The poet's use of *theotokos* in the *Metabole* suggests that it may have been written after the Nestorian controversy erupted, and Musaeus (late fifth century) seems to have been acquainted with Nonnos' paraphrase, so it is usually assigned a date of c. 450.[34] The 3650 hexameters of the work have been divided by editors into 21 books, ranging from 93 to 254 lines in length, one book for each chapter of the Gospel of John. Nonnos is an even more scrupulous paraphrast than Juvencus. He rarely deviates from the events and the order of events as they are presented by the evangelist. Insofar as the Gospel which he follows is a life of Christ, so is Nonnos' *Metabole*.

A collection of Homeric centos has come down to us under the names of Patrikios, Optimos, Eudokia (wife of the emperor Theodosius II), and Cosmas.[35] These fifty short poems take the reader through the life of

---

[32] Texts in *PG* 37, 480 ff. B. Wyss, "Gregor von Nazianz. Ein griechisch-christlicher Dichter des 4. Jahrhunderts," *Museum helveticum* 6 (1949), 177-210, provides a useful introduction to the poetry of Gregory.

[33] See, for instance, Rudolph Keydell's discussion in *RE* 17. 1, 919.

[34] See L. Schwabe, *De Musaeo Nonni imitatore liber* (Tübingen, 1876), p. vi.

[35] Edited by A. Ludwich (Leipzig, 1897). For a discussion of Eudokia in particular, see Ludwich's "Eudokia, die Gattin des Kaisers Theodosius II als Dichterin," *RhM* 37 (1882), 206-25.

Christ, beginning with the Son's descent to earth from heaven and ending with his ascension. They range from six to 111 lines in length. It is
impossible now to determine what each of the four authors' specific contributions to this collection may have been. Cosmas of Jerusalem lived
in the eighth century and was probably the editor of these poems. Like
many other poetic treatments of the life of Christ, the Greek centos avoid
discourses of Jesus such as the sermon on the mount and concentrate
instead upon miracles and the narratives surrounding the birth and death
of the Savior. It is interesting to note that an entire cento (44 lines) is
devoted to the harrowing of hell, a subject which finds no description in
the canonical Gospels. Like the *tituli*, the Homeric centos focus on single
episodes of the Gospels. Taken as a unit, on the other hand, they form
a fairly complete biography of Christ.

These are the major extant poems which make up the "life of Christ"
tradition in the Christian poetry of Late Antiquity. We should not
overemphasize their similarities. Their authors clearly have widely
divergent intentions, and these poems are not all of a kind. Some compositions are epics, others hymns, *tituli*, or mnemonic aids. But this is
clearly one of the strands—and an important one—of the larger literary
tradition to which Sedulius' *Paschale carmen* belongs. We cannot determine whether Latin poets knew Greek poets or whether writers of the
centos influenced other Christian authors. A Virgilian line in the *Paschale
carmen*, for instance, may have been taken from Proba's Virgilian *Cento*,
but Sedulius may also have borrowed directly from Virgil. All the same,
it is possible to discover distinct lines of continuity which connect the
Latin poets who wrote on the life of Christ. The importance of Juvencus,
in particular, as a source of influence and a formal model for the later
tradition cannot be overemphasized. Sedulius borrowed from
Evangeliorum libri quattuor extensively (Huemer counts some 30 echoes and
reminiscences) as well as from Prudentius' poetry. If Juvencus served as
the fountainhead, as it were, of the "Christiad" tradition in Late Antiquity, Sedulius himself became its most popular and influential representative. Of poets later than Sedulius, Rusticius Helpidius, Dracontius,
and the authors of *De evangelio*, *De Iesu Christo Deo et homine*, and *Miracula
Christi* are most likely indebted to him. Perhaps the greatest measure of
Sedulius' poetic achievement is that so few poets of Late Antiquity ventured
to write an epic life of Christ after him. According to a subscription in
a manuscript (*Aurelianensis* 295 [*CSEL* 72, xxx]) of Arator's *De actibus
apostolorum*, the sixth-century poet would have preferred to write on the
Gospels but decided to turn to Acts instead, because Juvencus and
Sedulius had already treated the Gospels in verse:

Qui, considerans Iuvencum et Sedulium scripsisse actus evangelicos, noluit eos iterum rescribere sed totum contulit ad actus Apostolicorum describendos.

Sedulius' verse treatment of the life of Christ cannot be fully appreciated except as read in the light of Juvencus' *Evangeliorum libri quattuor*. Salvatore Costanza has compared the first lines of the *Paschale carmen* with the proem of *Evangeliorum libri quattuor* and concludes that it would be "absurd" to imagine that Sedulius did not have Juvencus' work before him as he wrote.[36] Thematic parallels and verbal echoes abound. Like Juvencus, for example, Sedulius contrasts his new Christian poetry with the old pagan products, criticizes their lack of probity, and uses the formula *mihi carmen erit* to set up the introduction to the contents of his work. Like *Evangeliorum libri quattuor*, the *Paschale carmen* is written in hexameters and depends heavily on Virgil. No doubt Sedulius pays a tribute to the earlier Christian poet, too, in dividing the main body of the *Paschale carmen* into four books. Like Juvencus, Sedulius lays down an implicit challenge not only to the great epic poets of the past but also to the four evangelists themselves.

The similarity between the poetry of Juvencus and Sedulius did not go unnoticed by their readers in Late Antiquity and the Middle Ages. In his verse life of St. Martin (1. 14 ff.), for example, Venantius Fortunatus connects the two Christian poets:

> Primus enim docili distinguens ordine carmen
> maiestatis opus metri canit arte Iuvencus;
> hinc quoque conspicui radiavit lingua Seduli.[37]

In a line that has been attributed to Isidore of Seville (bishop from 602-636) the two poets are also mentioned in the same breath: *Ecce Iuvencus adest Seduliusque tibi*.[38] The hexameter poems of Juvencus and Sedulius were often published together, and their names continued to be linked in the Middle Ages. Alcuin, Theodulph of Orléans, Ermoldus Nigellus, Hrabanus Maurus, and Notker Balbulus, for example, all place the two side by side.[39]

Even though Sedulius owes more to Juvencus than any other Christian poet, there are still points of similarity between the *Paschale carmen* and other poems of the tradition which should not be overlooked. Like Proba's *Cento*, the first part of the *Paschale carmen* includes a consideration

---

[36] Costanza, "Da Giovenco a Sedulio," 262.
[37] In *MGH AA* 4, 1, 293-370.
[38] *PL* 83, 1110. See further C.H. Beeson, *Isidorstudien* (Munich, 1913), pp. 133-66.
[39] The epics of Juvencus and Sedulius were often published together in the Middle Ages and the Renaissance. See Chapter 7, n. 13, below.

of the Old Testament. Like Nonnos, who does not attach an epilogue of
his own invention to the *Metabole*, Sedulius simply paraphrases the last
verses of John's Gospel in the final lines of the *Paschale carmen* and adds
no further conclusion. Like the *tituli*, Sedulius' narrative has an
ecphrastic quality which is quite different from the steady kind of
paraphrastic flow that characterizes Juvencus' and Nonnos' longer
poems. Sedulius lingers lovingly over physical details in the episodes he
retells. Often he will react to the biblical stories as though he were
describing a plastic representation of the same.[40] Like the authors of
some of the summary poems, Sedulius is also quite selective as a biblical
paraphrast. As we have already seen, he includes only incidents from the
Gospels which suit his particular poetic program. This is different from
the practice of Juvencus, who tries for a fairly complete coverage of the
Gospels. Like Prudentius, for instance, in *Cathemerinon* 9, Sedulius skips
back and forth from Gospel to Gospel, selecting and discarding episodes
as he pleases.

Having noted the fifth-century poet's indebtedness to other Christian
poets, most obviously to Juvencus, we must now see how Sedulius may
be considered innovative as well as traditional in his poetic treatment of
the life of Christ.

iii. *The Thematic Design of the Paschale carmen*

Most discussions of the *Paschale carmen* have confined themselves to
describing its narrative subject. To understand the poem correctly, however, we must also take its thematic character into account. Sedulius used
the theme of the miraculous to solve a critical literary problem facing
him: how to tell the life of Christ in a unified way without sacrificing epic
scope. As we have seen, Christian poets before Sedulius (for example,
Prudentius) had concentrated on the miracles of Christ in shorter compositions, but Sedulius was the first to apply this thematic strategy to a
longer poem. It is the solution to this literary problem that constitutes
one of Sedulius' major poetic achievements. The application of a
thematic criterion to a given narrative subject marks the fifth-century
poet's epic life of Christ as essentially different from Juvencus'.

By choosing to concentrate on *miracula*, Sedulius eliminates many of
the details of the life and ministry of Christ which are recorded in the
Gospels.[41] The *Paschale carmen* has a greater sense of narrative leisure than

---

[40] For further discussion of vivid physical representation in the *Paschale carmen*, see
Chapter 6, n. 4, below.

[41] I disagree with Roberts' suggestion (p. 111) that "the poet's claim, in the first letter
to Macedonius, to have selected a few miracles from a large number available to him (*ex*

Juvencus' poem does. Sedulius has succeeded in making the story of the life of Christ more manageable. As a result, Sedulius is able not only to set that story in a broader setting than Juvencus' *Evangeliorum libri quattuor* but also to provide the poem with a tighter unity than the usual harmony of the Gospels or, indeed, the Gospels themselves possess.

Perhaps the best known example in Latin poetry of the employment of a theme to organize a large narrative subject is Ovid's *Metamorphoses*. The Augustan poet planned an ambitious work in which he set out to retell the whole of mythology, beginning with the creation of the world and ending with the apotheosis of Julius Caesar.[42] The problem facing Ovid was how to organize this unwieldy body of narrative subject matter. Ovid's solution presages Sedulius'. He proceeds chronologically and without omitting important stories, but his focus is on *metamorphosis*. Ovid is able to capture in his poem the panorama of mythic history from the very beginning to his own times, and his thematic emphasis helps him to preserve a tighter unity than he would have been able to achieve if he had tried to retell every myth in detail without the focus of *metamorphosis*.

Sedulius' use of the theme of *miracula* helps him, in the first place, to achieve a broader scope for the *Paschale carmen* than Juvencus' *Evangeliorum libri quattuor* is able to claim. The only comprehensiveness which Juvencus really achieves is that his epic retells practically every episode from the Gospels. Sedulius, on the other hand, devotes a considerable section of the first book of his poem to retelling miraculous incidents from the Old Testament which foreshadow the *miracula Christi* recorded in the Gospels. The fifth-century poet emphasizes the miraculous presence of Christ on earth long before his birth. Christ can be observed everywhere in the Old Testament. He is the creator of the world (*conditor orbis*)—here Sedulius picks up the emphasis of New Testament passages like Col. 1. 16—as well as its redeemer. His death and resurrection, therefore, represent the climax of a long history of concern on God's part with the salvation of mankind. By including Old Testament miracles (in which Christ participated in a subordinate role) in the first book of the *Paschale carmen*, Sedulius provides his readers with a sweeping view of the background for the incarnation. The life of Christ is placed in a panoramic context. Thus the *Paschale carmen* has a larger sweep and achieves greater cosmic significance than Juvencus' paraphrase of the Gospels.

---

pluribus pauca [sc. mirabilia] conplexus, 12. 5) cannot be taken seriously.'' Sedulius is surely not referring to a list of miracles which he has before him or in mind, but to all of the episodes of the Gospels which he could have included in the *Paschale carmen* but did not.

[42] On the plan of Ovid's epic, see Brooks Otis, *Ovid as an Epic Poet* (Cambridge, 1966), Chap. 3.

One specific example may help to demonstrate this point. When Sedulius describes Christ as *panis* in his retelling of the miracle of the feeding of the 4000 (3. 257-72) or when he tells of the risen Savior's appearance to his disciples on the shores of Galilee (5. 403), his readers are able to understand this metaphor against the Old Testament background which Sedulius has already provided for them in Book 1. In 1. 148-51 Sedulius retells the story of the miracle of manna in the wilderness and in 1. 159 the poet concludes: *Christus erat panis*. Later, in Book 3, in his account of the feeding of the 5000, Sedulius explicitly links this miracle with the provisioning of the Israelites:

> Cumque dehinc populum sese in deserta secutum
> ut typicus Moyses verusque propheta videret
> antiquam sentire famem, maioribus actis
> antiquam monstravit opem. (3. 207-10)

Again, in 5. 401-4, the poet links his description of Christ as bread to the presence of Christ in the eucharistic meal:

> Quisnam ambigat unam
> his rebus constare fidem, quippe est aqua piscis,
> Christus adest panis, sanctusque Spiritus ignis.
> Hinc etiam abluimur, hoc pascimur, inde sacramur.

Using these kinds of interconnections the author of the *Paschale carmen* permits and encourages the reader to look back to the past and forward to the present and the future. Sedulius sees the miraculous stories he retells, such as the multiplication of the loaves and fish, not only as foreshadowed by Old Testament incidents but also as types for contemporary church practice. The wondrous deeds of Christ belong to a continuum of miracles that goes back as far as the creation of the world and continues in the extension and application of Gospel events to Sedulius' own time.

Juvencus' paraphrase does not make such broad interconnections. True, the earlier poet will often paraphrase the evangelists' comments about an event in the life of Christ fulfilling the Scriptures. In his description of the slaughter of the innocents, for instance, Juvencus includes a reference to Jeremiah 31. 15, a passage which Matthew establishes as a prophecy of this event:

> Haec etiam caedes olim praescripta manebat,
> quam bonus Hieremias divino numine iussus
> conplorat, subolis misero pro funere matres
> horrendis graviter caelum pulsare querellis. (1. 263-6)

But this is the extent of Juvencus' Old Testament preparation. Unlike the *Paschale carmen*, Juvencus' epic does not give the reader appropriate Old Testament background in a separate, preliminary book.

Sedulius' use of *miracula* as a thematic criterion provides his *Paschale carmen* not only with panoramic scope but also with an independent, thematic unity. The miraculous is never far from Sedulius' mind, and it gives his poem on the life of Christ a focus of concentration and emphasis which *Evangeliorum libri quattuor* does not possess. In his retelling of the slaughter of the innocents, for instance, Sedulius seems almost to lose himself in his outburst of rage against Herod and his expression of pity for the dead infants and their mourning mothers:

> Quo crimine simplex
> turba perit? Cur qui vixdum potuere creari
> iam meruere mori? Furor est in rege cruento,
> non ratio; primosque necans vagitus et audens
> innumerum patrare nefas puerilia mactat
> milia plangoremque dedit tot matribus unum.
> Haec laceros crines nudato vertice rupit,
> illa genas secuit, nudum ferit altera pugnis
> pectus et infelix mater (nec iam modo mater)
> orba super gelidum frustra premit ubera natum.
> Quis tibi tunc, lanio, cernenti talia sensus?
> Quosve dabas fremitus, cum vulnera fervere late
> prospiceres arce ex summa vastumque videres
> misceri ante oculos tantis plangoribus aequor? (2. 117-30)

And yet the poet has not forgotten the miraculous in all of this. Even though absent (Mary and Joseph had taken him to Egypt), Christ was miraculously present in spirit, Sedulius tells us, suffering with the infants and the bereaved mothers because he had the capacity to feel *poenas alieno in corpore*:

> Extinctisque tamen quamvis infantibus absens,
> praesens Christus erat, qui sancta pericula semper
> suscipit et poenas alieno in corpore sentit. (2. 131-3)

In this passage and elsewhere in the *Paschale carmen* it is Sedulius' practice to insert miraculous events into Gospel stories or to lay special emphasis on the miraculous elements that are present in the evangelists' accounts. Sedulius uses the idea of the miraculous to unify the biblical episodes which he retells. Whether this poet is retelling stories from the Old or the New Testament, or episodes from Christ's life which deal directly with strictly miraculous acts such as healing and resurrection, or those events which are necessary for a fairly complete life of Christ, he only rarely fails to emphasize the miraculous, thus providing the *Paschale carmen* with a degree of unity which Sedulius' own Gospel sources themselves do not possess.

Juvencus, it is true, does handle the narrative sections of the Gospels fairly deftly—the fourth-century poet creates dialogues, for instance, which are particularly fluent—but he runs into difficulties when he tries to paraphrase the longer discourses of Jesus (e.g., the sermon on the mount, the parables, or the high-priestly prayer). Juvencus tries to include the most important of these but treats many others quite cursorily. By choosing to emphasize miracles, Sedulius sidesteps the problem by practically eliminating discourse altogether. He concentrates on the deeds rather than the words of the Savior.[43] Jesus does, of course, speak in the *Paschale carmen*. At the end of the second book, for instance, Sedulius relates the story of Christ's teaching his disciples how to pray, but the poet offers no explanation as to why he includes an event in his poem on miracles which is not strictly miraculous. Perhaps Sedulius considered the gift of prayer a miracle in itself. Perhaps he simply felt that it was necessary to include the Gospel background for such an important element in the liturgy of the church. But the few exceptions to the rule only serve to underscore the importance of the thematic criterion for the *Paschale carmen* in general. However loosely it may work, the theme of *miracula* does help to eliminate non-narrative material in the Gospels which would only add to the bulk of the poem and stand in the way of the unity which it has as it stands.

Actually, at a certain point, as the reader of the *Paschale carmen* will discover, Sedulius' theme and narrative unite. The entire life of Christ is miraculous whether he is performing actual miracles or not. The very presence of God on earth as man involves breaking the laws of nature. The poet makes this especially clear in the fifth book of the *Paschale carmen*. There are a number of miracles which take place during the passion, resurrection, and ascension of Christ. Dead men (including Christ himself) rise from the grave, and the sun is darkened, but Sedulius' overall emphasis in this last book is on the redemptive work of the Savior, not on miracles as such. While the third and fourth books relate one specific miracle after another, the fifth book is devoted to a larger, single miracle, the culmination of Christ's entire miraculous life, the redemption of the fallen world.

Already in the first book of the *Paschale carmen*, Sedulius had stressed the ability of God to do the impossible:

   . . . subditur omnis
   imperiis natura tuis, rituque soluto

---

[43] On *gesta* and *dicta*, see Jean Doignon, *Hilaire de Poitiers avant l'exil: Recherches sur la naissance, l'enseignement, et l'épreuve d'une foi épiscopale en Gaule au milieu du IVᵉ siècle* (Paris, 1971), 231-5.

transit in adversas iussu dominante figuras.
Si iubeas mediis segetes arere pruinis,
messorem producit hiems; si currere mustum
vernali sub sole velis, florentibus arvis
sordidus inpressas calcabit vinitor uvas;
cunctaque divinis parebunt tempora dictis. (1. 85-92)

The Old Testament miracles as well as the New all testify to Christ's
ability either as an aid to the Father or as assisted by the Father to do
the impossible. And in the fifth book Sedulius represents Christ as performing the greatest of impossible feats. He defies the most inexorable law
of nature by rising from the dead. Not only does he defeat death, but he
also overcomes sin, the cause of death. Thus, his life and death have
redemptive power for mankind. Sedulius makes these connections clear
in his apostrophe to death in Book 5:

Dic ubi nunc tristis victoria, dic ubi nunc sit
mors stimulus horrenda tuus, quae semper opimis
insaturata malis cunctas invadere gentes
poenali dicione soles? En pessima, non tu
pervenis ad Christum, sed Christus pervenit ad te,
cui licuit sine morte mori quique omnia gignens
omnia constituens te non formavit ut esses:
semine vipereo culpa genetrice crearis
et venia regnante peris. (5. 276-84)

The poem has been building up to this greatest of miracles. This is the
climactic point in the life of Christ, and Sedulius brings together narrative subject and theme here. Christ's entire life on earth as God in
human form, culminating in his death and resurrection in order to
redeem mankind (Sedulius refers to the subject of his poem in the last
lines as *facta redemptoris*), is the most miraculous of all the *miracula Christi*.

To sum up, then, Sedulius' choice of the life of Christ as the narrative
subject of a poem places him squarely within a Christian literary tradition which begins in the first part of the fourth century. (As we shall see
in a later chapter, the "Christiad" tradition—if we may call it that—
went on to become one of the most popular of the subcategories of the
biblical epic. Christian poets like Vida, Hojeda, Frénicle, Milton, and
Klopstock were still continuing, not without considerable popular success, to make the life of Christ the subject of their verse a thousand years
and more after the conception of the *Paschale carmen*.) Like Juvencus'
Evangeliorum libri quattuor, Sedulius' hexameter poem carries the reader
from Christ's birth to his ascension. But Sedulius' thematic strategy
enables the poet to be innovative in handling his narrative subject.
Although not the first to use *miracula Christi* as a theme, Sedulius was the
first Christian poet to put it to use in a longer hexameter poem. The

Paschale carmen combines, therefore, the comprehensiveness of Juvencus' epic poem on the life of Christ with the thematic unity and simplicity achieved by shorter poems such as Prudentius' ninth *Cathemerinon* hymn. The result is a new kind of "Christiad," an epic life of the Savior which is at the same time panoramic and focused in its vision of the miraculous life of the Savior of mankind.

CHAPTER FOUR

EPIC AND EVANGEL

Sedulius has been described with some accuracy as a "poet between two worlds."[1] His biblical epic not only harks back to the literary heritage of classical antiquity but also anticipates developments in European literature which come to full fruition in the Middle Ages and thereafter. Educated as they were in the schools of the *grammatici* and *rhetores*, it was difficult for Sedulius and most other Christian poets of Late Antiquity to think of using anything but traditional verse forms. At the same time, they were devoted to the truth of the Scriptures and felt ambivalent about or even hostile to pagan literature, especially its mythological content.[2] The result was that Christian poets of Late Antiquity followed a pattern, as Curtius puts it, "of keeping to the antique genres and filling them with Christian matter."[3] This is, in fact, pretty much the way in which Christian authors of Late Antiquity (e.g., Augustine and Jerome) justified their usurpation of the best of the classical cultural tradition.[4] The new Christian contents and contexts were supposed to "baptize" the pagan forms. For Christian authors the practice of borrowing from pagan authors like Virgil seemed as justifiable as the Israelites' spoiling of the Egyptians—an action performed at God's command—before they left for the promised land.

While there is much to be said for this analysis of the Christian poetry of Late Antiquity in general, Curtius' suggestion that Sedulius and other biblical poets merely filled the form of the pagan epic with Christian matter (as though the new content of the Christian epic did not affect its form in any way) is misleading. Sedulius' poem was intended to be an epic,

[1] For this expression, see Helene Homeyer, "Der Dichter zwischen zwei Welten: Beobachtungen zur Theorie und Praxis des Dichtens im frühen Mittelalter," *A&A* 16 (1970), 141 ff.

[2] On early Christian attitudes to pagan literature, see M.L.W. Laistner in *History* 20 (1935), 49-54, G. Ellspermann, *The Attitude of the Early Christian Latin Writers toward Pagan Literature and Learning* (Washington, 1949), and more recently C. Riggi, "Lo scontro della letteratura cristiana antica e della cultura greco-romana," *Salesianum* 39 (1977), 431-53. See also the excellent discussion in Roberts, *Biblical Epic*, p. 62, n. 5, and the relevant bibliography cited there.

[3] Curtius, *European Literature*, p. 459. Echoed by Hudson-Williams, "Virgil and the Christian-Latin Poets," 12.

[4] See Augustine, *De doctrina christiana* 2. 42 (*CC* 32, 76-7) and Jerome, *Ep.* 70. 2 (*CSEL* 54, 700 ff.). On Jerome's attitude towards pagan literature, see A.S. Pease's observations in *TAPA* 50 (1919), 150-67.

as we shall see, but it is also profoundly biblical and emphatically different from its pagan epic models not only in terms of content but in formal respects as well. The *Paschale carmen* is best understood as an early representative of a new literary form which is both biblical and epic, whose formal and material elements cannot be so glibly separated as Curtius' formula implies.

i. *The Gospel as Epic*

If Sedulius' first readers had been asked to identify the literary form of the *Paschale carmen* they would doubtless have declared it an epic. For one thing, Sedulius' poem was written in hexameters. In ancient literary theory specific meters were often associated with specific kinds of poetry. In *Inst.* 10. 1. 46-57, for instance, we find Quintilian lumping together under the category of epic a number of widely divergent authors who all happened to write in hexameters. The first-century rhetorician mentions Homer and Theocritus, two poets who differ in some very important respects, in the same breath. Quintilian evidently considers them both epic poets simply because they used hexameters. The connection between hexameters and the epic, which traditionally dealt with heroic subjects, was so well established that the hexameter was often simply described as "the heroic meter." Many of the earliest descriptions of the meter of Sedulius' poem (e.g., the "Gelasian Decree" and Isidore, *De viris illustribus* 20) term it "heroic," and the subscription in *Cod. Vind.* 85 describes Sedulius himself as having taught "the heroic meter" (meaning, no doubt, the *Aeneid*).

Of even more importance than Quintilian's statements on the epic, at least for our purposes, are the poetic theories of Diomedes, a grammarian more nearly contemporary with Sedulius, whose division of poetic genres in the fourth century was "of particular importance" for the Middle Ages.[5] According to Diomedes, there are three major kinds of poetry: *genus activum vel imitativum*, *genus enarrativum*, and *genus commune*. The genres are classified according to the person speaking. In the first the poet does not intrude at all; only the dramatic characters speak. Tragedy and comedy belong to this genre. In the second genre, only the poet speaks. To this category belong poems such as Lucretius' *De rerum natura* and Virgil's *Georgics* (with the exception of the Aristaeus episode in 4. 315-558). In the third genre both author and characters speak.

---

[5] Curtius, *European Literature*, p. 440. A text of Diomedes' *Ars grammatica* may be found in *GL* 1, pp. 299-529. For a general survey of ancient theories on the epic, see Severin Koster, *Antike Epostheorien* (Wiesbaden, 1970).

Diomedes subdivides the *genus commune* into two subordinate genres: *heroica species* and *lyrica species*. The *Iliad* and the *Aeneid* are examples of the former; the poetry of Archilochus and Horace belong to the latter. Even though it seems quite inadequate by modern standards, this system of genre classification had enjoyed a long life even before Diomedes popularized it in Late Antiquity. It goes back at least as far as Plato (*Republic* 3. 392-4), and Aristotle includes a brief description of the theory in his *Poetics* (3. 1-3). The theory had an immediate and lasting impact in Late Antiquity—Servius' classification of Virgil's *Eclogues*, for instance, apparently follows Diomedes' system[6]—and continued to be popular into the Middle Ages. If this view reflected typical fourth and fifth-century literary-critical attitudes, we may well imagine that Sedulius and many in his audience also thought of poetic *genera* along these lines. According to Diomedes' system of classification, Sedulius' poem would clearly have to be assigned to *genus commune* (as opposed to *genus activum* or *genus enarrativum*), since the poet interrupts his narrative frequently in order to address the reader or characters (see, for example, 1. 43-4; 5. 14-7), and since his characters also speak (e.g., 3. 298-304; 5. 6-8). To be even more precise, of the two categories into which Diomedes subdivides the *genus commune*, the *Paschale carmen* is representative of the *heroica species* (as opposed to the *lyrica species*), a distinction again made largely on the basis of meter.

The *Paschale carmen* has additional features besides its meter and mixed speaking voice which would have struck its earliest readers as characteristic of epic practice. Like most epic poets, Sedulius begins his poem with an invocation, an entreaty for divine guidance. An epic is usually an ambitious poem, and the epic poet traditionally asks for assistance from above before he or she begins. Like Juvencus, who turned for aid not to the Muses but to the Holy Spirit, requesting to be sprinkled with the water of the Jordan instead of the Muses' spring, Sedulius rejects the pagan objects of the usual epic invocation while preserving the form.[7] The entire first book of the *Paschale carmen* can be read as an unusually long invocation of God, asking him to lead the poet aright in his difficult assignment. In lines 79-81, Sedulius prays:

Pande salutarem paucos quae ducit in urbem
angusto mihi calle viam verbique lucernam
da pedibus lucere meis. . . .

---

[6] See, for example, G. Thilo, H. Hagen, eds., *Servii grammatici in Vergilii carmina commentarii* (Leipzig, 1887), 3. 1. 29.

[7] On the transformation of the invocation of the Muses in early Christian poetry, see Curtius, *European Literature*, pp. 235 ff.

Although Sedulius follows these lines by recounting Old Testament miracles and attacking pagans and heretics at some length, the atmosphere of prayer pervades the entire book. The petition that Sedulius begins at line 60 is resumed again in lines 334-50 as Sedulius prepares to ask anew for divine guidance:

> Interea dum rite viam sermone levamus
> spesque fidesque meum comitantur in ardua gressum
> blandius ad summam tandem pervenimus arcem.
> Hic proprias sedes, huius mihi moenibus urbis
> exiguam concede domum, tuus incola sanctis
> ut merear habitare locis alboque beati
> ordinis extremus conscribi in saecula civis.
> Grandia posco quidem, sed tu dare grandia nosti,
> quem magis offendit quisquis sperando tepescit. (1. 334-6; 345-50)

Finally in lines 351-4, Sedulius prays to Christ himself:

> Christe, fave votis, qui mundum in morte iacentem
> vivificare volens quondam terrena petisti
> caelitus, humanam dignatus sumere formam,
> sic aliena gerens, ut nec tua linquere posses.

Sedulius asks outright for divine help not only in composing his poem but also in his quest for salvation. Indeed, in the poet's mind the two seem to have become one. Like the pagan poet who hopes to gain immortality with his verse (e.g., Horace, *Odes* 3. 30), the Christian poet views his literary work as closely connected with his eternal salvation. Sedulius' predecessor, Juvencus, had also expressed hope of winning lasting glory through his poetic achievement:

> Nec metus, ut mundi rapiat incendia secum
> hoc opus; hoc etenim forsan me subtrahet igni
> tunc, cum flammivoma discendet nube coruscans
> iudex, altithroni genitoris gloria, Christus. (*Praef.* 21-4)

Like Juvencus, Sedulius asks for divine help in his immediate poetic journey as well as for the eternal reward which he hopes to gain by his literary endeavors. Unlike Juvencus, however, Sedulius devotes not a proem but several portions of an entire book to his invocation.

Like other epics of antiquity, the *Paschale carmen* is also a narrative poem.[8] Sedulius relates the story of the well-known deeds of an extraordinary individual. This is the proper subject of epic, according to Horace (*Ars poetica* 73-4):

> Res gestae regumque ducumque et tristia bella
> quo scribi possent numero, monstravit Homerus.

---

[8] Aristotle suggests that the hexameter is the meter most appropriate for narrative poetry in *Poetics* 24. 8-12.

Like the traditional heroes of epic, Christ is a *rex* and a *dux*, at least as
Sedulius describes him in the *Paschale carmen* (see 1. 338; 1. 85, 143).
Jesus came to earth, to be sure, to save men, not to destroy them (unlike
many epic heroes), but as Sedulius represents him in 4. 95-6 he is also
a great spiritual warrior, in combat not with physical enemies but with
Satan and his army: *cum pompis sociisque suis omnique nefandae agmine
militiae.* . . .

Epics are supposed to be about "arms and violent wars," as Ovid
observes in *Amores* 1. 1, and there are a surprising number of martial
images employed by Sedulius—the poet actually describes himself as a
soldier (*qui militat*) in 1. 339. The images abound in Sedulius' retelling
of the resurrection in the fifth book and help to give this book in particular a heroic tone. In 5. 319-22, for instance, in his description of the
day of resurrection, the poet describes Sunday as now endowed (since the
Lord rose from the dead on this day) with the "splendor of its own
trophy," a phrase with military connotations:

> Septima nam Genesis cum dicit sabbata, claret
> hunc orbis caput esse diem, quem gloria regis
> nunc etiam proprii donans fulgore tropaei
> primatum retinere dedit.

As Sedulius represents it, the resurrection is a kind of military victory,
with Christ (the triumphant warrior) trampling death (his vanquished
enemy) under his heel and terrifying the soldier who was guarding the
tomb:

> Illae igitur Dominum calcata vivere morte
> angelica didicere fide. Perterritus autem
> miles in ancipiti retinet discrimine vitam,
> deserta statione fugax testisque timoris
> vera refert gratis. . . . (5. 332-6)

The poet even refers to the grave clothes which Christ left neatly folded
behind him as *exuviae*, a word often used to refer to that which is stripped
off a fallen combatant and already applied by Sedulius (in 5. 200-1) to
the garment of Jesus for which the soldiers at the foot of the cross cast
lots. In that passage Jesus appears to have lost the battle with death. His
enemies are despoiling him:

> Huius in exuviis sors mittitur, ut sacra vestis
> intemerata manens a Christo scisma vetaret.

But when the word is used again in connection with Jesus' resurrection
in 5. 339-43, Sedulius changes the subject. Jesus is now despoiling his
own corpse. His grave clothes are no longer necessary since he has won
the battle with death:

Fare, inprobe custos,
responde, scelerata cohors, si Christus, ut audes
dicere, concluso furtim productus ab antro
sopitos latuit, cuius iacet intus amictus?
Cuius ad exuvias sedet angelus?

Like many epics in antiquity, the *Paschale carmen* also ends on a fairly
abrupt note. The narrative of Christ's life is carried up to the very end
of the poem. Jesus has just ascended into heaven. The disciples have
witnessed the event and "carry back the journey into the stars with eager
hearts and teach it to all men." Sedulius continues:

. . . testes nam iure fideles
divinae virtutis erant, qui plura videntes
innumerabilium scripserunt pauca bonorum.
Nam si cuncta sacris voluissent tradere chartis
facta redemptoris, nec totus cingere mundus
sufficeret densos per tanta volumina libros. (5. 433-8)

Not only does this ending honor the way in which John concludes his
Gospel, but its abruptness also resembles the endings of some of the best
known epics of antiquity (such as the *Aeneid*) which have very little in the
way of a conclusion or epilogue.[9] Perhaps Sedulius was consciously striv-
ing for this epic effect, too.

The Christian Aeneid

Of the pagan Latin poems with which Sedulius was evidently familiar,
it is Virgil's epic masterpiece, the *Aeneid*, which most influenced this
Christian poet.[10] That Virgil should have been a literary resource and
target for a Latin Christian poet is not surprising. For one thing, Virgil
was a popular schoolroom author who was seen by many believers as
practically a prophet of Christ, and, for another, he was easily the most
conspicuous of the poets of a religion and culture to which Christianity
was in many ways antagonistic.[11] Even though Sedulius does not
explicitly announce the fact of his *imitatio* or *aemulatio* of Virgil, his silence
means little. If, as the subscriptional evidence gives us reason to believe,
Sedulius was a *grammaticus*, he had very likely taught the *Aeneid* in school,

---

[9] See my discussion of the ending of the *Aeneid* and other ancient epics in "The Last
Line of the *Aeneid*," *CJ* 82 (1987), 310-13.

[10] Johannes Huemer devotes over 30 pages of his *De Sedulii poetae vita* (pp. 65-101) to
listing Sedulius' echoes and borrowings from Virgil, the majority of them from the *Aeneid*.

[11] On Vergil as a prophet of Christ, see Comparetti, *Vergil in the Middle Ages*, Chapter
7. For Christian interpretations of *Eclogue* 4, see the discussion of Stephen Benko,
"Virgil's Fourth Eclogue in Christian Interpretation" in *ANRW* 31. 1 (Berlin and New
York, 1980), pp. 646-705.

and even a casual reading of the *Paschale carmen* is enough to establish that the fifth-century poet knew Virgil extremely well. Sedulius draws heavily upon the language and ideas of the *Aeneid* and, one supects, may even have hoped that his Christian epic would rival the popularity and the authority of the greatest of all Latin epics.

Despite remaining unnamed, Virgil's presence is readily apparent in the preface and the opening lines of the *Paschale carmen*, in which Sedulius sets forth differences between his own and pagan poetry and establishes his right to sing of the miracles of Christ.[12] We can be certain, for instance, that Sedulius must mean for Virgil to be included in the ranks of the *gentiles poetae* with whom he takes issue in the opening lines of the first book:

> Cum sua gentiles studeant figmenta poetae
> grandisonis pompare modis, tragicoque boatu
> ridiculove Geta seu qualibet arte canendi
> saeva nefandarum renovent contagia rerum
> et scelerum monumenta canant, rituque magistro
> plurima Niliacis tradant mendacia biblis. . . . (1. 17-22)

After all, Virgil was the best known of the Latin pagan poets and the most popular of the schoolroom authors who had committed "their many lying tales to Egyptian papyri."[13] It is significant that the only pagan poet whom Sedulius does mention in the *Paschale carmen* is the one named here, Hosidius Geta, a second-century poet whose reputation rests solely upon his *Medea*, a Virgilian cento.[14] It would be difficult for Sedulius' readers not to be reminded of Virgil at this point, because without the Augustan poet's works Geta could not have written his poem. In the preface proper (1. 1-16) Sedulius may also have included another indirect reference to Virgil. In these lines the Christian poet warns his readers that the humble fare of his *Paschale carmen* will not be to the taste of the palate used to "the sweetness of great affairs:"

> Aut si magnarum caperis dulcedine rerum
> divitiasque magis deliciosus amas,
> nobilium nitidis doctorum vescere cenis,
> quorum multiplices nec numerantur opes. (*Praef.* 7-10)

---

[12] Hudson-Williams, "Virgil and the Christian Latin Poets," p. 13, remarks on the relationship between the Christian Latin poets of Late Antiquity and Virgil:
> Heavy as is their debt to Virgil, the poets are sparing in direct allusions to him. . . . The more sensitive, notably Prudentius, are significantly silent: it was a delicate relationship upon which it was unnecessary to dwell.

[13] For the prominence which Virgil enjoyed in the classrooms of Late Antiquity, see Comparetti, *Vergil in the Middle Ages*, pp. 24 ff.

[14] See now the Latin text and an Italian translation of the *Medea* by Giovanni Salanitro in the series *Bibliotheca Athena* 24 (Rome, 1981).

Throughout the opening lines of the *Paschale carmen* Sedulius echoes the
themes and language of the opening remarks of Juvencus' *Evangeliorum
libri quattuor*. In *Praefatio* 10, the fourth-century poet had spoken unforgettably of *dulcedo Maronis*, and it is possible that those in Sedulius' audience
familiar with Juvencus' poem may have detected an echo in *magnarum .
. . dulcedine rerum*.

But even if the first readers of the *Paschale carmen* failed to notice any
indirect allusion to Virgil in the opening lines of the poem, they surely
would have recognized the pervasive Virgilian tone of this Christian epic
in general. Echoes and reminiscences of the *Aeneid* abound. Some of the
borrowing on Sedulius' part may be unconscious—if he was a *grammaticus*, he probably knew much of the *Aeneid* by heart—but there are also
instances where it seems to be more than inadvertent. Although it has
sometimes been suggested that Christian poets like Sedulius made such
extensive use of Virgil because their own poetic abilities were deficient,
it is just as likely that Sedulius' borrowings were intended to suggest a
contrast between the famous pagan epic and his own Christian one.[15]

It sounds strange to modern ears to hear the God of the Bible
addressed as *tonans*, the adjective Virgil reserves for Jupiter. The biblical
concepts and the familiar classical forms seem too irreconcilable. As
Comparetti observes: ''The utter incompatibility that exists between
Christianity and paganism could not fail to put Christian poetry to great
inconvenience in its classical dress.''[16] Such criticism, however, fails to
reconstruct the probable intentions of the poet and the expectations of the
original audience for whom he wrote the poem. If Sedulius wanted his
challenge to the classical tradition to be unmistakable, his preservation
of so many characteristic features of the pagan epic was quite possibly
deliberate, intended to help his readers to see the difference between a
Christian and a pagan epic. At the very least, it must be admitted that
the incompatibility or tension between Christian content and pagan form
in the *Paschale carmen* did not stand in the way of the poem's immediate
popularity among its readers in Late Antiquity, who were evidently not
very offended by the clash between content and form to which modern
critics are so sensitive in this and other biblical epics of Late Antiquity.[17]

---

[15] The view that such reminiscences were not intended to evoke their original contexts
but were simply the product of an extensive borrowing of a convenient poetic idiom is
no longer commonly held. For an alternative perspective, see K. Thraede's discussion
of *Kontrastimitation* in ''Epos,'' *RAC* 5, 1039 ff.

[16] Comparetti, *Vergil in the Middle Ages*, p. 163.

[17] See Hudson-Williams, ''Virgil and the Christian Latin Poets'' (p. 21), for a description of the combination of Virgilian and biblical elements in the Christian Latin
poetry of Late Antiquity as ''grotesque and ridiculous.''

   Some of the Christian poet's borrowings are too startling and apt to
believe them entirely fortuitous. For example, Sedulius must have known
that his readers would be reminded of the Virgilian similes of lions and
their contexts when they read of Herod *ceu leo frendens* ordering the
slaughter of the innocents in his zeal to exterminate the infant Jesus.
Sedulius combines the Virgilian simile with the biblical (1 Peter 5. 8:
diabolus tamquam leo rugiens) to create a vivid picture of Herod as a cross
between Turnus and the devil:

> Ergo ubi delusum se conperit, impius iram
> rex aperit (si iure queat rex ille vocari,
> qui pietate caret, propriam qui non regit iram)
> ereptumque gemens facinus sibi, ceu leo frendens,
> cuius ab ore tener subito cum labitur agnus,
> in totum movet arma gregem manditque trahitque
> molle pecus, trepidaeque vocant sua pignera fetae
> nequiquam et vacuas implent balatibus auras:
> haut secus Herodes Christo stimulatus adempto
> sternere conlisas parvorum strage catervas
> inmerito non cessat atrox. (2. 108-17)

Herod is no more effective against that which has been willed of God
than Turnus, who is depicted as a bloody-mouthed lion in *Aeneid* 12. 4-8,
which attacks (*movet arma*) but cannot overcome Aeneas. Another
Virgilian passage from which Sedulius draws is *Aeneid* 9. 339 ff., where
a lion is compelled by his hunger to ravage the full sheepfolds:

> Impastus ceu plena leo per ovilia turbans
> (suadet enim vesana fames) manditque trahitque
> molle pecus mutumque metu, fremit ore cruento.[18]

Sedulius borrows imagery and language from this passage in 2. 108-17,
but the Christian poet emphasizes instead of the lion's hunger his frustra-
tion at losing the lamb that was already in his maw. It is this deprivation
which drives Herod to attack the tender flock. As it turns out, it is the
lambs (Christ and the innocents) which receive most of Sedulius' attention in his transformation of the Virgilian simile. Not only, therefore,
does Sedulius take advantage of the emotive power of a familiar epic
passage, but he complements Virgil's emphasis on the lion by laying
equal or greater emphasis on the lamb, a symbol laden with significance
for Christian readers and explicitly connected elsewhere in the *Paschale
carmen* (e.g., 5. 140) with the atoning death of Christ.
   Another example of such creative borrowing is Sedulius' account of
the storm on Galilee (3. 46-69). Jesus is presented here in a situation to

---

[18] I use the edition of R.A.B. Mynors (Oxford, 1969).

which Aeneas was accustomed, aboard ship in a storm (cf., e.g., *Aen.* 1.
81-123; 5. 1-34). Sedulius pieces together lines and phrases from storm
scenes in the *Aeneid* to construct a descriptive passage far more elaborate
than the simple New Testament narrative upon which it is based (cf. Mt.
8. 23-7). The Christian poet sacrifices the simplicity of the Gospel
account of the storm in order to impart an epic and Virgilian flavor to
this passage. The difference between Virgil's hero in the storm and
Sedulius' is that the unwarlike Jesus has power over the elements, like
Neptune or Aeolus in the *Aeneid*, whereas Aeneas, the renowned human
warrior, cannot control the weather (or his own destiny). The elements
are not actually threatening Jesus, Sedulius reassures his readers, but
simply expressing their joy with too much exuberance:

> Non erat illa feri pugnax audacia ponti,
> in Dominum tumidas quae surgere cogeret undas,
> nec metuenda truces agitabant flamina vires:
> sed laetum exiliens Christo mare conpulit imum
> obsequio fervere fretum, rapidoque volatu
> moverunt avidas ventorum gaudia pinnas. (3. 64-9)

Throughout the *Paschale carmen* Sedulius' application to Christ of the
language Virgil used to describe Aeneas suggests that he is setting off his
new hero, the immortal and resurrected Savior, against the background
of Virgil's mortal hero, Aeneas.[19] Virgil's hero is a model for Sedulius'.
Just as Aeneas leads his group of Trojan followers to a safe political haven
and a promising future in Italy, so Christ gives his followers freedom
(from sin and death) and leads them to a blissful new home (heaven). But
Aeneas is also a foil for Christ. The liberating hero of the *Paschale carmen*,
who guides all mankind (not just Romans) in the search for a spiritual
and eternal country, seems far more potent than Aeneas. Aeneas prays
for miracles; Jesus performs them. For many of Sedulius' contemporaries who could no longer believe in a Roman empire *sine fine* (the city
of Rome was sacked in 410 and again in 455), the *Paschale carmen*'s retelling of the origins of sin and the possibility of mankind's ultimate redemption must have represented a more cogent and credible exposition of their
own identity and destiny than Virgil's *Aeneid* was now able to provide.
   To anyone in Sedulius' audience familiar with his Christian poetic
precursors such a challenge to Virgil's *Aeneid* would have come as no surprise. As we have already seen, Juvencus makes a point of singling out

---

[19] In much the same way that Virgil set off his new responsible (*pius*) hero, Aeneas,
against the background of the egocentric Homeric heroes, Sedulius seems to invite his
reader to compare and contrast his Christian hero with Virgil's Roman one. (For a
discussion of the shift of values from Homer's epic heroes to Virgil's, see Maurice B.
McNamee, *Honor and the Epic Hero* [New York, 1960], pp. 51-74.)

the great Roman poet for mention in the preface to *Evangeliorum libri quattuor*:

> Sed tamen innumeros homines sublimia facta
> et virtutis honos in tempora longa frequentant,
> adcumulant quorum famam laudesque poetae.
> Hos celsi cantus, Smyrnae de fonte fluentes,
> illos Minciadae celebrat dulcedo Maronis. (*Praef.* 6-10)

Evidently the fourth-century poet viewed himself as an epic poet in the class of the great Publius Vergilius Maro (Juvencus clearly has the *Aeneid* and not the *Eclogues* or *Georgics* in mind, since he mentions Virgil in the same breath as Homer), with an even greater epic subject than that of the *Aeneid*. The Gospels' narrative of the life of Christ is to replace the false myths, the fictional *arma virumque* which are the subject matter of the famous pagan epic (see *Praef.* 15-20).

Proba, another poetic predecessor of Sedulius', also conceived of herself as an epic poet. In the prologue to her *Cento* she contrasts the traditional subject of an epic which she had already written with the subject (*pia munera Christi*) which she has chosen for her new epic:[20]

> Iam dudum temerasse duces pia foedera pacis,
> regnandi miseros tenuit quos dira cupido,
> diversasque neces, regum crudelia bella
> cognatasque acies, pollutos caede parentum
> insignis clipeos nulloque ex hoste tropaea,
> sanguine conspersos tulerat quos fama triumphos,
> innumeris totiens viduatas civibus urbes,
> confiteor, scripsi. . . . (1-8)

Like other epic poets Proba has an exalted sense of her poetic calling.[21] In line 12 she refers to herself as a *vatis*, and it seems that she, too, may have intended her Christian epic to rival the *Aeneid*. That, at least, was the way in which some of her earliest readers regarded her poem. In a preface which is attached to the *Cento*, an admirer of Proba claims that the poet's Christian work has changed Virgil for the better (*Maronem mutatum in melius*). Although few modern readers would agree with this judgment, we may be certain that there were many readers of the *Cento* in Late Antiquity who did not find the claim preposterous.

---

[20] On Proba's adaptation of Christ as an epic hero, see Elizabeth Clark and Diane Hatch, "Jesus as Hero in the Vergilian *Cento* of Faltonia Betitia Proba," *Vergilius* 27 (1981), 31-9.

[21] The seriousness of Proba's poetic enterprise has been called into question. In his study of "Theory and Practice in the Vergilian Cento," *ICS* 9. 1 (1984), 79-90, however, David Bright argues that Proba and Hosidius Geta "show both a seriousness and an ambition which set them far from any tradition of *nugae* and parody."

Like these Christian poets before him, Sedulius dared to challenge the most authoritative of the Latin poets largely because of his unbounded confidence in his subject matter. It only seemed natural to the first Christian Latin poets that an epic life of Christ should be read with the same degree of respect (or greater) and accorded the same privileged status as the *Aeneid*, because of the superiority of the truth of the Gospel over the false myths which are the subject of the *Aeneid*. Not only did the authors of biblical epics in Late Antiquity make such claims for their poetry, but their readers gave them credence. We know of at least one of Sedulius' readers in Late Antiquity who apparently held Sedulius' Christian epic in this kind of esteem. It is significant that Turcius Rufius Apronianus Asterius, the consul who produced an edition of Virgil's works in 494, should also have published an edition of the *Paschale carmen*. Quite possibly, as Roberts suggests, the consul thought of the two poets as "complementary." The two editions may, therefore, "represent a conscious programme by Asterius to produce reliable texts of the chief pagan and chief Christian poet of his day."[22] If Roberts' interpretation is right, the *Paschale carmen* was already something of a classic and Sedulius himself was being assigned Virgilian stature by the end of the fifth century. Whether or not this was Asterius' intention, we do know that in the centuries that followed there were many readers who put Sedulius on an equal footing with Virgil. The verses describing the contents of the library of Isidore, the seventh-century bishop of Seville, serve to illustrate the value which Christian readers of Late Antiquity and the early Middle Ages assigned to Sedulius and other Christian poets:

> Si Maro, si Flaccus, si Naso et Persius horret,
> Lucanus si te, Papiniusque tedet,
> par erat eximio dulcis Prudentius ore,
> carminibus variis nobilis ille satis.
> Perlege facundi studiosum carmen Aviti,
> ecce Iuvencus adest, Seduliusque tibi.
> Ambo lingua pares, florentes versibus ambo,
> fonte evangelico pocula larga ferunt.
> Desine gentilibus ergo inservire poetis,
> dum bona tanta potes, quid tibi Calliroen?[23]

For the reader who is bored with standard pagan verse, Sedulius is held forth as a preeminent Christian author whose work rivals or even excels

---

[22] Roberts, *Biblical Epic*, p. 78. We know of at least one other consul of Late Antiquity, Vettius Agorius Basilius Mavortius (527), who produced a parallel edition of a pagan and a Christian poet: Horace and Prudentius. See E.O. Winstedt, "Mavortius' Copy of Prudentius," *Classical Review* 18 (1904), 112-5, and "Mavortius and Prudentius," *Classical Quarterly* 1 (1907), 10-12.

[23] I use the text in *PL* 83, 1109-10.

that of such popular pagan poets as Horace, Ovid, Persius, Lucan, Statius, and even Virgil.

ii. *Sacra Poesis*

If the *Paschale carmen* is an epic, what distinguishes it from its pagan precursors? The most obvious difference—and this is noted by Sedulius and other Christian epic poets—is the new kind of epic subject:

> Cur ego, Daviticis adsuetus cantibus odas
> cordarum resonare decem sanctoque verenter
> stare choro et placidis caelestia psallere verbis,
> clara salutiferi taceam miracula Christi? (1. 23-6)

The Christian poet turns from the usual subjects of epic such as the great affairs of kings and generals and bitter wars (see *Ars poetica* 73) in order to concentrate on the deeds of Christ, his main character, who described himself as "meek and lowly in heart" (Mt. 11. 29). Sedulius observes in the preface to the *Paschale carmen* that the content of his Christian epic will not be to the taste of those who prefer tales of great exploits.[24] The author hastens to warn his readers to expect "humble fare," vegetables served in common earthenware:

> At nos exiguum de paupere carpsimus horto,
> rubra quod adpositum testa ministrat, holus. (*Praef.* 15-16)

If Sedulius' readers are expecting exotic, gourmet food, they are advised to look elsewhere. Other poets who are concerned with *magnae res* will provide more satisfying reading. Sedulius' disclaimer is not merely false humility. He knows that he cannot offer his readers exciting love scenes between princes and princesses or gory battle episodes. The only wars which the poet of the Gospels may describe are theological disputes or cosmic battles between spiritual forces of good and evil. Throughout the *Paschale carmen* Sedulius chooses not to emphasize the polemical and theologically controversial Jesus as he is presented in the Gospels. As we have seen, the poet does show him engaged in spiritual battle with Satan, but even when the Savior is casting out demons or facing his most difficult moments on earth, as, for instance, in the whole of his passion and death in Book 5, there is little indication of exertion or struggle on Jesus' part. As we have also seen, Sedulius concentrates on the action of the Gospels, the miracles and the major events of Christ's life, but in the final analysis the poet's hero is the prince of peace, and the *tristia bella*

---

[24] Quintilian in *Inst.* 1. 8. 5 speaks of the *magnitudo rerum* which is supposed to characterize heroic poetry.

which traditionally set the tone of the pagan epic are incompatible with a "heavenly poem" to be sung with "peaceful words" (1. 25). If there is something in his poem of whose greatness Sedulius is convinced, it is the salvation of mankind, but that, as he hints in the preface, is a treasure in earthen vessels (cf. 2 Cor. 4. 7). It will take a special kind of reader to discern its entertainment value.

There are other differences, however, between the Christian and the pagan epic, not as obvious as the change in content so often mentioned by the Christian poets themselves, but equally significant. It would, in fact, be a mistake to assume that the change in content does not affect formal aspects of Sedulius' Christian epic or to suggest that the *Paschale carmen* can simply be analyzed as new Christian content in an old pagan form. After all, the Gospels have their own style, their own narrative technique, their own set of familiar images, and Sedulius is as much a fifth-century evangelist as he is an epic poet in the tradition of Virgil.[25] In many ways, Sedulius' poem and Virgil's *Aeneid* are worlds apart—not only in content but also in form. In the pages that follow we shall examine three distinctively Christian aspects of the *Paschale carmen* which are functions of its new content, but which also affect its form: the poem's exegetical quality, the poet's persona as expressed in narrative intrusions, and the imagery of the *Paschale carmen*.

Exegesis

As a poet of the sacred book, Sedulius enjoys a different relationship with his subject from most pagan poets. He not only tells his story, he believes deeply in it. The Bible informs his life and his thought, and much of his creativity consists in his ability not only to retell but also to interpret the Scriptures. Sedulius' work is, therefore, an exegetical exercise as well as an epic, designed to explain to readers the meaning or meanings of the narratives which it relates.

It is instructive to compare Sedulius in this regard with the two other late antique Latin epic poets of the New Testament, Juvencus and Arator. The fourth-century author of *Evangeliorum libri quattuor* is relatively sparing in his overt interpretations, although he will intrude into the narrative on occasion, most often to utter some sort of a reaction to an episode which he is relating. He cannot resist, for example, a comment on the wickedness of Salome as she brings the head of John the Baptist to her mother: *Illa—nefas—matri scelerata ad gaudia portat* (3. 67). Some-

---

[25] On Sedulius' self-conception as an evangelist, see Witke, *Numen litterarum*, p. 218.

times, but only rarely, Juvencus does include indirect exegesis in
Evangeliorum libri quattuor, as in his description of the gifts of the Magi:

> Gaudia magna Magi gaudent sidusque salutant,
> et postquam puerum videre sub ubere matris,
> deiecti prono straverunt corpore terram
> submissique simul quaesunt; tum munera trina
> tus, aurum, murram regique hominique Deoque
> dona dabant. (1. 246-51)

Without abandoning the narrative mode completely, Juvencus includes
a simple explanation of why these three gifts were appropriate to give to
the child in Bethlehem. But he is seldom more explicit than this. It is safe
to say that exegesis is not one of Juvencus' primary poetic intentions.
    Sedulius' own handling of the same incident is an interesting contrast:

> Thensaurisque simul pro religione solutis,
> ipsae etiam ut possint species ostendere Christum,
> aurea nascenti fuderunt munera regi,
> tura dedere Deo, myrram tribuere sepulchro.
> Cur tria dona tamen? Quoniam spes maxima vitae est
> hunc numerum confessa fides, et tempora summus
> cernens cuncta Deus, praesentia, prisca, futura,
> semper adest semperque fuit semperque manebit
> in triplici virtute sui. (2. 93-101)

Like Juvencus, Sedulius demonstrates how the three gifts "illustrate
Christ." Gold is a proper gift for a king, incense for a god, and myrrh
for the dying Savior. But after relating briefly the fact and significance
of the respective gifts, Sedulius breaks off the narrative, addresses his
audience directly in the form of a rhetorical question—he is less concerned than Juvencus with keeping narrative distance—and proceeds to
exegize at some length on the number of the gifts. Sedulius sees the idea
of the triune God who always was, is, and will be as implicit in the three
gifts, and the Christian poet-exegete offers an animated five-line explica-
tion of the analogy.
    Sedulius' exegetical tendencies were carried to an extreme by Arator,
who, in effect, wrote a commentary in verse on Acts. A good example
of Arator's practice is his exegesis of the story of Peter's resurrection of
Dorcas (Acts 9. 36-43):

> Vocata redit lucique reducta
> se stupuit superesse sibi, quam protinus ipse
> prendit et erectam turbis gaudentibus offert.
> Illa manus meruit Petri contingere dextram
> pauperibus quae larga fuit, qua vita revertens
> cetera membra levat corpusque itura per omne
> hanc subiit quae causa fuit. Si iure movemur,

> instaurata dies animae patet apta figuris,
> quam nimis antiqui depresserat umbra pericli
> ad vocem conversa Petri: caput ante gravatum
> legis in obscurae gremio velut altera surgens
> ecclesia praesente levat, tenebrasque repellit
> lux operum comitata fidem, quae legis ab ore
> non fuerat promissa salus, quia fonte renatis
> gratia perpetuae coepit dare munera vitae. (1. 831-45)

The sixth-century poet, who sees Dorcas' resurrection as an allegory, has clearly become more interested in interpreting the event than in simply retelling it. Here (and elsewhere in *De actibus apostolorum*) Arator shows himself more concerned with *meditatio* than *narratio*. The raising of Dorcas from the dead suggests to the poet the conversion of the Old Testament church under the sway of the law to the new kind of salvation offered by grace in the New Testament era, and he devotes more energy to expounding this doctrine than he does to retelling the story of the life, death, and resurrection of Dorcas.

Sedulius occupies a middle ground between Juvencus and Arator. Narration and exegesis are of approximately the same importance to him. Often Sedulius will retell an episode without much explicit comment. In his description of the healing of Peter's mother-in-law, for instance, he shows himself capable of Juvencan-like reticence:

> Forte Petri validae torrebat lampadis aestu
> febris anhela socrum, dubioque in funere pendens
> saucia sub gelidis ardebat vita periclis,
> inmensusque calor frigus letale coquebat.
> At posquam fessos Domini manus adtigit artus,
> igneus ardor abiit, totisque extincta medullis
> fonte latentis aquae cecidit violentia flammae. (3. 33-9)

But just as often Sedulius will spell out exactly what he believes a passage to mean, as, for example, in his interpretation of the first petition of the Lord's Prayer:

> Sanctificetur ubi Dominus, qui cuncta creando
> sanctificat, nisi corde pio, nisi pectore casto?
> Ut mereamur eum nos sanctificare colendo,
> annuat ipse prior, sicut benedicier idem
> se iubet a nobis, a quo benedicimur omnes. (2. 244-8)

For most Christian exegetes of Late Antiquity (the Antiochene school was an important exception),[26] the Scriptures, even though historically and literally true, also contained a deeper truth which it was the exegete's

---

[26] On this point, see M.L.W. Laistner, "Antiochene Exegesis in Western Europe during the Middle Ages," *HTR* 40 (1947), 19-31.

task to discover. Each episode of the Bible and every detail of each episode had a kernel of spiritual significance which did not lie at the surface of the text and which could only be gotten at by means of exegesis.[27] We know that Sedulius was familiar with non-literal methods of biblical interpretation. In the *Paschale opus* (2. 17) he speaks of the *tripartitus intellegentiae sensus: secundum litteram . . . moraliter . . . spiritaliter.*[28] In the *Paschale carmen* Sedulius puts theory into practice, revealing himself to be quite adept at developing the non-literal sense of the Scriptural narratives which he retells.

The story of the return of the Magi to their homeland by a different route may serve to illustrate the way in which Sedulius does exegesis in the *Paschale carmen*:

> Tunc caelitus illi
> per somnum moniti contemnere iussa tyranni
> per loca mutati gradientes devia callis
> in patriam rediere suam. Sic nos quoque sanctam
> si cupimus patriam tandem contingere, posquam
> venimus ad Christum, iam non repetamus iniquum. (2. 101-6)

The poet retells the story line of Matthew 2. 12 ff. but is clearly interested in more than its literal meaning. According to Sedulius, the decision of the Magi to go directly home after their encounter with Christ in Bethlehem teaches all believers that they, too, should avoid evil after coming to faith in Christ. The poet's exegesis of the return of the Magi is, therefore, in part, moral interpretation. As Sedulius handles it, this story becomes more than an entertaining narrative. It is intended to have a salutary effect on his audience. This episode in Scripture is—like all of the Bible—"a mirror where man learns to know himself with his misery and sin, and the perfection to which God destines and calls him."[29] Like the wise men, Sedulius' readers are to shun the path of evil and stick to the narrow road which leads to salvation. This is a recurrent theme in the *Paschale carmen* (cf. 1. 80, 2. 293-7, 3. 330-3) as it is in Christian thought in general.[30] Sedulius links the story of the return of the Magi with this powerful Christian commonplace, thereby turning a relatively

---

[27] See *De doctrina christiana* 2. 6, for example, for Augustine's ingenious explanation of the true meaning of *Cant.* 4. 2 ("Your teeth are like a flock of shorn ewes that have come up from the washing, all of which bear twins, and not one among them is bereaved").

[28] For a general discussion of exegesis as practiced in the New Testament and the early church, see W.E. Gerber's article in *RAC* 6, 1211-29.

[29] Walther Burghardt, "On Early Christian Exegesis," *Theological Studies* 11 (1950), 104 ff., as quoted in William F Lynch, *Christ and Apollo* (New York, 1960), p. 230.

[30] See M.M. McKenna, "The 'Two Ways' in Jewish and Christian Writings in the Greco-Roman Period. A Study of the Form of Repentance Parenesis." Diss. University of Pennsylvania, 1981.

simple story into a profound one with obvious application to his readers' daily lives.

According to John Cassian, a close contemporary of Sedulius (c. 370-435), there were three levels of Scriptural interpretation besides the literal, namely, the tropological (i.e., moral), the anagogical, and the allegorical.[31] The story of the return of the Magi is well suited for tropological interpretation, as we have just seen, but Sedulius also gives it an anagogical treatment, that is to say, an interpretation which emphasizes the eschatological, "the last things, the celestial realities which are no longer the symbols of anything else."[32] One of the images most often used in anagogical exegesis is that of the heavenly Jerusalem, the church triumphant. Sedulius does not ignore the possibilities for an anagogical reading of Mt. 2. 12. Just as the three wise men returned safely home after shunning Herod, so, too, believers will arrive at their "holy fatherland" (*sanctam patriam*), namely, heaven, if they shun evil.

By far the most common type of interpretation which Sedulius uses in the *Paschale carmen* is the allegorical or typological. A good example is the story of the flood and the preservation of Noah and his family in the ark in 1: 73-8. Sedulius preserves the bare outline of the literal story but is more interested in its deeper, predictive significance. The Christian poet observes that the flood shows that the whole world would some day be washed with one baptism, just as it was once covered by the flood:

> . . . ut mystica virtus
> quod carnis delicta necant, hoc praesule ligno
> monstraret liquidas renovari posse per undas,
> totum namque lavans uno baptismate mundum. (1. 75-8)

The New Testament church's practice of baptism complements and fills out the significance of the Old Testament story, which is seen as a prophetic type or figure foreshadowing that which is to come later.

The Christian poet's exegetical practice affects the entire poem in a manner far more complex than the formula of new content in old form would suggest. Consider, for example, the resultant narrative style of the *Paschale carmen*. Sedulius' high degree of respect for the truth of his subject matter is, no doubt, behind his reluctance to use flashback (2. 144-8 is an exception) or prophecy as narrative devices. This voluntary restriction prevents Sedulius from enjoying the kind of narrative flexibility Virgil had. Part of the genius of the *Aeneid* derives from the way in which its

---

[31] *Collationes* 14. 8 (*PL* 49, 962 ff.). The hexameter summarization of the four levels of Scriptural meaning is well known:

> Littera gesta docet, quid credas allegoria,
> moralis quid agas, quo tendas anagogia (*PL* 113, 28).

[32] Lynch, *Christ and Apollo*, p. 230.

author manages to wrap up past, present, and future in one poem. In
Books 2 and 3, for instance, Aeneas tells of the past (the fall of Troy and
his wanderings), and in Books 6 and 8 he is given a glimpse of the future
of Rome. Sedulius is not able (or does not wish) to employ such narrative
finesse. The events of Scripture as Sedulius retells them are unfolded in
chronological order. The *Paschale carmen*'s narrative style is best described
as paratactic. The stories proceed like a succession of panels, such as the
mosaics in the nave of the church of Santa Maria Maggiore, which treat
of separate incidents within a larger Scriptural narrative.[33] Sedulius'
transitions are abrupt. He cares little about locating episodes in specific
temporal or scenic contexts.[34] The poet does not strive for continuity
between episodes, probably because the immediate and historical connections do not interest him so much as the larger spiritual meanings. It
is, in fact, the narrative style of the Gospels themselves which Sedulius
imitates. The evangelists, too, were not so interested in narrative continuity or in the precise chronological or geographical connections
between episodes as in the episode itself and its spiritual significance for
believers or prospective believers.

This is not to say that Sedulius eschews narrative sophistication
altogether. In a way, typology plays a role in the Christian epic similar
to that of foreshadowing in the *Aeneid*.[35] Just as Virgil will give the reader
some hint beforehand of impending doom for an individual, say, for
instance, the tragic queen Dido in Book 4 of the *Aeneid*, thus creating
suspense and heightening tension, so also already in Book 1 of the
Paschale carmen Sedulius points to the redemptive suffering of the
Messiah, which is only described in full in the last book. Throughout all
the books of the poem, Sedulius hints at what Jesus' fate will be, as he
does, for instance, in his retelling of the story of the Magi who bring
myrrh to the infant Christ as a present for his eventual burial (*myrram
tribuere sepulchro*). Sedulius uses the gift to remind the reader of an event
which he has hinted at before and will hint at again in the *Paschale carmen*
before he actually gets around to recounting it in detail: the Son of God
will die and be buried in a tomb.

Since the content of the biblical epics is given to such a large extent,
it is often assumed that the authors of poems like the *Paschale carmen* can-

---

[33] On the mosaics in Santa Maria Maggiore, see Heinrich Karpp, *Die frühchristlichen
und mittelalterlichen Mosaiken in Santa Maria Maggiore zu Rom* (Baden-Baden, 1966), and Beat
Brenk, *Die frühchristlichen Mosaiken in S. Maria Maggiore zu Rom* (Wiesbaden, 1975).

[34] Ilona Opelt makes this point in "Die Szenerie bei Sedulius," p. 109: "Sedulius ist
noch weit stärker als Iuvencus blind für die Landschaft des Heilgeschehens."

[35] See G.E. Duckworth, *Foreshadowing and Suspense in the Epics of Homer, Apollonius, und
Vergil* (Princeton, 1933), and Robert J. Rowland Jr., "Foreshadowing in Vergil, *Aeneid*
VIII, 714-728," *Latomus* 27 (1968), 832-42.

not attain the levels of meaning which a poet like Virgil is able to achieve in the *Aeneid*. The Augustan poet combines the heroic and the civilized, the Homeric past and the Roman future, the mythological and the historical in his masterpiece. His poem is a celebration of Augustus' greatness, but at the same time probably includes Virgil's own qualified view of Rome's imperial destiny. But the *Paschale carmen*, too, is a poem which offers its readers complex meaning. Sedulius rises above mere retelling. As an exegetical poet, he interprets his narrative in a variety of ways and expresses his own pious reactions to his subject material. Often Sedulius sets the stories of the Gospels against Old Testament contexts, viewing the life of Christ in its ultimate significance for mankind's redemption and hopes for heaven. Often the poet explains an episode's significance for his readers' daily life or salvation. Sedulius is as concerned with the dream as with the definite. He can and does retell narratives in a simple and straightforward style, but he also often strives to lead his readers to higher, more meditative and mystical levels of understanding.[36]

Authorial Intrusions

On occasion Sedulius will intrude into his narrative to address a character. This kind of authorial intrusion is not uncommon in the more traditional Latin epics. In the ninth book of the *Aeneid*, for instance, after he has told of the deaths of Nisus and Euryalus, Virgil addresses them both:

> Fortunati ambo! Si quid mea carmina possunt,
> nulla dies umquam memori vos eximet aevo,
> dum domus Aeneae Capitoli immobile saxum
> accolet imperiumque pater Romanus habebit. (9. 446-9)

One might suppose that Sedulius is simply following traditional epic practice in including authorial comments in the *Paschale carmen*. A closer examination, however, reveals the Christian poet's intrusions to be different both in degree and kind from Virgil's. Sedulius cannot, for instance, show moderation in his address of Judas:

> Tune cruente, ferox, audax, insane, rebellis,
> perfide, crudelis, fallax, venalis, inique,
> traditor inmitis, fere proditor, impie latro,
> praevius horribiles comitaris signifer enses?

---

[36] On the meditative function of Christian poetry in general, see Reinhart Herzog, ''La meditazione poetica: Una forma retorico-teologica tra tarda antichità e barocco'' in *La poesia tardoantica: Tra retorica, teologia e politica*, Atti del V corso della scuola superiore d. archeologia e civiltà medievali (Messina, 1984), pp. 75-101.

Sacrilegamque aciem, gladiis sudibusque minacem
cum moveas, ori ora premis mellique venenum
inseris et blanda Dominum sub imagine prodis?
Quid socium simulas et amica fraude salutas?
Numquam terribiles aut pax coniurat in enses,
aut truculenta pio lupus oscula porrigit agno. (5. 59-68)

In comparison with this heated diatribe, Virgil's apostrophe of Nisus and
Euryalus seems relatively detached. Sedulius feels more than a twinge of
sympathy or antipathy for the characters in his narrative; he lives in a
passionately hot and cold relationship with these Gospel personalities. In
this respect, the Christian poet has broken with the epic poet's traditional
detachment from his subject. Virgil's intrusions are less extreme, one
suspects, because his subject, for instance, the death of Nisus and
Euryalus, is more literary and less historically real to him.[37]

If he hates Judas for betraying Christ, Sedulius loves Mary, the
mother of the Lord. He cannot mention her role as *theotokos* without
bursting into an ecstatic hymn of praise:

Salve, sancta parens, enixa puerpera regem,
qui caelum terramque tenet per saecula, cuius
nomen et aeterno conplectens omnia gyro
imperium sine fine manet. . . . (2. 63-6)

Sedulius does more here than simply mimic the kind of narrative intrusion characteristic of his epic models. His Christianity has transformed
the intrusion device. The poet does not restrict himself to a simple comment or two; he bursts into an impassioned hymn of praise to the mother
of God, which breaks entirely out of the narrative mode usually
associated with the epic. In fact, *Salva sancte parens* (1. 63 ff.) was eventually taken over for use in the Roman liturgy. Lines 63-4 were adapted
with a few small changes as the Introit for the Common of feasts of Mary.
Lines 67-8 became part of the second antiphon of Christmas Lauds and
line 69 was used in the Magnificat antiphon on the feast of the Presentation of Mary.[38]

The description of Sedulius by some of his Renaissance editors as *poeta
Christianissimus* is most apt.[39] Sedulius is clearly a Christian poet, as

---

[37] It should be observed that the vehemence of Sedulius' reactions to his narrative does
have some precedent in the Latin epic tradition, if not in Virgil. The first-century poet
Lucan, who dealt with a historical subject close to his own time (the war between Pompey
and Caesar), also intrudes frequently and passionately into his narrative. See Gordon
Williams, *Change and Decline: Roman Literature in the Early Empire* (Berkeley, 1978), pp. 233-
5. (I owe this reference to Professor Roberts.)

[38] For more extensive discussions, see Joseph Connelly, *Hymns of the Roman Liturgy*
(New York, 1957), p. 57, and A. Bastiaensen, "L'antienne *Genuit puerpera regem*, adaption
liturgique d'un passage du *Paschale carmen* de Sedulius," *RB* 83 (1973), 388-97.

[39] See, for example, Chapter 7, n. 41.

opposed to a poet who also happens to be a Christian (like, for example, the fourth-century Ausonius). This Christian poet's persona penetrates the fabric of the entire poem, emerging most clearly in narrative intrusions. As Sedulius describes the abuse of Jesus by the servants of the high priest, for instance, he confesses that he may be unable to continue:

> Heu mihi quantis
> inpedior lacrimis rabidum memorare tumultum
> sacrilegas movisse manus! (5. 94-6)

We feel ourselves in the presence of a highly devotional poet, one who is filled with his own religious emotion and who elicits it from his readers. Sedulius' God has died, not just a literary character invented by himself or inherited from an earlier poetic tradition. Yet another example: when Sedulius describes Jesus' trial before the tribunal of Pilate (5. 152-3), he turns to his audience and asks: *Credite iam Christum, pro cunctis credite passum. / Quid dubitatis adhuc?* It is most unusual for the epic poet to address his readers so directly. Indeed, in this narrative intrusion, Sedulius resembles a Christian preacher as much as he does an epic poet. His aim here is to convert and edify as well as to entertain. Sedulius asks unbelieving or uncommitted readers how they can still hestitate to come to faith in Christ after witnessing his suffering for all mankind. Once again, therefore, the formula of new content in an old form is at best a half truth. The narratives which Sedulius retells elicit responses from him, authorial intrusions in the manner of the traditional epic poet, but they are transformed under the Christian poet's handling into polemical tirades, deeply devotional hymns, and passionate conversion appeals.

Imagery

We turn now to the imagery of the *Paschale carmen*. While it is important to recognize that Sedulius borrows a great deal from Virgil, including his imagery, we should not ignore the important function which Christian images play in this poem. One such example in the *Paschale carmen* is the recurrent figure of the snake. Sedulius often borrows from Virgil's well known descriptions of serpents (e.g., *Aeneid* 2. 204 ff.; 5. 84 ff.). In so doing he manages to capture some of the feeling of size, danger, and sinister beauty which Virgil's readers have discovered in his snakes. But the biblical connotations of the serpent are just as potent in this Christian poem as its Virgilian associations. The snake is the form which Satan is often described as taking in the Bible when he tries to deceive or overmaster mankind, and there is a wealth of Christian associations connected with the figure of the snake. At the same time that he uses familiar Virgilian language, Sedulius also makes the most of the biblical ideas behind the serpent figure as he incorporates this image into the narratives of the *Paschale carmen*.

The poet first introduces his readers to the *saevissimus anguis*, the *perfidus draco*, in Book 2. 1-6 as he tells of how the serpent tempted the first humans to eat of the forbidden fruit in the garden of Eden, which led to their exile from this first paradise. While still in the garden, however, God swore enmity with the snake and promised Eve that a descendant of hers would crush the serpent's head, although his own heel would be bruised in the process. When he describes the encounter of Christ and Satan in the wilderness in Book 2, Sedulius reminds the reader of the tempter's Old Testament identity by describing him again in serpentine language:

> . . . labefactus et amens,
> altera vipereis instaurans arma venenis
> cum Domino montana petit cunctasque per orbem
> regnorum monstravit opes. . . . (2. 185-8)

In his exposition of the third petition (also in the second book) Sedulius again identifies the enemy of man as the *saevus hydrus* (2. 259), and in his account of one of Christ's miracles of healing the poet describes the blind and dumb man as in the power of the *lubricus chelydrus*:

> En iterum veteres instaurans lubricus artes
> ille chelydrus adest, nigri qui felle veneni
> lividus humano gaudet pinguescere tabo,
> quodque per alternos totiens disperserat aegros
> virus in unius progressus viscera fudit. (3. 189-93)

In 4. 94-7 we find *ille nocens anguis* again possessing a man, this time leading an array of demons into warfare with Christ, and in 4. 145-9 we learn that it is the same *squameus anguis* who has had Mary Magdalene in his power:

> . . . sed squameus anguis
> imperiosa sacri fugiens miracula verbi
> corde tuo depulsus abit volucresque per auras
> in chaos infernae lapsus penetrale gehennae
> septem ingens gyros, septena volumina traxit.

In the last book of the poem, Sedulius now describes the serpent who has been shut out of paradise as "groaning" to live in it again (5. 226). The repentant thief on the cross, on the other hand, has gained entrance to paradise, led by the Lord as a lamb by a shepherd (5. 217 ff.). Here, at last, the sheep are safe from the attacks of the snake:

Quem Dominus ceu pastor ovem deserta per arva
colligit errantem secumque abducere gaudet
in campos, paradise, tuos, ubi flore perenni
gramineus blanditur ager, nemorumque voluptas
inriguis nutritur aquis, interque benigne
conspicuos pomis non decipientibus hortos
ingemit antiquum serpens habitare colonum. (5. 220-6)

The door to paradise has been reopened by the death and resurrection
of Christ. By rising from the dead, Christ has overcome death, itself a
function of the Devil and described by Sedulius in 5. 283-4 in serpentine
terms: *semine vipereo culpa genetrice crearis, / et venia regnante peris.* If it had
not been for the serpent, man would never have tasted of death in the
first place. But since he ate of the forbidden fruit, he had to die. Christ's
battle, then, is with death, and in 5. 332-3 we see the final identification
of death with the serpent. Christ, predicted in Gen. 3. 15 as the crusher
of the serpent's head, has trampled death underfoot: *Illae igitur Dominum
calcata vivere morte / angelica didicere fide.* The ancient and most deadly
enemy of mankind has finally been defeated.

The imagery of the snake informs the *Paschale carmen* at a number of
levels. Linked together are the ideas of the deceptive snake in the garden
of Eden and the author of misleading philosophy. Sedulius contrasts the
Attica doctrina of *Cecropii veneni* (1. 40) with the simple but pure food of
Christian doctrine.[40] The serpent is a liar and the father of lies (see John
8. 44), who tricked Adam and Eve into losing paradise and is thus
responsible for introducing death into the world. Thematically, it is quite
an appropriate image to be featured prominently in a poem which deals
so often with *salus*, reminding the reader, as it does, of the urgent
necessity of salvation. The destructive snake poses a serious threat to the
sheep and can only be warded off by the shepherd. The good shepherd,
Christ, is the representative of true philosophy, who overcomes the
deceitful prince of this world, destroys death, his weapon, and opens
paradise to all believers.

Sedulius borrows heavily from the language with which Virgil so
unforgettably describes snakes in his poetry. *Paschale carmen* 4. 149 (*septem
ingens gyros, septena volumina traxit*), for instance, is taken *in toto* from *Aeneid*
5. 85. But the Christian poet does more than just borrow. Sedulius shows
considerable freedom and poetic skill in incorporating the serpentine
image into the *Paschale carmen*, and the result is a complex and unified network of distinctively Christian imagery. Sedulius' snakes have Virgilian

---

[40] Compare the description of dialectic in Martianus Capella, *De nuptiis Mercurii et
philologiae* 4. 328 ff. (ed. J. Willis [Leipzig, 1983]): *in laeva quippe serpens gyris immanibus
involutus. . . .*

overtones, but they are also laden with profound Christian significance for any reader who finds the serpent not only a fascinating and deadly animal but a symbol of an evil force which sickens human life and casts a pallor of sin and death over the universe.[41]

We have seen, in conclusion, that the *Paschale carmen* was most likely intended to be an epic, quite possibly, in fact, intended to rival the *Aeneid*. Sedulius was a self-conscious epic poet, who, as Witke observes, did not "leave the resources of the epic form untouched to any great degree in his effort to write his poem."[42] On the other hand, the *Paschale carmen* is also a poem with uniquely Christian content which not only fills but stretches, as it were, the traditional epic form. Sedulius tells the Gospel story as an epic, but the resultant product is "susceptible to the formal changes which his story suggests."[43] The *Paschale carmen* is an exegetical work, a composition filled with Christian praise and exhortation and shot through with distinctively Christian imagery. To be understood properly, therefore, the *Paschale carmen* cannot be viewed solely against the background of biblical sources on the one hand or epic models on the other. Sedulius' poem is, rather (for want of a better term), a biblical epic, an early example of a new literary form which combines inextricably formal and material elements from the epic and the biblical traditions—whose own tradition finds fullest expression in the Middle Ages and the Renaissance.

---

[41] On the serpent as a Christian symbol in patristic writings, see A. Quacquarelli, *Il leone e il drago nella simbolica dell'età patristica*, Quad. di vet. Chr. 11 (Bari, 1975).

[42] Witke, *Numen litterarum*, p. 218.

[43] Witke, *Numen litterarum*, p. 218.

CHAPTER FIVE

STRUCTURE AND MEANING

Of Claudius Marius Victor's *Alethia*, J. Lindsay observes: "Like other such poems of this period . . . it lacks cohesive structure and philosophic unity."[1] While this observation may be true of some of the biblical epics of Late Antiquity, it is not really applicable to the *Paschale carmen*. An examination of the structure of the *Paschale carmen* reveals that Sedulius does in fact use a number of different and complex schemas to organize his work into a cohesive whole. One of these structures is temporal and related to "salvation-history;" another is atemporal and architectonic in the way in which it functions within this Christian epic. The *Paschale carmen* does not, as Lindsay seems to assume, simply reflect the structures of the biblical originals upon which it is based. Sedulius is a poet with a "message," and his poem is a carefully organized work which is designed in such a way as to help the Christian poet make his Christian point.

i. *Temporal Structure*

The temporal structure of the *Paschale carmen* is more complicated than it appears at first glance and requires some explanation here. As we have seen, the narrative of the life of Christ provides Books 2-5 of the poem with a natural chronological structure. Book 2 begins, after an introduction to the subject of the incarnation, by retelling the story of the angel's annunciation of the birth of Jesus to Mary. Book 5 ends with the disciples' return to Jerusalem after they have witnessed the last event of Christ's earthly life, his ascension. The structure of Books 2 through 5, therefore, takes on many of the same contours as the Gospels themselves. Matthew and Luke both begin their works with the events preceding and accompanying the birth of Christ. Although he does not mention the immediate circumstances surrounding Christ's birth, John prefaces his Gospel with an introductory prologue which puts the incarnation into a general theological setting. Mark plunges into the ministry of John the Baptist, which preceded that of Christ's. The climax of each of the Gospels is also quite clearly the climax of Christ's life: his passion and death. Each of the four Gospels (Matt. 26-27, Mark 14-15, Luke 22-23,

---

[1] Jack Lindsay, *Song of a Falling World* (London, 1948), p. 179.

John 13-19) retells the events surrounding Christ's death in detail, and each of the evangelists is careful, too, to direct the reader's attention in earlier chapters towards the impending death and resurrection. The passion, death, and resurrection of Christ come close to the end of each of the Gospels. Events after the resurrection, such as Christ's ascension, function as a kind of anticlimax.

The four books into which Sedulius divides the life of Christ help the poet further to organize the Gospel narrative. Book 2 is devoted to early events in Christ's life. Books 3-4 concentrate on Christ's miracles. The last book of the poem is concerned with the events surrounding Christ's death. The Christian poet follows the Gospels' sequence of events in the life of Christ fairly faithfully, but the division of his material into four books helps to give Sedulius' life of Christ a structure which the Gospels themselves do not have. Christ's early career (e.g., his birth, visit to the temple as a twelve-year old, and baptism) are all handled in one book. Christ's miracles are collected into Books 3 and 4. They begin with the "beginning of miracles" (John 2. 11) and conclude with the raising of Lazarus, the last miracle which Jesus performed before entering Jerusalem to suffer and die. The last book of the poem is devoted entirely to the last events in Jesus' life. It begins with an intimation of the coming passion:

> Has inter virtutis opes iam proxima paschae
> coeperat esse dies, Domini cum gloria vellet
> ponere mortalem vivamque resumere carnem,
> non aliam, sed rursus eam, quam munere plenam
> lucis ab infernis relevans ad sidera duxit. (5. 1-5)

And it ends with Christ's last act on earth, his ascension into heaven after his death and resurrection. Sedulius' treatment of Christ's early life (Book 2) and the poet's consideration of his death (Book 5) frame the two books in which his miracles are recounted.

To be sure, the poet's organization of the events of Christ's life into books does not prevent the reader from being carried along with the flow of the narrative of the life of Christ from birth *usque ad passionem et resurrectionem ascensionemque*. As Sedulius indicates in his letter to Macedonius, this is one of his primary intentions:

> Quatuor igitur mirabilium divinorum libellos, quos ex pluribus pauca conplexus usque ad passionem et resurrectionem ascensionemque Domini nostri Jesu Christi quatuor evangeliorum dicta congregans ordinavi, contra omnes aemulos tuae defensioni commendo.

The structure of the narrative of Books 2-5 does approximate the temporal structures of the four Gospels, beginning, as they all do, with the first events and the background of Christ's life on earth, climaxing in his death and resurrection, and ending with his ascension into heaven. But Sedulius uses the framing device to help separate the early life of Christ (Book 2) from the later events (Book 5) and to distinguish the strictly miraculous (Books 3-4) from the biographical (Books 2 and 5).

What is the structural function of the first book of the *Paschale carmen*? Even though Book 1 does not tell directly of the life of Christ, Sedulius uses it to help the reader fit the life of Christ into another, bigger temporal structure. The first book of the *Paschale carmen* is not only prefatory, but programmatic for the following books, as in traditional Christian theology the Old Testament is for the New. Without the Old Testament background, the events of Christ's life have somewhat limited relevance. It is only, for instance, if believers realize that man has been cast out of paradise that they will appreciate the full significance of Christ's death and the restoration of Eden. As read against the background of the first book, therefore, the second through the fifth books of the poem present the reader with much more than a biography of a Jewish rabbi and miracle worker who lived and died in the first century. Sedulius, like the evangelists, connects Jesus with the Messiah prophesied in the Old Testament, and he uses Book 1 to prepare the reader for this identification:

> Indicio est antiqua fides et cana priorum
> testis origo patrum, nullisque abolenda per aevum
> temporibus constant virtutum signa tuarum. (1. 93-5)

As Sedulius proceeds to tell of the life of Christ in Books 2-5, he keeps this Old Testament background before the eyes of his readers. In the fifth book, for instance, Sedulius introduces us to Jesus as a lamb before the tribunal of Pilate, drawing the imagery of the sheep dumb before its shearers from Isaiah 53. 7:

> At Dominus patiens cum praesidis ante tribunal
> staret, ut ad iugulum ductus mitissimus agnus
> nil inimica cohors insontis sanguine dignum
> repperiens, regem quod se rex dixerit esse
> obicit et verum mendax pro crimine ducit. (5. 139-43)

Even if unfamiliar with the passage from Isaiah, the reader of the *Paschale carmen* will remember the poet's description of the ram which was slain instead of Isaac in Book 1 (114-20). In this connection Sedulius had already observed that Christ (of whom the ram caught in the bushes was a type) was the *pius agnus*, who would shed his blood for the human race (*pro humana gente*).

The number of books into which Sedulius divides the poem illustrates the close connection between the Old and New Testaments in the poet's mind. Sedulius' reference to "four books" in his letter to Macedonius makes clear his intention to write a poem whose structure would remind the reader of the four Gospels and Juvencus' *Evangeliorum libri quattuor*. But the prefatory book containing Old Testament episodes brings the total number of books in the poem to five, the number of books in the Pentateuch, the authoritative Torah of Moses. The *Paschale carmen* can be seen as a version not only of the Gospels, but also of the Christian Bible, with its two Testaments. Sedulius' biblical epic is divided into two unequal parts, the first representing the Old Testament, the second the New. There is a constant tension and interplay between the Old and New Testament parts of the *Paschale carmen*, as Sedulius tells his story of the life of the Savior who came to lead mankind from the Law to the Gospel, from promise to fulfillment, from the ruined garden to the new order of salvation and eternal paradise.

The first book of the poem is a book of beginnings. It describes the earliest events in the history of the world, such as creation, the fall into sin, and the flood. It also, however, includes many hints of the end of all things temporal and points the reader to the world to come. In lines 334 ff., for instance, Sedulius points out to his readers the anagogical significance of the story of the life of Christ:

> Interea dum rite viam sermone levamus
> spesque fidesque meum comitantur in ardua gressum,
> blandius ad summam tandem pervenimus arcem.

Both the poet and his ideal reader are pilgrims on their way to the heavenly citadel (*summam arcem*), where Sedulius prays that he may be given at least a small house (*exiguam domum*) in which to live. The author presents his own writing as well as the reader's reading of the Paschal story as symbolic of the Christian pilgrim's quest, which will be completed only at the end of time.[2] Sedulius continues to remind his readers throughout the poem that the end is drawing near. It can hardly be an accident that every book of the *Paschale carmen* concludes with an "intimation of the last day," the author's vivid reminder to his readers that just as the books of his poem, and, indeed, the poem itself must come to an end, so also they will soon come to the end of their earthly lives and arrive at their ultimate and eternal destination.[3]

With its Old Testament background and its eschatological overtones, therefore, the first book of the *Paschale carmen* provides the poem with a

---

[2] See Barbara Lewalski, *Milton's Brief Epic: The Genre, Meaning and Art of Paradise Regained* (Providence, 1966), p. 47.

[3] Lewalski, *Milton's Brief Epic*, p. 47, makes this observation.

temporal structure which spans all of sacred history. Christ's life (Books 2-5) fits into a bigger temporal framework, namely, the entire history of salvation (*Heilsgeschichte*), which begins with the creation of the world, in which Christ was intimately involved, and ends with its end and the establishment of the kingdom of Christ, which, as Sedulius describes it in 2. 250-4, has no temporal limit (*fine carens*) and is beyond the realm of time (*nescit tempus habere*).

ii. *The Good Shepherd*

Like Virgil and other Latin poets, Sedulius pays special attention to numbers. In 1. 359-63, for instance, the Christian poet comments on the numerological significance of four (as connected with the evangelists) and twelve (the number of Jesus' disciples):

> Quatuor hi proceres una te voce canentes
> tempora ceu totidem latum sparguntur in orbem.
> Sic et apostolici semper duodenus honoris
> fulget apex numero, menses imitatus et horas,
> omnibus ut rebus totus tibi militet annus.

The evangelists imitate the four seasons, according to Sedulius, while the number of the disciples reflects the months of the year and the hours of the day. Given Sedulius' interest in numerology in general, it is possible that he was not unaware of the number of lines and books in his poem and that he strove, as Latin poets before him also did, to achieve architectonic structures based on numbers within the *Paschale carmen*. If so, the location of the figure of Christ, the good shepherd, at a position in the poem whose centrality is determined by the number of lines in the book and the number of books in the poem may be more than a coincidence.

In his retelling of Matthew's account of the commission of the twelve disciples (3. 158-75), Sedulius passes over the first fifteen verses of the tenth chapter of Matthew quite summarily and concentrates his paraphrastic energies on Jesus' warning to his followers: *Ecce ego mitto vos sicut oves in medio luporum.* Matthew's *oves* offers the poet the opportunity to introduce the figure of the good shepherd into the middle of the third book. Matthew himself does not refer to Christ as the good shepherd anywhere in his Gospel, but Sedulius pulls the metaphor out of its Johannine context (John 10. 11) and inserts it here into Matthew's story-line. As he gives the disciples their last-minute instructions, Jesus refers to them as sheep. If they are sheep, then Jesus, their leader, must be a shepherd. Matthew does not make this connection explicit, but Sedulius does:

Ac velut hoc dicens: ego vobis quippe ministris
servandos conmitto greges, ego denique pastor
sum bonus et proprios ad victum largior agros:
nemo meis ovibus quae sunt mea pascua vendat. (3. 166-9)

For Sedulius' purposes the remaining 26 verses of Matthew's account of
the commissioning are of little importance. Instead of paraphrasing them
he lauches into a simile on the apostles. According to the poet, they are
like the four rivers which flowed from one source in the garden of Eden
(cf. Gen. 2. 10-14):

Haec in apostolicas ideo prius edidit aures
omnipotens, ut ab his iam sese auctore magistris
in reliquum doctrina fluens decurreret aevum:
qualiter ex uno paradisi fonte leguntur
quatuor ingentes procedere cursibus amnes,
ex quibus in totum sparguntur flumina mundum. (3. 170-5)

Just as the fountain in Eden is the source for the four rivers, so also the
sheep-disciples—and the Christian church along with them—trace their
mission back to the good shepherd.

It seems very probable that the insertion of the good shepherd into the
story of the commissioning of the 12 did not happen by accident. The
figure of the shepherd standing at line 167 of Book 3 of the *Paschale carmen*
occupies the center of the entire poem. Of the 333 lines of the book,
Christ the shepherd appears in the precise center, line 167. Of the 27 sections into which this book naturally divides itself, lines 158-175 represent
the central one, the 14th.[4] Among the five books in the *Paschale carmen*,
the third is, of course, central.

If Sedulius did mean to locate a prominent figure centrally in his epic,
his practice was not without poetic precedent. Students of Augustan
poetry have noted that it was not unusual for poets like Virgil and Horace

---

[4] I follow the paragraphing of Huemer's edition. Confusingly enough, Huemer
includes the numbering for the spurious lines 176-181 in the third book, although he does
not include the lines themselves in the text proper. Thus, the final line in the third book,
according to the count in his edition, is 339. The six lines in question are found only in
early printed editions, not in any of the MSS or the commentary of Remigius of Auxerre.
The problems concerning the number of books in the *Paschale carmen* also warrant further
explanation here. Sedulius' work was handed down through the Middle Ages and the
Renaissance in four (in many MSS) and perhaps three books (if we can trust the witness
of Isidore in *De viris illustribus* 20). The division of the poem into four books, however,
is probably based upon a copyist's misunderstanding of Sedulius' own remarks about the
number of books in the *Paschale carmen* in the prefatory epistle to Macedonius. There
Sedulius does speak of four books but only with reference to those which contain Gospel
subject material: *quatuor igitur mirabilium divinorum libellos, quos . . . quatuor evangeliorum dicta
congregans ordinavi.* The two earliest MSS of the *Paschale carmen* both appear in the five-
book format. For a more detailed discussion, see Huemer, *De Sedulii poetae vita*, pp. 39-41.

"to place the great names precisely in the center" of their poems.[5] In his first *Eclogue*, for example, Virgil places his homage to Octavian (*hic illum vidi iuvenem, Meliboee, quotannis / bis senos cui nostra dies altaria fumant*) exactly in the center of the poem. And in the third *Eclogue* Virgil positions Pollio and the *nova carmina* at the precise center of the amoebean contest between the two herdsmen.[6] Nor was Sedulius the first Christian poet to have the idea of positioning the good shepherd prominently in a work. In his eighth *Cathemerinon* hymn, Prudentius locates the good shepherd in the central panel of this twenty-stanza hymn. The four stanzas (lines 33-48) in which Prudentius describes the good shepherd, the lost sheep, and paradise are at the center of the hymn.[7]

Even more striking analogies may be found in the Christian art of Late Antiquity. No one who has visited the Roman catacombs can have failed to notice the prominence enjoyed by the good shepherd in catacomb art. Often the figure of the shepherd is positioned centrally in the ceilings of cubicula, as it is, for example, in the Catacombs of Praetextatus, Priscilla, and Lucina.[8] Early Christian sarcophagi, too, often feature the good shepherd in a central position.[9]

It is generally agreed that the centrally placed good shepherd serves more than a decorative function in early Christian art. One of the fundamental ideas behind the good shepherd in early Christian thought in general is that of salvation (in Latin *salus*, in Greek *soteria*).[10] In *Protrep-*

---

[5] Otto Skutsch, "Symmetry and Sense in the *Eclogues*," *HSCP* 73 (1969), 157. See E. Coleiro, *An Introduction to Vergil's Bucolics with a Critical Edition of the Text* (Amsterdam, 1979), pp. 97-8, for a review of the "overall numerical schema" of the *Eclogues*.

[6] See C.P.E. Springer, "Aratus and the Cups of Menalcas: A Note on *Eclogue* 3. 42," *CJ* 79 (1983-4), 133.

[7] Willy Evenepoel, *Zakelijke en Literaire Onderzoekingen Betreffende het Liber Cathemerinon van Aurelius Prudentius Clemens*, Verhand. Acad. voor Wetensch., Lett. & Schone Kunsten van België, Kl. der Lett. 41, No. 91 (Brussels, 1979), p. 127, makes this observation: "Deze hymne is concentrisch opgebouwd: de strofen 9-12 vormen op betekenisvolle wisze het central gedeelte."

[8] For illustrations see Joseph Wilpert, *Die Malereien der Katakomben Roms* (Freiburg, 1903), tables 17 and 35. 1-2.

[9] For examples see Joseph Wilpert, *I sarcofagi cristiani antichi* (Rome, 1929-36), tables 1. 1-3. One of the most striking sarcophagi, with three good shepherds, one in the middle flanked by two others on either end of the front of the sarcophagus, can be seen in the Museo Pio Clementino in the Vatican. For an illustration, see André Grabar, *Early Christian Art from the Rise of Christianity to the Death of Theodosius*, trans. Stuart Gilbert and James Emmons (New York, 1968), pl. 287.

[10] Th. Kempf, *Christus der Hirt: Ursprung und Deutung einer altchristlichen Symbolgestalt* (Rome, 1942), argues that the good shepherd is more closely connected with the idea of the *logos*. Johannes Quasten in "Das Bild des Guten Hirten in den altchristlichen Baptisterien und in den Taufliturgien des Ostens und Westens," in *Pisciculi: Studien zur Religion und Kultur des Altertums* (Münster, 1939), 220 ff., connects the good shepherd with baptism. But the idea of salvation may underlie both of these concepts. Anton Legner's observations in *Der Gute Hirt* (Düsseldorf, 1959), p. 12, are worth quoting here:

ticus 116. 1, for example, Clement of Alexandria comments on the good shepherd and his function as rescuer of the flock: "It is always the purpose of God to save the herd of mankind. For this reason, our good God sent the good shepherd to the world."[11] A source more contemporary to Sedulius, Peter Chrysologus, also links Christ's role as good shepherd with his salvific activity on behalf of mankind (in *Sermo* 168):

> Homo habens oves centum Christus est. Pastor bonus, pastor pius, qui in una ove, hoc est, in Adam, posuerat totum gregem generis humani. . . . Hanc ergo Christus veniens quaerere in mundum, in utero virgineae regionis invenit. Venit suae nativitatis in carne, in crucem levans humeris suae imposuit passionis, et gaudens toto resurrectionis gaudio per ascensum ad coelestem tulit et pertulit mansionem.[12]

In early Christian art the most popular themes used by catacomb painters and sarcophagus sculptors were taken from the Old Testament, and predominant among them were stories involving divine salvation, such as Jonah and the whale, the three men in the fiery furnace, Daniel in the lion's den, and others. The good shepherd is often found represented together with such "signal instances of the deliverance of God's faithful servants in an hour of need."[13] The centrality of the figure suggests that it provides the key to the interpretation of the other biblical scenes represented. One good example of the thematic centrality of the good shepherd in early Christian art may be seen in a wall painting from the Dura Europus baptistery, where we find the good shepherd and Adam and Eve in the "most central spot in the room, the niche of the *chevet* (behind the font)." André Grabar observes:

> Images representing the essential dogmas of original sin and redemption are made central by their location; and furthermore, for obvious reasons, it is the image of redemption in the form of the Good Shepherd and His Flock, that predominates.[14]

Adam and Eve are at the bottom occupying only a corner of the niche while the good shepherd is much larger and stretches over the entire wall. Even though Adam and Eve are in desperate straits, the artist seems to suggest, they have not been forgotten by the good shepherd. Christ, the

---

Aus der breiten Grundlage der Vorstellungen vom Guten Hirten . . . war das die Zeit so sehr beschäftigende Thema übernommen, um in seiner Verbildlichung den Gedanken der *Soteria* auszudrücken. Nicht weil der Hirte der Logos ist, ist er im christlichen Bereich dargestellt worden, sondern weil der Logoshirte den Menschen die *Soteria* bringt.

[11] My translation is based on the text in *GCS* 12, 81.

[12] *PL* 52, 641.

[13] Grabar, *Early Christian Art*, p. 102.

[14] André Grabar, *Christian Iconography: A Study of its Origins*, trans. Terry Grabar (Princeton, 1968), p. 20 and illustration 40.

saving shepherd of lost sheep, is the way by which mankind, cast out of the garden of Eden, may reenter paradise.

It is significant that the good shepherd should occupy such a central place in early Christian funereal art in particular. Early Christians believed that it was the good shepherd who could make best sense not only of their lives but especially of their deaths. As a salvific figure, the good shepherd would be featured centrally on a sarcophagus or in a cubiculum because he was thought of as the one most able to rescue the sheep-believer from death and bring him to safe pasture (paradise). J. Kollwitz makes this point admirably and his conclusions are worth quoting here:

> Von hier aus versteht sich auch der besondere sepulkrale Sinn der Darstellung: der Christus-Hirt als Bringer der Erlösung (*Soteria*) wird zur Hoffnung auch am Grabe. Daneben spielt auch der Gedanke mit an die Errettung der Seele aus den Gefahren der Jenseitswanderung.[15]

The good shepherd is a *psychopompus*, a divine figure standing between this life and the next, prepared to assist mortals in making the difficult transition.

It seems likely, then, that the figure of the good shepherd was located centrally in early Christian painting and sculpture in order to help interpret the biblical events represented. The good shepherd is a symbol of salvation reminding the viewer of another, safer world which lies above the world of drowning prophets and men in danger of being burned alive.[16] The good shepherd assumes central importance especially in Christian funereal art, where the need for rescue from death and rest after one's earthly pilgrimage is most readily apparent.

As in early Christian art, so also in Sedulius' poem the good shepherd in its central position may be seen as serving a kind of interpretative role. The narrative structure of the *Paschale carmen* climaxes, as we have seen, in Book 5 with the death and resurrection of Christ. This is the point towards which the events of all of the books have been driving. By placing the good shepherd in the center of the poem, however, Sedulius provides his readers with a counterbalance to the narrative thrust of the *Paschale carmen*. The good shepherd is connected with paradise, the green pastures where believers will come after they traverse the less pleasant terrain of earthly life. The repentant thief on the cross, for instance, who had certainly experienced his share of troubles in life (not the least of which was

---

[15] J. Kollwitz, "Christusbild" in *RAC* 3, 6.

[16] The good shepherd was a popular subject in early Christian art up until the first half of the fifth century, when it began, mysteriously, to disappear from the monuments. See the observations of Boniface Ramsey in *HTR* 76 (1986), 375-8.

his mode of death), receives paradise as the reward for his labors (*Paschale carmen* 5. 222-3). Paradise is the home of the divine Christ, who left it to come to earth at the beginning of Book 2 and returned to it when he ascended out of the view of his disciples at the end of Book 5. Christ has always been there, before he created the world, before his incarnation. Christ is timeless (cf. John 8. 58), and he reigns in heaven into eternity. This atemporal realm of ideas is kept before our eyes as we follow the development of the Gospel narrative. Although for the moment Christ is bound to time and place, mocked, beaten, and even killed, the vision of the good shepherd placed centrally in the poem reminds the reader that this same Jesus now reigns eternally triumphant in heaven. The events of the Gospel swirl below the figure of the good shepherd, who floats serenely, as it were, at the apex of this poem. On earth mankind is always locked in combat with the forces of the serpent (4. 90-8), but in paradise the good shepherd keeps the serpent out (5. 226), and the sheep are forever safe from danger. At the same time as the poet outlines before our eyes the suspenseful progress of Christ's life on earth, he also reminds his readers that the events of the Gospel have already happened. This architectonic structure produces a beatific and restful vision of the good shepherd, the Savior of mankind, which suggests to the poem's readers that they may now rest confident in their faith as they will most surely rest some day in paradise.

iii. *The Meaning of the Paschale carmen*

The figure of the centrally placed good shepherd provides the viewer with a key to understanding the entire *Paschale carmen*. No other symbol could better sum up the "philosophic unity" of this Christian poem than the good shepherd, the source of *salus*. The message of salvation is, finally, the real point of the *Paschale carmen*. Sedulius includes so many miracles in his poem not in order to supply his readers with a convenient list—this apparently was Gregory of Nazianzus' intention—but because they so clearly illustrate divine salvation in action. All of the 18 Old Testament miracles which Sedulius chooses to retell involve rescue. *Salus* is the theme which binds together the stories of Jonah in the whale's belly, the three men in the fiery furnace, Daniel in the lion's den, and others. The miracles of the Gospels, too, as Sedulius retells them, are intended not only to awe his readers but to provide evidence of the Lord's saving power. The miracles of healing, in particular, with their distinctive conflation of the language of "physical health and Christian Salvation,"[17] reinforce the theme of *salus*. This was the purpose of the

---

[17] Roberts, *Biblical Epic*, p. 152.

miraculous life and redemptive death of Christ: the salvation of the world. As a symbol of *salus* reaching back to the fall of man (2. 1-34) and looking forward to paradise (5. 220-6), the good shepherd dominates this poem of rescue and redemption and integrates the poem's narrative components: Old Testament miracles, Christ's miracles, and the life and death of the Savior.

In the *Paschale carmen* Sedulius lays more emphasis on Christ as *salutifer* than on his ethical teaching or his supreme example of compassion and self-sacrifice. The poet's soteriological interests are revealed in the first lines of the poem, when he declares his intentions to sing of the "famous miracles of the saving Christ," and indeed the idea of *salus* may be said to inform the entire *Paschale carmen*. Let us single out three distinct aspects of the idea which are especially apparent. The first of these is the salvation of the author and his reader. As we have seen, Sedulius plays upon the traditional pagan concept of earning immortality by composing enduring literature. The actual composition of his poem becomes equivalent to and interchangeable with the path to salvation. The two arduous tasks begin to meld for the poet. In the first appearance of the good shepherd in the *Paschale carmen*, he is shown in connection with the poet himself, who is being led down the path to the completion of the poem and to paradise:

> Pande salutarem paucos quae ducit in urbem
> angusto mihi calle viam verbique lucernam
> da pedibus lucere meis, ut semita vitae
> ad caulas me ruris agit, qua servat amoenum
> pastor ovile bonus, qua vellere praevius albo
> virginis agnus ovis grexque omnis candidus intrat. (1. 79-84)

The act of writing this poem has become a literary metaphor for the narrow road to salvation. Christ as Muse can save the poem; as Messiah he can save the poet. By implication, even if he does not state it outright, Sedulius also suggests that the reader of the *Paschale carmen* will be taking steps in the right direction towards his or her own salvation, too, by reading his poem.

A second aspect of the idea of *salus* as presented in the *Paschale carmen* is that of Messianic salvation. In Books 2-5, as we have seen, Sedulius shows us Jesus in the context of salvation-history, as the word incarnate, the Messiah prophesied by the Jewish Scriptures. Jesus' life and miracles occurred against an Old Testament historical-theological background and preparation; the evangelists emphasize this point and Sedulius follows them in this regard. Christ's death on the cross in the fulness of time is the culmination of sacred history (cf. Galatians 4. 4-5). The cross itself, as Sedulius points out, is a four-sided figure of completeness which embraces not only Palestine but all the quarters of the world:

Neve quis ignoret speciem crucis esse colendam,
quae Dominum portavit ovans, ratione potenti
quattuor inde plagas quadrati colligat orbis.
Splendidus auctoris de vertice fulget Eous,
occiduo sacrae lambuntur sidere plantae,
Arcton dextra tenet, medium laeva erigit axem,
cunctaque de membris vivit natura creantis,
et cruce conplexum Christus regit undique mundum. (5. 188-95)

It is this climactic moment in the history of salvation and this universal symbol to which Jew and Gentile alike must look for the foundation of their relationship with God the Father. This is salvation in the historical and cosmic sense.

The third aspect of the idea of salvation in the *Paschale carmen* is connected with the church. In word and sacrament alone is salvation to be found. In baptism, for instance, the believer will find assurance of the forgiveness of sins, life, and salvation. Throughout the poem Sedulius reminds his readers of the true catholic church to which he and most likely they also belong. By participating in its sacraments the believer becomes part of the mystical body of Christ (cf. Eph. 4. 4, 12 and 1 Cor. 12. 12-27). Here stress is laid upon the salvation of the community rather than the individual. For example, close to the end of the poem Sedulius describes Jesus preparing a meal of bread and fish for his disciples who have been fishing all night on Galilee without success. When the fishermen came ashore to eat, they are described as "seeking the table:"

Tunc epulis praeceptor eos invitat edendis
alloquiis de more piis, mensamque petentes
unanimes nota Domini bonitate fruuntur
et Christum sensere suum. (5. 405-8)

Undoubtedly Sedulius intends to convey here the connotations of the eucharistic meal. The disciples have no food themselves to eat, but they are invited to a dinner provided by Christ; they enjoy "the goodness of the Lord" (cf. Psalm 34. 8). In this connection, just a few lines from the end of the poem, Sedulius once again introduces Christ as a shepherd. Over breakfast Jesus asks Peter whether he loves him. Peter replies that he does and the "loving shepherd," as Sedulius calls Jesus, enjoins Peter to feed his "white flocks" (*nitentes greges*):

Modicoque paratu
postquam victa fames et surrexere relictis
rite toris, an corde Petrus se diligat alto,
explorat Dominus; Petrus annuit. Ergo nitentes

pastor amans augere greges operario in omni
parte bono commendat oves, commendat et agnos. (5. 408-13)

The simple meal on the sea shore has become a rite of forgiveness. Peter who has denied his Lord three times is restored to *salus*. Like his Savior, he, too, is to become a shepherd of souls.

Salus is not a simple idea, and in the *Paschale carmen* the reader is given but a sampling of some of its flavors. Still, it is a single idea, and the biblical figure of the good shepherd sums up many of its individual aspects. The good shepherd is a cumulative image, which knits together many of the strands of ideas which run through the *Paschale carmen*. They are so intertwined that it is impossible to untangle the network of connected ideas and images completely. For example, Sedulius places a great deal of emphasis on the idea of the disciples as shepherds. The poet makes a point of the good shepherd handing over pastoral responsibilities to the disciples. They become shepherds, too. In Matthew 10. 16, they are simply sheep. According to Sedulius, it is they who have handed down true Christian doctrine, as the simile of the rivers flowing from a common source suggests. The Christian poet's stress on the role of the disciples and the special emphasis in particular which he places on Peter are no doubt influenced by the doctrine of the apostolic succession. One imagines that Ursinus, the *antistes* in the circle of Macedonius, and Macedonius himself, of whose ministry Sedulius speaks in pastoral language, would have been pleased by such an emphasis.[18]

Sedulius also connects the image of the good shepherd with that of Christ the lamb. The Paschal meal had lamb as its main course, and in the preface to the poem Sedulius elaborates upon the metaphor suggested by his title. The reader is invited to read the poem as though he were being invited to a meal. Sedulius' poetry is food, because the subject of his poem is Christ, the Paschal lamb.[19] So Christ is not only shepherd but sheep, a paradoxical idea which Sedulius develops further in 1. 119 ff. (the ram substituted for Isaac is really a type of the lamb of God) and in 5. 356, where Sedulius makes the connection explicit: *victima quae dabitur, cum victima pastor habetur?*[20]

---

[18] In the prefatory epistle to Macedonius, Sedulius describes the priest as a shepherd (*CSEL* 10, 11):

> Quibusdam exemplum factus es ad salutem: alios intra septa tui gregis aspiciens oves fecisti: alios enutristi. . . .

[19] In the epistle to Macedonius Sedulius also refers to 1. Cor. 5. 7, a passage in which Paul calls Christ "the Pascha sacrificed for us:"

> Huic autem operi favente Domino Paschalis carminis nomen inposui, quia Pascha nostrum immolatus est Christus, cui honor et gloria cum Patre et Spiritu sancto, per omnia saecula saeculorum. Amen.

[20] See *PG* 52, 827 ff. for the same paradox of Christ as shepherd and sheep in a sermon attributed to John Chrysostom.

We have seen, in conclusion, that the *Paschale carmen* is a structured work. Sedulius' poem is designed to take the reader not only from the manger to the cross but also from the beginning of time to the end of time and beyond. These temporal structures of the poem are complemented by another structural feature of the *Paschale carmen*, namely, the centrally placed good shepherd. This figure of salvation which is featured so prominently can be seen as offering the reader a key to the *Paschale carmen*'s ultimate meaning. The stories of God's wondrous deeds in the Old Testament, the miracles of Christ, and indeed his entire life are brought together in the figure of the good shepherd as Savior of mankind. The idea of salvation was, of course, not Sedulius' own. To some extent it was inherent in the biblical texts whose stories the poet was retelling. All the same, it must be said that the Christian Gospel had never been expressed in quite this way before. In any event, whether or not Sedulius' message was entirely new, it is clear that this Christian poet had a serious point to make. The central figure of the good shepherd, which overarches the narrative structures of the *Paschale carmen* and helps to integrate the disparate elements of the poem, sums up most eloquently its ultimate soteriological significance.

CHAPTER SIX

SOUND AND SENSE

So far in our analysis of the *Paschale carmen* we have considered larger aspects of the poem's composition. Now let us enter the poet's workshop, as it were, and examine his craft in more detail. How does Sedulius go about retelling a specific biblical episode in verse? In this chapter we shall concentrate on a single passage of the *Paschale carmen* (3. 1-11) in order to discover some of the particular elements which contribute to Sedulius' poetic artistry. Sedulius' version of the wedding at Cana will be contrasted, first of all, with the Gospel's account. We shall consider 1.) the poetic effects achieved in the selection and arrangement of traditional material and the insertion of new material, 2.) the restructuring of the episode, 3.) diction, and 4.) meter and other devices of sound. The second part of the chapter compares and contrasts Sedulius' version of the wedding at Cana with other Christian poetry of Late Antiquity which retells the same story. The distinctiveness of Sedulius' artistry will be more evident when viewed against the background of contemporary or near contemporary Christian Latin poetry.

i. *The Artistry of Paschale carmen 3. 1-11*

This is how Sedulius retells the story of the wedding at Cana:

> Prima suae Dominus thalamis dignatus adesse
> virtutis documenta dedit convivaque praesens
> pascere, non pasci veniens, mirabile! Fusas
> in vinum convertit aquas: amittere gaudent
> pallorem latices, mutavit laeta saporem
> unda suum largita merum, mensasque per omnes
> dulcia non nato rubuerunt pocula musto.
> Implevit sex ergo lacus hoc nectare Christus:
> quippe ferax qui vitis erat virtute colona
> omnia fructificans, cuius sub tegmine blando
> mitis inocciduas enutrit pampinus uvas. (3. 1-11)

The Vulgate's translation—the Latin version of the Bible with which Sedulius was probably best acquainted—reads as follows:[1]

---

[1] According to Mayr, *Studien zu dem Paschale carmen*, p. 95, who observes that not many traces of the influence of the *Itala* can be found in the *Paschale carmen*, Sedulius most likely used Jerome's version of the Gospels:
Die von Hieronymus im Jahre 383 begonnene und noch im gleichen Jahre

Et die tertio nuptiae factae sunt in Cana Galilaeae et erat mater Iesu ibi
2. vocatus est autem ibi et Iesus et discipuli eius ad nuptias 3. et deficiente
vino dicit mater Iesu ad eum vinum non habent 4. et dicit ei Iesus quid mihi
et tibi est mulier nondum venit hora mea 5. dicit mater eius ministris quod-
cumque dixerit vobis facite 6. erant autem ibi lapideae hydriae sex positae
secundum purificationem Iudaeorum capientes singulae metretas binas vel
ternas 7. dicit eis Iesus implete hydrias aqua et impleverunt eas usque ad
summum 8. et dicit eis Iesus haurite nunc et ferte architriclino et tulerunt
9. ut autem gustavit architriclinus aquam vinum factam et non sciebat unde
esset ministri autem sciebant qui haurierant aquam vocat sponsum
architriclinus 10. et dicit ei omnis homo primum bonum vinum ponit et
cum inebriati fuerint tunc id quod deterius est tu servasti bonum vinum
usque adhuc 11. hoc fecit initium signorum Iesus in Cana Galilaeae et
manifestavit gloriam suam et crediderunt in eum discipuli eius. 12. Post
hoc descendit Capharnaum ipse et mater eius et fratres eius et discipuli eius
et ibi manserunt non multis diebus.[2]

Abbreviation, Amplification, and Innovation

The reader learns from Sedulius' version of the wedding at Cana only
that Christ's first miracle took place at a wedding where Jesus changed
six jugs filled with water into wine. Sedulius omits to mention when and
where the miracle took place and who else was present. The poet does
not tell of Mary's observation that the supply of wine was low nor of the
rebuke which Jesus addressed to her. Indeed, he never mentions her
presence at all. Nor are Mary's instructions to the servants included.
Sedulius does not mention why the jugs were there or how much they
held. Jesus' instructions to the servants are left out, and we do not learn
of the steward's reaction to the better wine. Sedulius also fails to record
the effect of the miracle on the disciples and what happened afterwards.
On the other hand, the Christian poet elaborates at some length on
specific details of the Gospel account and includes material in *Paschale
carmen* 3. 1-11 which does not derive from John's original. These decisions to retain, omit, expand, condense, and add to the elements of John
2. 1-12 are consistent with Sedulius' poetic practice elsewhere in the
Paschale carmen and will help us better to understand the rationale which
underlies his handling of traditional narrative material in general.

In his retelling of the story of the wedding at Cana, Sedulius retains
only the details from the Gospel account which are necessary for the

---

vollendete Revision des Neuen Testaments fand auch in der abendländischen Kir-
che willige Aufnahme. Bei Sedulius ,,, gehören Nachwirkungen der Itala des Neuen
Testaments zu den Seltenheiten.

[2] I use the sparsely punctuated edition of *Biblia sacra iuxta vulgatam versionem*, ed. R.
Weber, 3rd ed. (Stuttgart, 1983).

recognition of the original story or which suit his own poetic purposes. Since the poet is retelling biblical stories to an audience which evidently knows them fairly well, he can afford to concentrate on the narrative kernel. Sedulius probably retains John's observation that this was the first (*initium*) of miracles because the poet wants to make it clear to his readers at the beginning of Book 3 that he is now beginning a long catalogue of Christ's miracles. The Christian poet also follows the evangelist in mentioning the fact that the miracle took place at a wedding and that there were six jugs in all. The latter observation may be included to help give some idea of the impressiveness of the miracle. The Lord created more than a few glasses of wine. As Sedulius retells them, Jesus' miracles are supposed to sound impressive, and numbers help to suggest magnitude. Sedulius is also careful to mention, for instance, the number of baskets of crumbs collected after the feeding of the 4000 and the 5000 (3. 217 ff. and 270 ff.).

With respect to Sedulius' omissions, as has been observed, the poet is never very interested in locating his episodes in time and space. Sedulius most often will begin an episode with a vague *dehinc* (3. 207), *praeterea* (4. 31), or *post* (4. 64). In 3. 1-11 the poet ignores the evangelist's fairly precise setting for the event (*die tertia* and *Cana Galilaeae*). Here as elsewhere in the *Paschale carmen* Sedulius' concern is with inner landscape, the mystical realm rather than the physical.

Sedulius leaves the mother of Jesus out of the episode entirely, even though Mary plays an important role in the Gospel account. According to John, she notices that the wine supply is low, and brings it to Jesus' attention, thus earning a stern rejoinder from her son. She then instructs the servants to do whatever Jesus tells them. Sedulius probably deletes Mary because her presence is not essential for the story and also because he does not want to tell of her rebuke. The poet views her as close to divine and such a slight accords ill with the honor "the mother of the Father" is given elsewhere in the *Paschale carmen* (cf., e.g., 2. 63 ff.). Nor does Sedulius usually cast Christ in so human a role. As we have seen, Sedulius consistently avoids representing Christ in anger. Jesus' words to his mother may sound too much like an angry human rebuke to correspond with Sedulius' vision of the divinely serene lord of all creation, who is not really very subject to human emotions.

Sedulius also declines to mention why the six stone jugs were ready to hand. Some of the evangelist's first readers may well have known that there would have been purificatory water vessels present at a Jewish feast (cf. Mark 7. 3-4) and that stone jars were preferred to earthen because if ritually contaminated they could be cleansed (cf. Lev. 11. 29-38). The fifth-century poet, however, is addressing an audience who might be concerned about the symbolical significance of the number six, but who would probably have been unfamiliar with (or simply not interested in) the intricacies of Jewish ceremonial customs.[3]

Sedulius' account is focused on Christ and his actions. The reader of the *Paschale carmen*'s account of the wedding at Cana never learns of the existence of servants, a steward (*architriclinus*), or even a bridegroom. Sedulius leaves out any mention of the servants' role in filling the jugs with water and carrying the wine to the steward to test. Nor are we told of the steward's reaction to the wine and his observation to the bridegroom that the best wine should be served first, not last. The steward has the last spoken word in the evangelist's account (v. 10), and the disciples of Jesus are the subject of the last clause in John's own summary of the event (v. 11). In John's account the miracle at the wedding at Cana is important because of its spiritual effect on those around Jesus. The disciples believed in Jesus as a result of this first miracle. It was an early turning point for their faith in their leader. The Gospel account eventually brings the reader's attention back to Christ in vv. 11-12, but the story of the miracle itself concludes by focusing not on Christ but on the steward and the bridegroom. As elsewhere in the *Paschale carmen*, Sedulius is less concerned with minor characters in the Gospels, even the disciples, than he is with Christ, who moves through a world rendered somewhat remote by his divine superiority. The disciples are little different from the water, which, in Sedulius' view, exists only to marvel at and rejoice in the Savior.

Unlike the evangelist (cf. John 2. 12), Sedulius does not really care where Jesus went next, who was with him, or how long he stayed there. The fifth-century poet is only concerned with setting up the next miracle. *Post* (3. 12) suffices to explain the transition. Jesus' brothers (mentioned by John in 2. 12) concern Sedulius even less than his disciples. Indeed, the poet had already suggested earlier that Mary was always a virgin (2. 44-7). The relationship of Jesus to his brothers, which was of some interest to the evangelist (cf. John 7. 1-10), must have seemed a detail not only of little consequence but even a trifle awkward to the Catholic poet.

While Sedulius sketches out the narrative outline of the story of the wedding at Cana in the most cursory fashion, the poet devotes con-

---

[3] Cf. Augustine, *In Iohannis Evangelium tractatus* 9. 6 (*CC* 36, 94), for example, for a symbolical explanation of the number six. The bishop of Hippo considers this number a sign of the imperfection of the Old Testament era:

Sex ergo illae hydriae, sex aetates significant, quibus non defuit prophetia. Illa ergo tempora sex, quasi articulis distributa atque distincta, quasi vasa essent inania, nisi a Christo implerentur.

siderable effort to elaborating on the Gospel's account and introducing material which is not to be found in the original.

The first innovation to strike the reader of Sedulius' account is the poet's reaction to John's *vocatus est autem Iesus* (v. 2). The paradoxical nature of this situation strikes his fancy. A guest attends a feast expecting to be wined and dined but ends up playing the host: *convivaque praesens / pascere, non pasci veniens* (3. 2-3). Although the evangelist emphasizes such paradoxes elsewhere, as, for instance, in his consideration of the blind man who can "see" and the Pharisees who are blessed with physical sight but are "blind" in Chapter 9 of his Gospel, he does not highlight the paradoxical in this account. Sedulius, by contrast, rarely fails to make the most of such paradoxical situations (cf. 5. 356), as he does here, because they help to confirm a point which he makes throughout the poem—the miraculous Christ upsets and reverses the usual order of things (cf. 1. 220 ff.).

Nature does not resent this intrusion but rather celebrates Christ as its deliverer. Sedulius describes the water as rejoicing to be turned into wine:

> . . . amittere gaudent
> pallorem latices, mutavit laeta saporem
> unda suum largita merum (3. 4-6)

The poet adds a touch to the story here which is quite different in spirit from anything in the Gospel's account. The evangelist would never personify an element of nature in this way. Sedulius' detail underscores Christ's power to reverse the laws of nature and contributes to a theme which recurs throughout the *Paschale carmen*, namely, the idea of nature rejoicing when confronted with its creator (cf. 3. 46-69).

Sedulius informs us, too, that the "cups blushed upon all the tables with sweet wine, newly made." Such elaborate description does not characterize the evangelist's style. It is important for the readers of the Gospel to know where Jesus was and when, but John does not care to lavish attention on the physical for its own sake. Sedulius, on the other hand, has more of a painterly instinct. He feels it necessary to include such a colorful and descriptive passage in the episode and lingers lovingly over the sensual scene which he has created. The reader can practically see the drinking cups and the sparkling red wine on the tables.[4] Although Sedulius is not much interested in providing specific temporal or geographical contexts for his episodes, he does give them an immediate and vivid generic setting. Of the effect of the miracle, John mentions only

---

[4] On *illustratio* and *evidentia*, vivid description of detail, see Quintilian, *Inst.* 6. 2. 32.

the steward's reaction and the disciples' faith; the poet gives us a glimpse of the gala party which must have followed.

Finally, Sedulius concludes these eleven lines with an allusion to John 15. 1 ff. The last three lines (3. 9-11) are truly innovative insofar as they cannot be said to amplify any specific detail of the original directly. It is simply the Savior's close connection with wine in John 2. 1-12 which suggests to the poet's mind the metaphor of Christ as vine. It is characteristic of the poet's practice to illustrate his episodes with references to other biblical passages (cf. 1. 107-20), and Sedulius shows a special interest elsewhere in the epithets attached in the Gospel of John to Christ (e.g., the good shepherd). Here Sedulius explains that Christ is capable of performing the miracle of turning water into wine because he is not only the vine, the source of wine, but also—and here the poet makes a leap—the source of all fertility: *virtute colona / omnia fructificans*. Christ the vine also serves, the poet adds, as a protective shelter for its crop of grapes against the sun: *cuius sub tegmine blando / mitis inocciduas enutrit pampinus uvas*.

Structure

Sedulius' poetic version of the wedding at Cana, with its combination of traditional and new material, assumes quite different narrative contours from those of John 2. 1-12. Most conspicuous is the transposition of the evangelist's summary sentence which comes near the end of his account (2. 11) to the head of Sedulius' version of the story. As suggested above, Sedulius takes this opportunity to begin the long catalogue of miracles in Books 3 and 4 with the observation that the wedding at Cana was the first of the miracles. Appropriately, the first word in the catalogue (as well as the first word in the episode) is now *prima*. This is how John ends his account of the miracle, but Sedulius has a different conclusion in mind (Christ as the true vine) and so moves the indication of the miracle's primacy to first place in his account.

The shape which this episode takes is characteristically Sedulian. A distinctive kind of narrative rhythm is achieved as the poet moves back and forth between the old and the new. The pattern is accentuated by alternations between simple and dense language. It helps Sedulius to tell the details of the story, as he does in lines 4 and 8, with great clarity and speed, but it also gives the poet ample opportunity to include his own elaborations.

The entire episode as it is restructured by Sedulius is built up around lines 4 and 8. In 3. 1-3 Sedulius gives some background for the miracle by observing that it was the first and by remarking about what an unusual sort of guest the Lord turned out to be. Then, in just five words, he conveys the essential facts of the story: *fusas in vinum convertit aquas*. In the lines that follow (4b-6) Sedulius rhapsodizes on the water's delight at losing its natural qualities and ends the period with a vivid description of the wine blushing on the tables. Line 8 recapitulates the key event in the Gospel account with the addition of the detail of the six jugs. The last three lines of the episode are devoted to the flowery elaboration of the idea of Christ as a fecund and protective vine. Sedulius' structuring of the episode could be outlined in the following way:

> 1-3 Christ as a guest.
> 4a Narrative of the miracle.
> 4b-6 The reaction of the water.
> 7 The description of the wine.
> 8 Recapitulation of the miracle.
> 9-11 Christ as a vine.

The poet frames the miracle itself with his introduction to the idea of Christ as guest (1-3) and the concluding metaphor of Christ as vine (9-11). He also surrounds the water (4b-6) and the wine (6b-7) with simple, single-clause descriptions of the miracle (4 and 8). This is in evident contrast with the evangelist's more rambling narrative structure. John begins and ends the episode with signals of temporal and geographical location, never actually says that the water was changed into wine, and devotes more attention to Mary, the servants, and the steward, than to Jesus himself. Sedulius concentrates the focus of his gaze on Christ (in the frame) and his miracle (the center), the twin subjects of this episode and of his poem (cf. 1. 26). All else is extraneous.[5]

Diction

Since Sedulius retains so little of the substance of John's account, it should not surprise us that very few of the significant words of the Vulgate's version appear here. Sedulius retains only four: *implevit, vinum, aqua, sex*. The most conspicuous substitutions are: *prima documenta dedit virtutis* for John's *hoc fecit initium signorum*; *thalamis* for *ad nuptias*; *dignatus adesse* for *vocatus est*; *latices* and *unda* for *aqua*; *lacus* for *hydrias*; *fusas aquas*

---

[5] Similar narrative and descriptive patterns can be observed elsewhere in the *Paschale carmen*, as, for instance, in the story of the raising of Lazarus in 4. 271-90. In four lines (271-4) Sedulius sets up the story, giving all the essentials in clear, concise language. Then in 275 ff. the poet develops the theme of mourning. What did it mean that Jesus wept? Why did Mary and Martha doubt his divine powers? It takes Sedulius only a line and a half to tell the rest of the story. The last seven lines of the passage are devoted to a lengthy comment on the breaking of the law of death and the paradoxical situation of Lazarus, whom Sedulius describes as a *vivens cadaver*.

for *implete hydrias aqua*; *nectar, mustum, merum* instead of *vinum*; *Christus* and *Dominus* for *Iesus*.

The author of the *Paschale carmen* often chooses a "poetic" word or expression to replace a more prosaic or biblical one. "The first document," for instance, is Sedulius' metaphorical periphrase of the less colorful *initium*. *Thalamis* (3. 1), derived as it is from the Greek, is a more exotic word than *nuptias*. In the plural especially it seems to be confined to poetic use.[6] (In his prose paraphrase of the passage in the *Paschale opus*, Sedulius uses *nuptiis*.) Water is never just water for our poet. John is content to repeat *aqua* and *vinum* every time it is necessary to speak of these elements (he refers to wine four times and water three times). Unlike the evangelist, however, Sedulius strives for variety in his diction. First he uses *aqua*, but then *latices*, followed by *unda*. *Vinum*, too, is used only once. After that Sedulius refers to the fruit of the vine as *merum, mustum*, and finally *nectar*. The poet refers to the jugs themselves as *lacus*, a more high-flown word than the prosaic *hydriae* (retained in the *Paschale opus*).[7] Of interest, too, is Sedulius' reluctance to use the name of Jesus here as well as throughout the poem. The evangelist uses the proper name six times in John 2. 1-11. Sedulius uses *Dominus* once and *Christus* once but not *Iesus*, a name which must have sounded too intimate (or too humble) to his ear. In general, the fifth-century poet strives for a loftier tone than the evangelist and seems to prefer the more respectful titles for his Lord. According to John, Jesus was simply invited (*vocatus est*) to the wedding feast. The poet, by contrast, has Jesus "deign to be present" (*dignatus adesse*). Sedulius considers it an honor for the wedding party to have the Lord attend the festivities.

At least one of Sedulius' changes in wording helps him to accelerate the narrative. Sedulius compresses John's version of Jesus' command to the servants by attaching a proleptic adjective to the noun *aquas*. Instead of spelling out Jesus' instructions as the evangelist does and then reporting on the fulfillment of the command, the poet condenses the entire action, command and fulfillment, into a single word: *fusas*. The evangelist, by contrast, does not mind being narratively redundant. His narrative style, whether by design or not, resembles the painstaking repetitiveness of Old Testament narrative patterns (cf., e.g., 2 Kings 8. 8-9).[8]

Sedulius adorns the *Paschale carmen* generously with figures of speech and thought (noticeably absent in the Gospels). John does use an occa-

---

[6] See *A Latin Dictionary*, C. Lewis and C. Short, eds. (Oxford, 1958), p. 1866.

[7] See the discussion of *lacus* in *TLL* 7, 060 ff.

[8] On repetition in biblical narrative in general, see the fifth chapter of Robert Alter, *The Art of Biblical Narrative* (New York, 1981).

sional metaphor, but the Gospel narratives on the whole are relatively unadorned with such rhetorical devices. The Sedulian passage before us, by contrast, contains examples of antithesis, exclamation, oxymoron, and a number of other figures. The idea of the guest who provides nourishment instead of taking it, for instance, calls forth an antithesis from our poet: *convivaque praesens / pascere non pasci veniens*[9] followed by an exclamation (*mirabile!*), as the narrator is carried away in his admiration for the paradox of the guest playing host. At the thought of the water turning into wine, Sedulius permits himself a particularly flamboyant poetic fancy. In a striking pathetic fallacy, the poet imagines the water as rejoicing to lose its pale color, happy to change its flavor. Sedulius marks the end of this first period fittingly with a "golden line," a verse in which two nouns and two adjectives are separated by a verb: *dulcia non nato rubuerunt pocula musto.*[10]

The poet saves his choicest poetic devices, however, for the extended metaphorical passage with which he concludes the episode. The story of the wedding at Cana culminates in three lines filled with Virgilian overtones. Christ can perform this miracle which involves wine because he is a vine. The metaphor, of course, is not Sedulius' own, but he is the first Christian poet to apply it to this story. And Sedulius does more than simply rephrase the Johannine figure here. The subject of Christ the vine moves him to allegory. When he speaks of "the enduring grapes," Sedulius is undoubtedly thinking of the church and its members (cf. John 15. 5). His description of the vine "with cultivating power" is suggestive of the wine of the eucharistic meal which nurtures believers. Sedulius' delight in paradox is evident throughout the *Paschale carmen*, and it manifests itself here in the form of an oxymoron: *vitis colona*. Christ is the vine which is not cultivated, but the cultivator. Sedulius piles up nouns and descriptive adjectives as he adorns this idea. There are Virgilian echoes (cf. *Georgics* 1. 448) in the last line, and Sedulius follows Virgil's example in using a golden line (*mitis inocciduas enutrit pampinus uvas*) to round off the period.[11] To the poet's ear, this is the kind of emphatic coda which the episode deserves.

[9] See *Ad Herennium* 4. 45. 58 for a discussion of this figure. On Augustine's use of antithesis, see Henri Marrou, *St. Augustin et la fin de la culture antique*, 2nd ed. (Paris, 1949), p. 80.

[10] Dryden's definition of the "golden line" in the Preface to his *Sylvae* is most memorable: "Two substantives and two adjectives with a verb betwixt to keep the peace." For the citation, see L.P. Wilkinson, *Golden Latin Artistry* (Cambridge, 1963), p. 215.

[11] On Virgil's use of the golden line to round off periods, see Wilkinson, *Golden Latin Artistry*, p. 216.

While Sedulius' language quite clearly verges on the "magnilo-quent"[12] (*Paschale carmen* 3. 1-11 contains some typical examples of Sedulius' "baroque" diction), it should be observed that this Christian poet is also capable of achieving simplicity. Sedulius knows how to make the most of the Latin language's ability to say a great deal in very few words. His dense and lofty diction is often offset by lines of exquisite simplicity and clarity, such as *in vinum convertit aquas* or *implevit sex ergo lacus hoc nectare Christus*. The poet strives for humbleness of style (as he suggests in the preface to his poem) as well as epic overtones, and the two disparate styles live in a balance or tension with each other in the *Paschale carmen*. To be sure, Sedulius' sense of artistry is far more rhetorical and sophisticated than the evangelists', but despite the way in which it is often described by critics Sedulius' language is not altogether rhetorical, artificial, or bombastic. The *Paschale carmen* contains numerous examples of *sermo humilis* as well as "purple patches."

Meter

The very fact that Sedulius' version is written in hexameters con-stitutes a major difference between the style of the poet and that of the evangelist. John does not use meter or other devices of sound inten-tionally in 2. 1-12. There was, of course, such a thing in Antiquity as rhythmical prose. The Gospels, however, do not usually contain such studied effects of sound, although rhythmically balanced passages are to be found (e.g., Mt. 5. 1-12). Even though the boundaries between prose and poetry were not so clearly demarcated in the literature of Antiquity as they are now, it is safe to say that in general the balancing of sound and sense was more characteristic of verse than prose. In the ranks of the Christian paraphrasts of Late Antiquity, to be sure, we do find versifiers who seem content to render prose into verse without much concern for metrical artistry, but Sedulius should not be included in their number. In the *Paschale carmen* Sedulius uses meter successfully not only to create "verbal music" but also to facilitate understanding and enhance meaning.

It should be observed that Sedulius' mastery of the hexameter is fairly complete. Unlike Commodian and other Christian poets who tend towards accentual verse, Sedulius is capable of writing a correct quan-titative hexameter line.[13] But even though Sedulius' verse has a distinc-

---

[12] Curtius, *European Literature*, p. 148.
[13] For a discussion of Commodian's accentual poetry, see Raby, *Christian-Latin Poetry*, pp. 11 ff.

tively traditional tone, there is also much that is new and characteristically Sedulian about it. The most conspicuous feature is the abundance of leonine rhymes. Several occur in this passage. In line 7, for example, the first syllable of the third foot and the last syllable of the last foot rhyme.[14] Sedulius' verse also shows signs of conscious metrical planning and artistry. Let us consider, for example, the patterns of "homodyne" and "heterodyne" lines and caesura and diaeresis.[15] The first line of Sedulius' version of the wedding at Cana is dactylic, contains three heterodynes, and has no diaeresis. The episode, therefore, begins with a line which is fast and filled with tension. The reader feels impelled to move on without lingering. In the following lines, the number of heterodynes declines and homodynes increase until the seventh line, which is almost entirely homodyne: *dulcia non nato rubuerunt pocula musto*. The verse ictus and the prose accent coincide in all of the words in the line except for *nato*. Similarly, the number of caesurae declines and the diaereses increase until in line 7 there are three diaereses (after *dulcia*, *rubuerunt*, and *pocula*) and only two caesurae (after *non* and *nato*). The effect of the diaereses is to fill the line with emphatic stops, to slow the reader down. This is a significant line, the end of the period. The wine has been made, the party is back in full swing, and the reader is supposed to breathe a sigh of relief and come to a full stop. Sedulius emphasizes the effect by resolving the metrical tension. Again, in lines 8-10, caesurae and heterodynes increase until Sedulius again relaxes the tension in yet another line in which homodynes outnumber heterodynes and diaeresis occurs as frequently as caesura. The episode is over. In both lines 7 and 11, Sedulius also combines "golden lines" with relaxed metrical tension.

It is not only metrical artistry which concerns Sedulius but other aspects of the sound of his verse as well. Most obvious is the alliteration in line 5 as the poet uses *l*'s to capture the liquid sound of the water turning into wine: *Pallorem latices, mutavit laeta saporem*. The assonance of phrases like *unda suum largita merum* (or even more noticeably *mitis inoc-*

---

[14] For other rhymes, see lines 6 and 11. By all accounts, Sedulius played an important role in the development of European rhymed poetry. See, for example, *Die Genese der europäischen Endreimdichtung* (U. Ernst, P. Neuser, eds.), Wege der Forschung 444 (Darmstadt, 1977), *passim*.

[15] For "heterodyne" and "homodyne," see W.F. Jackson Knight, *Accentual Symmetry in Vergil* (Oxford, 1950). Jackson Knight was the first to apply these terms to the two "waves" in the hexameter lines, which coincide when stress and ictus fall on the same syllable and fail to coincide when they do not (see p. 13). For a discussion of caesura and diaeresis, see C.G. Cooper, *An Introduction to the Latin Hexameter* (Melbourne, 1952), p. 21. Diaeresis is when a word in a line of poetry ends simultaneously with a foot. Caesura is when the word ends before the foot is complete. Cooper observes that "diaeresis ... disrupts verse. Caesura ... binds verse together" (p. 21).

ciduas enutrit pampinus uvas) helps to emphasize the lilting and happy quality of lines 6 and 11.

ii. *A Comparative Analysis*

To appreciate the distinctiveness of Sedulius' handling of the wedding at Cana in *Paschale carmen* 3. 1-11, it will be useful to compare and contrast Sedulius' version with other poetic accounts which have come down to us from Late Antiquity. The poets considered below are not all of a kind but are brought together here in order to provide a background for our consideration of Sedulius' treatment of this miracle. The story of the turning of water into wine was a favorite among Christian poets of the period. Juvencus, Hilary of Poitiers (if he is the author of *Hymnum dicat turba fratrum*), Prudentius in the *Dittochaeon* and in *Cathemerinon* 9, Sedulius (*A solis ortus cardine*), Dracontius in *De laudibus Dei*, Rusticius Helpidius in his *Tristicha*, and the authors of *De Iesu Christo Deo et homine* and *Miracula Christi*—all retold the story in Latin verse.

The Texts

The Latin texts of the other poetic versions of the wedding at Cana follow:

1. Juvencus, *Evangeliorum libri quattuor* 2. 127-52:

Interea thalamis conubia festa parabant
in regione Chanan, ubi clari mater Iesu
nato cum pariter convivia concelebrabat.
Vina sed interea convivis deficiebant.
Tum mater Christum per talia dicta precatur:
Cernis, laetitiae iam defecisse liquorem?
Adsint, nate, bonis ex te data munera mensis.
Olli respondit terrarum gloria Christus:
Festinas genetrix; nondum me talia cogit
ad victus hominum tempus concedere dona.
Mensarum tunc inde vocat laetata ministros
mater et imperiis nati parere iubebat.
Sex illic fuerant saxis praepulchra cavatis
vascula, quae ternis aperirent ilia metretis
haec iubet e fontis gremio conplere ministros.
Praeceptis parent iuvenes undasque coronant
conpletis labiis lapidum; tum spuma per oras
conmixtas undis auras ad summa volutat.
Hinc iubet, ut summo tradant gustanda ministro.
Ille ubi percepit venerandi dona saporis
nescius, in vini gratum transisse liquorem
egestas nuper puris de fontibus undas,

increpat ignarum sponsum, quod pulchra reservans
deteriora prius per mensas vina dedisset.
His signis digne credentum discipulorum
perpetuam stabili firmavit robore mentem.

2. *Hymnum dicat turba fratrum* (lines 25-6):

Vinum quod deerat hydriis mutuari aquam iubet,
nuptiis mero retentis propinando populo.

3. Prudentius, *Cathemerinon* 9. 28-30:

Cantharis infusa lymfa fit Falernum nobile,
nuntiat vinum minister esse promptum ex hydria,
ipse rex sapore tinctis obstupescit poculis.

4. Prudentius, *Dittochaeon* (lines 125-8):

Foedera coniugii celebrabant auspice coetu
forte Galilei, iam derant vina ministris.
Christus vasa iubet properanter aquaria lymfis
inpleri, inde meri veteris defunditur unda.

5. Sedulius, *A solis ortus cardine* (lines 49-52):

Novum genus potentiae:
aquae rubescunt hydriae,
vinumque iussa fundere
mutavit unda originem.

6. Dracontius, *De laudibus Dei* 2. 140-1:

Vertit aquas, ut vina fluant, mirabile donum:
pocula sunt latices et fluminis ebriat unda.

7. Rusticius Helpidius, *Tristicha* (lines 55-7):

Insipidi quondam laticis elementa saporem
flagrantis sumpsere meri; nam providus auctor
munera laetitiae virtutum exordia fecit.

8. *De Iesu Christo Deo et homine* (lines 33-4):

. . . fluvios in vina refundens
hoc donum sponsale dedit. . . .

9. *Miracula Christi* (lines 5-6):

Permutat lymphas in vina liquentia Christus,
quo primum facto se probat esse Deum.

Comparisons and Contrasts

Perhaps the most striking difference between Sedulius' version of the wedding at Cana and those of other Christian Latin poets of Late Antiquity is with respect to length. The other poets deal with the story either more extensively or more briefly than Sedulius. Juvencus' version is the longest. The other poetic treatments are much shorter, ranging from one to four lines and from eight words to 23. In terms of its length, Sedulius' version falls somewhere between Juvencus' treatment of the passage and the summary versions. Sedulius uses 66 words and 11 lines, while Juvencus takes 155 words and 26 lines to retell the same story.[16]

Juvencus includes more details of the original than Sedulius. He tries, for instance, to locate the episode in time and space *(interea, Chanan)*. Even though he does not mention them at first, Juvencus also includes Jesus' disciples later in the episode. Mary, too, plays an important role in Juvencus' account. Her conversation with Jesus and her instructions to the servants are included. Like Sedulius, Juvencus tells how many jugs were present but does not say why they were there. In general, it is Juvencus' practice to Romanize or simply ignore much of the Jewish background of the Gospel narratives. Juvencus does include Jesus' instructions to the servants, the steward's reaction to the new wine, and his criticism of the bridegroom. Although he mentions the effect which the event had on the disciples, Juvencus does not indicate that this was the first miracle. This is not surprising, since, according to *Evangeliorum libri quattuor*, the stilling of the storm (2. 25-42) and other miracles of Christ precede the wedding at Cana.

The shorter versions naturally all tell of the turning of water into wine. But only the author of *Miracula Christi* and Rusticius Helpidius tell us that it was Jesus' first miracle. Most of the summary versions do mention that it took place at a wedding, but only the author of *Hymnum dicat turba fratrum*, Sedulius (in *A solis ortus cardine*), and Prudentius remember the jugs, and none of them specifies their number. With only two exceptions, the shorter versions omit all of the details which Sedulius does in the *Paschale carmen*. In the *Dittochaeon* Prudentius gives a specific location for the wedding *(Galilei)* and in *Cath.* 9 he tells of the steward's reaction to the wine.

The other Christian poets add less material of their own invention to the story than Sedulius does. This is not surprising in the case of the summary poets, who are interested in communicating the essence of the story rapidly. Juvencus does amplify his original, but his additions to the story line are less far-ranging than Sedulius'. Consider, for example, Juvencus' amplification of the Gospel's *et impleverunt eas usque ad summum*:

---

[16] This is quite typical. Consider, for example, the respective number of lines which the same Christian Latin poets devote to the story of the raising of Lazarus: Juvencus 97, Sedulius 20, *A solis ortus cardine* 4, *Dittochaeon* 4, Rusticius Helpidius 3, *De Iesu Christo Deo et homine* 3, Dracontius 2, 9th *Cathemerinon* 2.

> Praeceptis parent iuvenes undasque coronant
> conpletis labiis lapidum; tum spuma per oras
> conmixtas undis auras ad summa volutat.

Juvencus is primarily interested here in rephrasing a single detail of the original. Sedulius' expansion of John's *vocatum est autem et Iesus*, on the other hand *(convivaque praesens, pascere non pasci veniens, mirabile!)*, does not limit itself to stylistic periphrasis but actually introduces a new idea into the narrative. The fifth-century poet helps the reader to anticipate the outcome of the episode by suggesting in a pregnant expression what the guest (who is also a host) will do before the wedding is over. Juvencus ventures forth less often on such imaginative flights of invention.

The differences between Sedulius and the other Latin poets who retell the story of John 2. 1-11 become even clearer in a consideration of the ways in which they reshape the episode. Juvencus is evidently interested in following the narrative outline of the original and adheres to its order with some strictness. The structure of his version of the episode is essentially the same as John's. In *A solis ortus cardine, Miracula Christi*, the *Dittochaeon*, and the *Tristicha*, where the episode occupies a single stanza, there is also little reshaping of the episode. Prudentius' *Dittochaeon* follows the evangelist in telling of the wedding first and its locale, the absence of wine, and the filling of the water jugs, before considering the actual transformation of water into wine in the last line. In his hymn Sedulius' water vessels begin to blush in the second line, but only in the last line is the change made explicit. Like John, Rusticius Helpidius follows the mention of the miracle with an indication of the miracle's primacy. *Miracula Christi* also mentions the change first and the primacy of the miracle second. In the other versions where the episode is handled in only one or two lines, the changing of the water into wine is the first item to be mentioned. Then follows the statement of the wedding context, the fact of the miracle's primacy, or the reaction of the steward. In his treatment of the miracle in the *Paschale carmen*, Sedulius is unique among the Christian Latin poets in the liberties which he takes in restructuring the episode. He alone moves John's belated observation that this was the first miracle to first place. Sedulius' conclusion, too, is quite unusual. Every other poet ends by mentioning the steward's reaction, the fact of the miracle, or the disciples' faith. Sedulius is the only poet to make a connection with John 15.

As far as diction is concerned, it should be observed that both Juvencus and Sedulius substitute ''poetic'' words and expressions for ''unpoetic'' ones. Thus, for Juvencus, the *hydriae* of the original become *saxis praepulchra cavatis vascula*. *Mulier* becomes *genetrix*; *ad nuptias* becomes *thalamis*. Most of the other poets, too, use a more traditional poetic vocabulary than the Vulgate's translation of John 2. 1-11. Water becomes *lymfa* in Prudentius' *Cathemerinon* 9 and *Miracula Christi* or *unda* in Dracontius' *De laudibus Dei*. Marriage is *foedera coniugii* in the *Dittochaeon*. Prudentius' jugs are *vasa aquaria* or *canthari*. The conspicuous exceptions to the rule are the hymns *A solis ortus cardine* and *Hymnum dicat turba fratrum*, whose authors retain more of the vocabulary of the Gospel. Sedulius keeps *aqua*, *vinum*, and *hydriae* in his hymnic version of the story. Hilary retains *nuptiae*, *vinum*, *aqua*, and *hydriae*.

Juvencus does not use nearly so many figures of speech as Sedulius. *E fontis gremio* (2. 141) could be understand as personification, but it is probably just a faded metaphor. The epic language of the crowning of the wine contains another personification *(labiis lapidum)*. But Juvencus does not employ the extravagant anaphoras, the lengthy apostrophes, and impassioned exclamations which Sedulius loves to use. Most of the summary versions, too, are more restrained and less colorful than Sedulius' version. Simplicity of language and clarity predominate. Prudentius and Dracontius do include figures of speech in their versions of the story. Prudentius' *Falernum nobile* is an example of metonomy, and Dracontius describes the water as "drunken." In general, however, the authors of the summary versions do not wax quite so eloquent as Sedulius.

Five of the other nine versions of the wedding at Cana besides the *Paschale carmen* also use hexameters. *Miracula Christi* is written in elegiac distichs; *A solis ortus cardine* is in iambic dimeters—the meter made famous by Ambrose for its use in hymns—and Hilary and Prudentius (*Cath.* 9) employ trochaic tetrameters. This last meter had long been a favorite with Roman soldiers[17] and became increasingly popular in later Latin poetry.[18] Juvencus uses hexameters in *Evangeliorum libri quattuor*, but his lines are heavier than Sedulius', whose favorite hexameter pattern is DSDSDS (D-Dactyl, S-Spondee). According to George Duckworth, the pattern appears in about 16% of the lines of the *Paschale carmen*, giving Sedulius' hexameters an "Ovidian" rather than a "Virgilian" sound.[19] The pattern provides for lilting lines and a lively effect in *Paschale carmen* 3. 1-11 and elsewhere. Sedulius uses DSDSDS in four of the eleven lines in his retelling of the wedding at Cana. Juvencus, by contrast, prefers more ponderous lines and includes three examples of SSSSDS in 2. 127-52. Perhaps Juvencus intended the spondaic

---

[17] See Suetonius, *Galba* 6.

[18] It is used, for example, in the *Pervigilium Veneris* (of uncertain date and authorship but written not earlier than the second century AD).

[19] George Duckworth, *Vergil and Classical Hexameter Poetry* (Ann Arbor, 1969), pp. 132-4.

preponderance to add to the solemnity of his subject. Prudentius (in the *Dittochaeon*), Dracontius, Rusticius Helpidius, and the author of *De Iesu Christo Deo et homine*, on the other hand, use more dactyls than either Juvencus or Sedulius.

Other differences: Juvencus, Prudentius, and Rusticius Helpidius use elision in their versions of the wedding at Cana, while Sedulius studiously avoids it here and elsewhere in the *Paschale carmen*. The author of the *Paschale carmen* also makes frequent use of a three-syllable word accented on the antepenult and followed by a two-syllable word to end his hexameter lines (e.g., *pocula musto*, *nectare Christus*, *tegmine blando*, *pampinus uvas*). Such endings occur less frequently in Juvencus' hexameters.[20] Sedulius also makes greater use of rhyme than his fourth-century predecessor. Several examples of rhyme appear in Juvencus' lines, but it is hard to tell whether they are intentional or not since accidental rhymes are common in an inflected language (cf., e.g., Propertius, *Carmina* 4. 3. 4). Rhyme occurs with such high frequency in Sedulius' poetry, however, that there can be no mistaking its deliberate use. The effect of the abundance of leonine rhymes is to give Sedulius' verse a distinctly unclassical ring. More so than Juvencus, then, Sedulius blends the old with the new in constructing the sound of his verse. Rhyme is a premonition of the European poetry of the future, just as the hexameter is an echo of the epic and the classical past.

Some of the other poets who treat of the wedding at Cana use alliteration but not with the same effect as Sedulius. See, for instance, the predominance of the letter *c* in Juvencus' *nato cum pariter convivia concelebrabat* (2. 129) or *p* in *praeceptis parent iuvenes undasque coronant* (2. 142). Prudentius also uses the device in the *Dittochaeon* (*foedera coniugii celebrabat auspice coetu*) and in *Cath.* 9 (*cantharis infusa lymfa fit Falernum nobile*). But these examples do not contribute so notably to the sense as the alliterative suggestion of flowing water in *Paschale carmen* 3. 5.

It should be observed, in conclusion, that we have compared Sedulius' verse version of the wedding at Cana with those of other Christian Latin poets of Late Antiquity not in order to suggest that his is "better" but rather to illustrate some aspects of Sedulius' uniqueness as a poet. It is clear from this comparative study that Sedulius possesses a distinctive poetic style. The sound of his verse, for instance, is unmistakable. The Sedulian hexameter, with its avoidance of elision, abundant use of leonine rhyme, and fondness for the DSDSDS pattern, bears the metrical fingerprint, as it were, of this poet. It is clear also that Sedulius is a com-

---

[20] In their versions of the wedding at Cana, Juvencus has five in 26 lines; Sedulius four in 11 lines.

petent poetic craftsman, who manipulates sense and sound, skillfully juggles content and form, and uses diction and meter as effectively as other contemporary Christian poets.

A comparison of Sedulius' poetic handling of a specific Scriptural episode with the versions of other Latin poets of Late Antiquity also suggests, despite the critics, that Sedulius is a poet possessed of a degree of "original talent," who has at least some "trace of the creative faculty."[21] From our analysis of his handling of John 2. 1-12, Sedulius appears to be more than a mechanical versifier interested only in turning prose into hexameters. Rather, it is more accurate to describe the narrative essence of the Gospel's story of the wedding at Cana as a seed planted in the poet's mind which has produced an entirely new organism, if you will, bearing only the remotest resemblance to the evangelist's account or that of any other Latin poet of Late Antiquity.[22]

How well the classical and the biblical elements in Sedulius' poetry are reconciled or integrated is another question. One might criticize Sedulius and other biblical epic poets of Late Antiquity, as Curtius does, for even attempting to blend such opposite elements as biblical narratives and epic diction and style. It is undeniable that the *Paschale carmen* reflects the tension which exists between Jerusalem and Athens. We should note, however, that this is a tension which no subsequent biblical epic (including Milton's masterpiece), was able fully to resolve either. Once the limitations inherent in this particular literary tradition are acknowledged, however, we should not fail to give Sedulius (and other early practitioners of this kind of poetry) credit for achieving the poetic effects they desired to achieve within the constraints which they imposed upon themselves.[23]

---

[21] Raby, *Christian-Latin Poetry*, p. 36.

[22] The comparative analysis also suggests that despite critics who have implied that the Christian poets of Late Antiquity are all of a kind—Comparetti (*Virgil in the Middle Ages*, p. 126), for example, dismisses Prudentius, Juvencus, Sedulius, Avitus, Paulinus of Nola and others as "a motley crew of writers of the vilest sort"—there is, in fact, quite a diversity in style and technique among them.

[23] This survey, although representative, is by no means exhaustive. The reader might also, for example, consider with profit lines 13-20 of the hymn *Inluminans altissimus*, which may have been written by Ambrose.

CHAPTER SEVEN

POPULARITY AND INFLUENCE

The following chapter surveys the history of the reception of Sedulius'
Paschale carmen. We shall examine the status which Sedulius' poem
enjoyed as a popular school text in the Middle Ages and the Renaissance
and consider its influence on biblical epics written as late as the 16th and
17th centuries. This survey is not intended to be an exhaustive study of
such an extensive subject and will focus on only three critical periods:
Late Antiquity, the Carolingian period, and the 16th and 17th centuries.
It will be of value if it offers the reader some sense of the kind of appeal
Sedulius had for generations of readers and the importance of his poem
for the history of European literature.

i. *Sedulius and his Earliest Readers*

Sedulius' biblical epic met with early and enthusiastic approval.
Within the century in which it was written, Christian poets were borrowing and echoing lines and phrases from the *Paschale carmen*. Paulinus of
Pella, Paulinus of Périgueux, Rusticius Helpidius, Dracontius, and the
authors of *De evangelio*, *De Iesu Christo Deo et homine*, and *Miracula Christi*,
all probably knew the *Paschale carmen*. By the end of the fifth century Turcius Rufius Apronianus Asterius had produced his own prestigious edition of the poem. The consul of 494 held this Christian poet in the highest
regard. In an epigram of his own composition, included in some Sedulian
manuscripts, Asterius (inspired perhaps by Sedulius' own claims in
Paschale carmen 1. 17-26) describes Sedulius as *iustus* and *verax poeta*:[1]

> Sume sacer meritis, veracis dicta poetae
> quae sine figmenti condita sunt vitio,
> quo caret alma fides, quo sancti gratia Christi,
> per quam iustus ait talia Sedulius.
> Asteriique tui semper meminisse iubeto,
> cuius ope et cura edita sunt populis.
> Quem quamvis summi celebrent per saecula fastus
> plus tamen ad meritum est, si viget ore tuo.

By the beginning of the sixth-century the *Paschale carmen* was well enough
known not only to be included in the "Gelasian Decree" but to receive

---

[1] I use the text provided by Huemer in *CSEL* 10, 307.

high praise there. The Decree describes Sedulius as *venerabilis* and a poet worthy of "conspicuous praise" *(insigni laude)*.[2]

In the sixth century we find Cassiodorus (c. 485-c. 580) quoting from the *Paschale carmen* in his influential *Institutiones* as well as in the *Expositio in Psalterium*, where he describes Sedulius as *poeta veritatis*.[3] Cassiodorus assumes that his readers are quite familiar with *Paschale carmen* 1. 349-50; he refers to the passage as "those well-known lines of Sedulius" (*Sedulii versus illi*). Venantius Fortunatus (c. 540-c. 600), bishop of Poitiers and himself a prolific poet, praises Sedulius on two occasions. In *Carmen* 8. 1 Fortunatus describes the poet as "sweet:"[4]

> Quod tonat Ambrosius, Hieronymus atque coruscat,
> sive Augustinus fonte fluente rigat,
> Sedulius dulcis, quod Orosius edit acutus
> regula Caesarii linea nata sibi est. (8. 1. 57-60)

In his life of St. Martin (1. 18) Venantius Fortunatus also speaks highly of the fifth-century poet's abilities *(hinc quoque conspicui radiavit lingua Seduli)*.[5]

In the seventh century, as we have already seen, Isidore thought enough of Sedulius to include his name in his catalogue of "illustrious men,"[6] and the *Paschale carmen* is praised enthusiastically in a description of Isidore's library as a healthy Christian literary alternative for readers tired of pagan authors like Virgil.[7] Among the doubtful writings ascribed to Ildephonse of Toledo (c. 610-667), according to Huemer, there is an enthusiastic description of the author of the *Paschale carmen* as: *bonus ille Sedulius, poeta evangelicus, orator facundus, scriptor catholicus*.[8]

In his *Historia Francorum* (5. 44), Gregory of Tours (bishop from 573-94) tells of Chilperic (d. 584) and his attempts at writing verse. According to Gregory, it was Sedulius' example which inspired Chilperic to write a prose and a verse version of the same work: *Scripsit alios libros idem rex versibus, quasi Sedulium secutus; sed versiculi illi nulli penitus metricae conveniunt rationi*.[9] According to the Venerable Bede (c. 673-735), Sedulius' double work *(opus geminatum)* also served as the model for the *De virginitate* of Aldhelm, bishop of Sherborne (c. 640-709). Aldhelm wrote two versions

---

[2] For a discussion of the problem of dating the Gelasian Decree, see above, Chapter 2, n. 9.

[3] *Expos. in Psalt.* 113. 12 (*CC* 98, 1032).

[4] *MGH AA* 4, 180.

[5] *MGH AA* 4, 296.

[6] *PL* 83, 1094.

[7] *PL* 83, 1110.

[8] Quoted in Huemer, *De Sedulii poetae vita*, p. 52.

[9] *PL* 71, 361-2. On the poetry of Chilperic, see Dag Norberg, *La poésie latine rythmique du haut Moyen Age* (Stockholm, 1954), pp. 31 ff.

of the work, one in prose and one in verse. No doubt Bede himself and Alcuin, too, both of whom also wrote such double works, were influenced by the example of Sedulius' *Paschale carmen* and *Paschale opus*. So besides receiving considerable attention for his authorship of the *Paschale carmen*, Sedulius was also given credit for establishing a literary tradition which enjoyed a considerable vogue among Anglo-Latin writers of the seventh and eighth centuries.[10]

In Britain in the early Middle Ages Sedulius was especially popular.[11] Bede in particular knew Sedulius very well. The eighth-century polymath quotes from the *Paschale carmen* in his *De arte metrica*, *De orthographia*, *In libros regum quaestiones 30*, and *In Lucae evangelium expositio*, where he praises the beauty of the *Paschale carmen* (*Sedulius in paschali carmine pulchre versibus dixit. . .*).[12] From manuscripts and other sources we know that Sedulius' *Paschale carmen* enjoyed wide circulation in early Anglo-Saxon England, where it was evidently part of a poetical "school canon." Alcuin (c. 735-804) mentions Sedulius along with Juvencus and Arator in his *Versus de patribus, regibus, et sanctis Euboricensis ecclesiae* (v. 1551), a poem which commemorates the school in which Alcuin had studied and taught.[13]

The *Paschale carmen* was highly respected by its first readers in Late Antiquity and the early Middle Ages. Unlike the mixed reviews with which Proba's *Cento* was greeted (e.g., Jerome, *Ep.* 53. 7. 3), the responses to the *Paschale carmen* which survive from its first centuries of existence are uniformly positive.[14] It used to be commonly believed, on the basis of Sedulius' own dedicatory letter to the *Paschale opus*, that the

---

[10] On the *opus geminatum*, see Peter Godman, "The Anglo-Latin *opus geminatum* from Aldhelm to Alcuin," *Medium aevum* 50 (1981), 215-29, and *Alcuin: The Bishops, Kings, and Saints of York* (Oxford, 1982), pp. lxxviii ff. See also Roberts, *Biblical Epic*, p. 82.

[11] Columban (543-615) knew Sedulius, according to W.F. Bolton, *A History of Anglo-Latin Literature, 597-1066* (Princeton, 1967) I, p. 43. Neil Wright discusses the influence of Sedulius on the *Hisperica famina* in *Cambridge Medieval Celtic Studies* 4 (1982), 61-76.

[12] *CC* 120, 401.

[13] Godman, *Alcuin* (p. lxix), remarks that "the late Antique poets whom Alcuin knew and cited in similar proportions are Caelius Sedulius, Arator, and Juvencus. Familiar to both Bede and Aldhelm, the works of these three writers formed a core of Biblical epic poetry which enjoyed a wide circulation in early Anglo-Saxon England. . . ." Elsewhere (p. lxx) Godman also observes: "The group of late Antique and early Medieval Latin poets whom Alcuin lists at vv. 1551-3 and from whom he quotes repeatedly—Caelius Sedulius, Arator, Juvencus, Paulinus of Nola, and Venantius Fortunatus—form a coherent whole. They correspond to texts contained in a number of composite manuscripts of the early ninth century . . . which are among our major witnesses to a poetical 'school canon.'"

[14] As Roberts (*Biblical Epic*, p. 4, n. 12) observes, it was probably "the element of literary *jeu d'esprit*, typical of the cento, that aroused the opposition" of Jerome to Proba's poem.

Paschale carmen originally met with a hostile reception from Macedonius. In that letter Sedulius speaks of Macedonius as "instructing" him to rewrite the text of the *Paschale carmen* in prose because it displeased (*offenderit*) him as it was.[15] For a long time scholars had seen in this "opposition" to the *Paschale carmen* a reflection of the traditional Christian suspicion of pagan literature. Macedonius, it was assumed, did not care for the poem because it was so redolent of Virgil. It was Curtius, however, who rightly observed that Sedulius' claim to be writing the *Paschale opus* only in response to the commands of a superior is a *topos* commonly found in literary prefaces, which need not be accepted at face value.[16] Macedonius was probably no more displeased with the *Paschale carmen* than any of its other early readers. Indeed, the issuing of a prose version of the poem is most likely a solid indication of the *Paschale carmen*'s popularity with its first audience.

ii. *Sedulius and the Carolingians*

Sedulius continued to enjoy enormous popularity and prestige throughout the early Middle Ages. Carolingian scholars and poets, in particular, accorded the author of the *Paschale carmen* the highest esteem. Alcuin, the influential adviser of Charlemagne, was much indebted to Sedulius.[17] He quotes from the *Paschale carmen* frequently in his letters and other writings, and the taste which he had for Sedulius' poetry was typical of the times. Among the ninth-century intellectual lights who knew of and admired the *Paschale carmen* we must include: Theodulf of Orléans (d. 821), who describes Sedulius as "brilliant" (*rutilus*), Smaragdus (d. after 825), Claudius of Turin (d. 827), Dungalus Reclusus (d. after 827), Jonas of Orléans (d. 843), Hrabanus Maurus (d. 856), Notker Balbulus of St. Gall (c. 840-912), Eulogius of Córdoba (c. 810-859), and many others.[18] Sedulius was not only widely read during this period but respected as having close to patristic authority. In *De partu*

---

[15] For a succinct review of the history of scholarship on the problem, see Roberts, *Biblical Epic*, pp. 79-81. Herzog's suggestion that the *Paschale opus* represented a new "edition" of the *Paschale carmen* has been correctly rejected by Roberts, *Biblical Epic*, p. 83, n. 86.

[16] Curtius, *European Literature*, pp. 461-2. In the preface to his *Epitome*, as Curtius observes (p. 462, n. 43), Lactantius also claims that he has been "commanded" to write his work. For parallels in other Latin prose prefaces, see Janson, *Latin Prose Prefaces*, pp. 116-41.

[17] See Huemer, *De Sedulii poetae vita*, pp. 53-4, and J.D.A. Ogilvy, *Books Known to Anglo-Latin Writers from Aldhelm to Alcuin (670-804)* (Cambridge, Mass., 1936), pp. 79-80.

[18] See Huemer's list, *De Sedulii poetae vita*, pp. 53-6. I am also indebted to the exhaustive references in the indices to Max Manitius, *Geschichte der lateinischen Literatur des Mittelalters* in *Handbuch der Altertumswissenschaft* 9 (Munich, 1911-31).

virginis, for example, Paschasius Radbertus (c. 785-c. 860) claims that Sedulius' description of the virgin birth was unsurpassed for clarity even by the church fathers: *Nihil ergo apertius dicere queunt, nihil manifestius hic sancti doctores de partu Virginis.*[19] The fifth-century poet was quoted as an authority in a number of doctrinal disputes. In a discussion of the Trinity, for example, Gottschalk of Orbais (c. 803-c. 869) cites *Paschale carmen* 1. 324 as an authoritative text and praises Sedulius as a *fidelis poeta.*[20] Interestingly, Gottschalk's deadly opponent, Hincmar of Reims (845-882), demonstrates equal respect for Sedulius as a doctrinal authority and quotes him often in his rebuttal of Gottschalk's arguments.[21]

For the Carolingians Sedulius enjoyed a reputation as a poet equal or even superior to Virgil. This is clear from Carolingian manuscripts, where (as Huemer observes) Sedulius' works often follow directly after Virgil's, and from the schools, where Sedulius was evidently considered as important an author as the Augustan poet.[22] One text which survives from the ninth century, *Codex Laudunensis* 468, a guide to Virgil and Sedulius in particular and the liberal arts in general, illustrates the point.[23] Ninth-century manuscripts of the *Paschale carmen* abound. Their production was probably due, at least in part, to a demand for texts of the *Paschale carmen* for use in schools. Although the oldest extant Sedulian manuscripts, *Taurinensis* E. IV. 42 and a palimpsest, *Ambrosianus* R. 57, are dated to the seventh century, many more survive from the ninth.[24] *Karoliruhensis* 217, *Turicensis* C. 68, *Sangallensis* 877, *Montepessalanus* 362 and *Parisinus* 9347, 14143, 13337, for example, are all dated to the ninth century. *Bernensis* 267, *Carnotensis* 58, and *Sangallensis* 197 are from the ninth or tenth centuries. At least one commentary on the *Paschale carmen* from this period also survives, that of Remigius of Auxerre (c. 840-908).[25]

The Carolingians considered Sedulius to be one of the most preeminent of the Christian Latin poets. Ermoldus Nigellus places Sedulius first

---

[19] As quoted by Huemer, *De Sedulii poetae vita*, p. 56.

[20] *PL* 125, 479.

[21] See Huemer, *De Sedulii poetae vita*, p. 55.

[22] Huemer, *De Sedulii poetae vita*, p. 8, n. 1.

[23] See now the edition of John Contreni in the series *Armarium codicum insignium* 3 (Turnhout, 1984).

[24] For a discussion of *Taurinensis* E. IV. 42 and a facsimile from fol. 20ᵛ, see E.A. Lowe, *Codices latini antiquiores*, Part IV (Oxford, 1947), pp. 12-13.

[25] Edited (in part) by Huemer, *CSEL* 10, 316-59. Sedulius is also quoted in a ninth-century *florilegium versuum* (*Sangallensis* 870), where he enjoys the heady company of such well known Latin poets as Lucretius, Martial, Ovid, and Virgil. See the discussion in Arthur Patch McKinlay, *Arator: The Codices* (Cambridge, Mass., 1942), p. 62.

in a list of Christian poets which he compiled for Louis the Pious, the son
of Charlemagne:

> Non ego gestorum per singula quaeque recurram,
> nec fas, nec potis est, nec valet ingenium,
> si Maro, Naso, Cato, Flaccus, Lucanus, Homerus,
> Tullius et Macer, Cicero sive Plato,
> Sedulius, nec non Prudentius atque Iuvencus
> seu Fortunatus, Prosper et ipse foret:
> omnia famosis vix possent condere cartis
> atque suum celebre hinc duplicare melos.
> Ast ego lintre rudi rimoso navita remo
> inmensi pelagi aequor adire volo.[26]

For Carolingian poets, Sedulius possessed something of the same
authority which Virgil had for the poets of Late Antiquity. Alcuin, Paul
the Deacon (c. 730-799?), Paulinus of Aquileia (c. 750-802), Angilbert
(c. 750-814), Florus of Lyons (d. 860), Walafrid Strabo (c. 808-849), and
others, all borrowed from Sedulius' verse.[27] Sometimes the borrowing is
almost verbatim, as, for instance, in line 11 of Florus' poem on Matthew
(*inde quater denis ieiunans ipse diebus*), which is very close to *Paschale carmen*
2. 175-6 (*inde quater denis iam noctibus atque diebus* / *ieiunum dapibus...*).
Florus depended heavily on the *Paschale carmen* not only for his poems on
the Gospels of Matthew and John but also for his *Gesta Christi Domini* and
Oratio cum commemoratione miraculum. Another Carolingian poet, whose
name is unknown, devoted his talents to recasting the *Paschale carmen* into
quatrains. Only a fragment of this effort survives.[28] For the Carolingians, as for many medieval readers of the *Paschale carmen*, it seemed
that its author had surpassed—if not in his art, then certainly in his
overall product—the greatest of the *veteres poetae*. A short poem in *Codex
Ambrosianus* J. 35 sums up this response to the *Paschale carmen*:

> Scripsit Sedulius carmine nobili
> laudes, Christe, tuas gestaque caelica
> Lucani similis versibus arduis.
> Iam cedant veteres: nam superat novus
> hic, hic Sedulius carmine nobili,

---

[26] The last lines, of course, are based on a passage from Sedulius' first epistle to
Macedonius:
> . . . utpote qui nulla veteris scientiae praerogativa suffultus tam inmensum paschalis
> pelagus maiestatis et viris quoque peritissimis formidandum parva tiro lintre
> cucurrerim.

[27] For a recent (and sympathetic) treatment of Carolingian poetry, see Peter Godman,
Poetry of the Carolingian Renaissance (Norman, Oklahama, 1985).

[28] In *Paris.* 9347 f. 4a. Discussed by Manitius, *Geschichte der lateinischen Literatur* II, p.
492.

dum te, Christe, canit, optime, maxime,
qui cum patre tenes regna perennia,
cum sancto pariter flamine iugiter,
cui sit laus et honor saecla per omnia.[29]

Even though Sedulius would never enjoy this degree of respect and influence again, his work continued to be read and quoted throughout the
next centuries by such diverse figures as Pope John VIII (pope from 872-
882), Odo of Cluny (c. 879-942), Ratherius of Luttich, Jotsald of Cluny,
Joannes Canaparius, Aimoin of Fleury, Dudo of St. Quentin, and Bern-
ward of Hildesheim (c. 960-1022), to mention just a few names.[30]
Sigebert of Gembloux (c. 1032-1112) includes an entry for Sedulius in his
De viris illustribus; Honorius of Regensburg (c. 1085-1156) mentions
Sedulius in *De luminaribus ecclesiae*. John of Salisbury (c. 1115-1180), who
quotes *Paschale carmen* 1. 66-7 in his *Policratus*,[31] and Engelbert of Admont
(d. 1331) also knew of the fifth-century poet.[32]

The *Paschale carmen* evidently continued to be read in schools throughout the medieval period.[33] Around 1075, Winrich of Trier compiled a
catalogue of authors to be read in school, in which he included Sedulius
along with eight other Christian authors. Aimeric of Angoulême, a
French grammarian, includes Sedulius in his *Ars lectoria* of 1086, and
Conrad of Hirsau (c. 1070-1150) mentions Sedulius in a listing of 21 curriculum authors in his *Dialogus super auctores*. Eberhard the German (fl.
before 1280) includes the author of the *Paschale carmen* in a list of 37 school
authors.[34]

Medieval poets outside the circle and beyond the time of the Carolingian poets also read and borrowed from Sedulius. The *Paschale carmen*
has been shown, for instance, to have had an influence on Otfrid's
Evangelienbuch, a ninth-century verse paraphrase of the Gospels written in
the Franconian dialect. Like Sedulius' poem, Otfrid's work is also in five
books and retells the story of the life of Christ with many exegetical

---

[29] I use the text provided by Huemer, *De Sedulii poetae vita*, p. 8.

[30] For these references and others, see Manitius, *Geschichte der lateinischen Literatur* II,
passim.

[31] See Joseph B. Pike, *Frivolities of Courtiers and Footprints of Philosophers: Being a Translation of the First, Second, and Third Books and Selections from the Seventh and Eighth Books of the
Policratus of John of Salisbury* (Minneapolis, 1938), p. 94.

[32] Huemer, *De Sedulii poetae vita*, p. 58.

[33] Zachary of Besançon, master of the cathedral school from 1131-4 and a canon of
the Praemonstratensian priory of St. Martin at Laon about 1157, quotes *Paschale carmen*
1. 355-8 (on the four symbols of the evangelists). See Beryl Smalley, *The Gospels in the
Schools c. 1100-c. 1280* (London and Ronceverte, 1985), pp. 30-2.

[34] For these and other lists of curriculum authors, see Curtius, *European Literature*, pp.
48-51, 260, 464-7.

touches.[35] Sedulian echoes and borrowings have also been detected in *Ecbasis captivi* and the poetry of Hrosvita.[36] Odo of Cluny wrote a meditation on sacred history from creation to doomsday in 7 books of 5560 hexameters, a work which bears a number of resemblances to the *Paschale carmen*.[37] The Old Saxon poem known as the *Heliand* (written in the first half of the ninth century), which retells the entire Gospel story including sermons and parables, may also have been indebted to the *Paschale carmen*. Biblical narrative poetry continued to be written throughout the Middle Ages and in languages other than Latin. It is possible that the authors of such Old English works as *Christ and Satan* and *The Dream of the Rood* as well as such later compositions as *The Passion of our Lord*, *The Southern Passion*, *The Harrowing of Hell*, and *The Northern Passion* of the 13th and 14th centuries knew of the *Paschale carmen*, even though they do not explicitly acknowledge the fifth-century master. We do know that Sedulian manuscripts continued to be produced throughout western Europe all through the Middle Ages.[38] If Sedulius was a "curriculum author," many medieval biblical poets must have made the acquaintance of the *Paschale carmen* in schools. It would be surprising if they were not at least indirectly influenced by its author.

iii. *Sedulius in the Renaissance*

The *Paschale carmen*'s popularity continued without abatement in the Renaissance period. Sedulius was as well known as he had ever been during the Middle Ages, although criticisms of his poetic style now began to appear with greater frequency. Among the influential Renaissance figures who appreciated Sedulius, we find Johannes Trithemius (1462-1516), who included a discussion of Sedulius in his *Catalogus scriptorum ecclesiasticorum* of 1494, in which he refers to Sedulius as "a man well versed in the divine Scriptures and most learned in secular letters, outstanding either at verse or prose, who shone forth brilliantly in the city

---

[35] See C. Marold, "Otfrids Beziehungen zu den biblischen Dichtungen des Juvencus, Sedulius, Arator," *Germania* 32 (1887), 385-411. Ulrich Ernst, *Der Liber Evangeliorum Otfrids von Weissenburg: Literarästhetik und Verstechnik im Lichte der Tradition* (Cologne and Vienna, 1975), also considers the influence of the late antique biblical epics on Otfrid. See also Kartschoke, *Bibeldichtung*, pp. 290-3.

[36] Manitius *Geschichte der lateinischen Literatur*, I, p. 617 and p. 631.

[37] See Manitius' article in *ZOG* 52 (1901), 227.

[38] For his edition of the *Paschale carmen*, Huemer compiled a list of over 30 MSS ranging from the seventh to the fifteenth century, but there are a number of others which have been discovered since that time or which Huemer simply overlooked (see above, Chap. 1, n. 2).

of Rome with his amazing teaching.''[39] The famous Venetian printer,
Aldus Manutius, featured the *Paschale carmen* prominently in his influential collection, *Poetae christiani veteres* of 1501-04, only one of over 30
separate editions of Sedulius' poetry which survive from the 16th century. The German reformer, Martin Luther (1483-1546), translated the
first stanzas of *A solis ortus cardine* into German and praised Sedulius as
''a most Christian poet'' in *De divinitate et humanitate Christi*.[40]

16th-century editors heaped praise upon the fifth-century poet.[41] One
edition of the *Paschale carmen*, which appeared in Lyons in 1553, describes
Sedulius as ''celebrated no less for his elegance than for his purity'' (*non
minus elegantia quam puritate clarus*).[42] A prefatory puff to another 16th-
century edition of Juvencus, Sedulius, and Arator recommends these
biblical epics as good antidotes to the impious songs which find their
origins ''in stinking stews'' (*fornicibus putentibus*) and praises Sedulius
along with Juvencus as deservedly famous (*quos merito claros asservere
viri*).[43] Yet another enthusiastic introduction (in Jac. Thanner's 1517 edition of the *Paschale carmen*) is even more extravagant in its praise of the
work, describing the *Paschale carmen* as a *praeclarissimum opus* and assigning
its author the epithet *divus*.[44]

The *Paschale carmen* continued to enjoy wide use as a school text
throughout the 16th century. Aldus Manutius produced his edition of the
Christian poets, at least in part, for pedagogical reasons:

---

[39] The translation is based on the text of Peter Quentel's 1546 edition (published in
Cologne):
   . . . vir in divinis scripturis exercitatus et in secularibus literis eruditissimus, carmine excelens et prosa . . . in urbe Roma mirabili doctrina clarus effulsit.

[40] *WA* 39. 2, 95.

[41] Jacobus de Breda refers to Sedulius as *poeta christianissimus* in the introduction to his
1509 edition. (For brief descriptions of this and a number of other early printed editions
of Sedulius, see *BMGC*, 218, p. 296.)

[42] *C. Iuvenci, Coelii Sedulii, Aratoris sacra poësis* (Lyons, 1553).

[43] For this edition of Theodor Poelmann (published in Basel sometime after 1537),
Reinhard Lorichius wrote a dedicatory epistle and an epigram which concludes with a
hearty commendation of the poetry of Juvencus and Sedulius:
   Talia proiecit portenta Iuvencus, et aestu
   Sedulius pepulit talia monstra pari.
   Casta salutiferi duo nam sacraria verbi,
   impuros quae non passa fuere modos.
   Carmina fornicibus putentibus impia quadrant,
   conveniunt sacris organa sancta viris.
   Hinc divina pio cecinere poemata versu,
   laurigeris compti tempora laeta comis.
   Excipite ergo duos almi virtute poetas,
   quos merito claros asservere viri.

[44] *BMGC* 218, p. 296.

. . . statui Christianos poetas cura nostra impressos publicare, ut loco fabularum, et librorum gentilium infirma puerorum aetas illis imbueret, ut vera pro veris, et pro falsis, falsa cognosceret. . . .

John Colet (1467?-1519) included Sedulius along with other "Cristyn auctours [such as Lactantius, Prudentius, and Juvencus] that wrote theyre wisdome with clene and chast laten other in verse or in prose" in his statutes for St. Paul's School in London.[45] In Germany, Georg Fabricius (1516-71), who played an important role in the organization of schools in Saxony, included Sedulius in his popular collection, *Poetarum veterum ecclesiasticorum opera christiana et operum reliquiae ac fragmenta* (Basel, 1562), and commended Sedulius to his readers as a *vir maximus* and *pientissimus*. Ludovicus Vives, in his instructions for the education of Princess Mary, praises the Christian poets of Late Antiquity most highly, who "in many places," he writes, "might compare with any of the ancients—I speak of the elegancies of verse." Vives adds of these poets that "whilst they discuss matters of the highest kind, for the salvation of the human race, [they] are neither crude nor contemptible in speech."[46] We know that Sedulius continued to be read in some English schools into the latter part of the sixteenth century. The Statutes at St. Saviour's, Southwark, of 1562 mention Sedulius, as do the Statutes of St. Bees two decades later.[47]

All of this is not to suggest that Sedulius did not have his share of critics. As early as the 12th century, we find Sextus Amarcius pointing

---

[45] T.W. Baldwin, *William Shakspere's Small Latine and Lesse Greeke* (Urbana, 1944) I, p. 128.

[46] Baldwin, *Small Latine and Lesse Greeke* I, p. 187 and p. 191. An edition of the *Paschale carmen* (Turin, 1516) survives which was produced expressly for use in private instruction. The author of the preface observes to his patron:

Sed et illud me invitavit: quod cum Io. Baptistam filium non postremae idolis habeas quem litteris et virtuti tenellum ad huc me praeceptore adhibes: quem etiam per sacra dogmata deduci iubes. . . . Per hanc igitur ipsam pietatis viam et tuo exemplo et praeceptorum lectionibus si ducatur filius cum historicis documentis et Ciceronianis libris quod iam fieri coeptum est: erit utique ut tua integritas et non venalis fides: quae apud divinum tuum ducem eo quo sedes fastigio evexerunt id omnino promerentur.

[47] Baldwin, *Small Latine and Lesse Greeke* I, p. 424 and p. 433. One early edition of the *Paschale carmen*, with a commentary by Aelius Antonius Nebrissensis (Toledo, 1520), seems clearly designed for use in the schools. A prefatory poem to the reader declares:

Haec legite o iuvenes divini carmina vatis:
haec versate pia nocte dieque manu.
Non hic monstra canit priscis conficta poetis:
non hic centauros oedipodasve leges.
Veia salutiferi narrat monumenta tonantis:
et sacrum e sancto defluit ore melos.
Quae quoniam Antoni ingenio patefacta videre
quisque potest: laetus perlege quisquis ades.

out respectfully that the biblical epics of Late Antiquity are not highly
polished masterpieces:

> Alchimus, Arator, Sedulius atque Iuvencus
> non bene tornatis apponunt regia vasis
> fercula: miror eos, non audeo vituperare.[48]

Petrarch (1304-74) is less cautious. In *Eclogue* 10. 311 ff., the 14th-
century humanist observes:

> Longe ibi trans fluvium, regum inter busta seorsum,
> unus erat rutilus divini ruris arator
> qui pinguem scabro sulcabat vomere campum.
> Huic comes, hinc prudens, hinc sedulus alter aranti
> certabant rigido glebas confringere rastro.
> Terra fera, fessique boves et laurea nusquam,
> nusquam hedere, aut mirtus, viridis non gloria serti,
> non studium Muse, fragilis vox.[49]

Petrarch puns on the names of Sedulius and other Christian poets of Late
Antiquity without mentioning them outright and implies that they
worked with fertile material but failed to distinguish themselves as poets
(*non studium Muse, fragilis vox*). In the 16th century as well, the biblical
epics of Late Antiquity came in for their share of criticism. Even though
we find Erasmus expressing his admiration for Christian poets like
Juvencus in a letter of 1496 (*Ep.* 49, 85 ff.), later in life the Dutch
humanist was less than enthusiastic about much of the Christian poetry
of Late Antiquity. By 1511 in *De ratione studii* he was calling Prudentius
(who did not write a biblical epic) "the one really stylish poet among
Christian authors."[50] Even in the adulatory prefaces to editions of the
Paschale carmen and other biblical epics, it is apparent that devotees of the
biblical poets of Late Antiquity had been put on the defensive. In his
remarks on Juvencus and Sedulius in an edition which appeared
sometime between 1537 and 1561, Reinhard Lorichius concedes that
these Christian poets may not be in the first rank of authors, although
he quickly adds that they are not the worst either.[51] Admitting that the
style of the biblical epics of Late Antiquity is not the best, Lorichius
remarks that poets like Sedulius do not always "sound forth with

---

[48] *Sermones* 3, 270-2. I use the edition of Karl Manitius (Weimar, 1969), p. 136.

[49] The text of the *Eclogue* is taken from Thomas G. Bergin, *Petrarch's Bucolicum Carmen* (New Haven and London, 1974), pp. 172-5.

[50] I use the translation of Brian McGregor in *Collected Works of Erasmus* (Toronto, 1978) 24, p. 675. See also Erasmus' objections in *Opera* (1703-6) Vol. IX, p. 93, C, D (as cited in Baldwin, *Small Latine and Lesse Greeke* I, p. 85, n. 27).

[51] The Latin original reads: "*In quorum numero si non primas ferunt, Iuvencus hic noster, ac Sedulius, certe (mea sententia) non tamen in postremis erunt.*"

impressive verbal skill or excessive elegancies which flatter and charm more because of the refinement of discourse than the pursuit of edification,'' but they do ''compensate richly for this lack by the very rich fruit they bear in the way of outstanding truth and piety.''[52]

However critical the 16th century may have been of Sedulius and the *Paschale carmen*, the biblical epic was to become one of that century's most popular literary forms, and the life of Christ emerged as a favorite poetic subject. The Renaissance biblical epic poets were not unfamiliar with the antiquity of their literary tradition. They frequently referred to Sedulius' *Paschale carmen* and other biblical epics of Late Antiquity in attempting to justify their own attempts to write biblical poetry. In 1499, for instance, in a preface to his *De triumpho Christi*, Macarius Mutius cites Sedulius (along with other Christian poets of Late Antiquity) as a good model for contemporary poets, whom he accuses of laziness:

> Nemo fere exercet; nemo excitat. Ecce florent nostra tempestate ingenia; vigent studia. Quotusquisque tamen est qui ad illustrandas sacras litteras stilum accommodet?

Mutius suggests that Christian poetry like that of Sedulius, for which he has the highest praise, has fallen into decline *(sed obsolevit id genus Camoenarum iampridem et in tenebris iacet)*. There are further recommendations for the resuscitation of the Christian muse in both of the prefaces attached to the work, and Mutius applies his theories to practice in a short poem (317 hexameters) on Christ's triumphant descent into hell. Mutius' remarks about the poverty of Christian poetry in his own time are somewhat exaggerated. We know of a number of 15th-century examples of biblical poetry, the most famous perhaps being *Parthenice Mariana*, the life of Mary from the conception of her famous son to her assumption, in three books of hexameters, written by the Carmelite monk Giovanni Battista Spagnuoli (Mantuan) and first published in 1481. Like Macarius Mutius, Mantuan holds up Christian poetry of Late Antiquity, for example, the *Evangeliorum libri quattuor* of Juvencus, as providing good precedent for his own efforts in this direction. Erasmus himself, who at least early on in life was much interested in the possibility of a *poesis docta ac sacra*, also composed religious poetry as a young man, including a hexameter poem on Christ's triumphant descent into hell.[53]

---

[52] The Latin text follows:
Qui si non undique pomposo verborum apparatu intonantes, delicatis nimium, quae magis elegantia sermonis, quam studio pietatis, sibi blandiuntur ac perplacent ingeniis satisfacere videbuntur: omnia compensabunt uberrimo conspicuae veritatis et sanctimoniae fructu.

[53] See C. Reedijk, *The Poems of Desiderius Erasmus* (Leiden, 1956).

Macarius Mutius would have been gratified by the rapid development of Christian poetry in the 16th century. His, of course, was not the only appeal for more and better Christian poetry. It seems clear that Aldus Manutius' publication of *Poetae christiani veteres* in the first years of the 1500s was intended to present "models for contemporary imitation."[54] In any event, whatever the exact stimulus, the 16th century witnessed a flowering of interest in setting sacred matter to hexameters in general and a veritable spate of epic lives of Christ in particular. These include: 1. Antonio Cornazano's *La vita e passione de Christo* (1518), in three books of terza rima; 2. Alvarus Gomez de Ciudad Real's massive *Thalichristia* (1522), in 25 books relating the story of the Fall, Old Testament types, and the life and death of Christ, before concluding with a discussion of the founding of the church; 3. Jacobus Bonus' *De vita et gestis Christi* (1526), in 16 books; 4. Teofilo Folengo's *La humanità del Figlivolo di Dio* (1533), in 10 books of ottava rima; 5. Marcus Hieronymus Vida's *Christiad* (1535), in 6 books of hexameters, the most famous of the Latin biblical epics of the Renaissance, a work commissioned by Leo X; 6. Jacobus Strasburgus' *Oratio prima* and *Oratio secunda* (1565), hexameter treatments of the temptation of Christ and a parliament in heaven; 7. Charles Godran's *Encomium crucis dominicae* (1565), a close paraphrase of John 18-19; 8. Michel Foucqué's *La vie, faictz, passion, mort, résurrection, et ascension de nostre seigneur Jésus Christ* (1574), in 8 books of decasyllables; 9. Abraham Fraunce's *Countesse of Pembrokes Emanuel* (1591), in 2 books of rhyming hexameters, and others.[55]

Not every biblical epic poet of the Renaissance explicitly acknowledged Sedulius or other pioneers in the tradition, and the 16th-century poets certainly showed far more independence and boldness than Sedulius in adopting Virgilian narrative devices such as *in medias res* or flashback. They invented dialogue and action, created elaborate councils set in heaven or hell, and avoided traditional exegesis as much as possible. Sedulius was respected but not slavishly imitated. One important similarity between the style of the *Paschale carmen* and many of the 16th-century Gospel poems, however, is their agreement on the discreet use of pagan mythology. As Mario Di Cesare observes, Mutius' discussion of biblical poetry in the introduction to *De triumpho Christi*, in which he rejected pagan mythology and "all its trappings," did "set the tone for much of the following decades, Sannazaro excepted."[56] As he declares in the preface to *De triumpho Christi*, Mutius plans to sing (like other epic

---

[54] Lewalski, *Milton's Brief Epic*, p. 54.

[55] For these and other examples, see Lewalski, *Milton's Brief Epic*, pp. 53-67 and the lists in Watson Kirconnell, *Awake the Courteous Echo* (Buffalo, 1973), pp. 315 ff.

[56] Mario Di Cesare, *Vida's Christiad and Vergilian Epic* (New York, 1964), p. 79.

poets) of the descent of his hero into the underworld, but he also makes it clear that the hell which Christ visited would have been barely recognizable to Heracles: *Non belluam hic trifaucem eduxit, sed patres illos amplissimos antiquae legis ab umbris Erebi liberavit.*[57] Save for an occasional reference to hell as Tartarus or Erebus, Mutius avoids allusions to figures from classical mythology such as Cerberus or Charon, whom Virgil had immortalized as denizens of the underworld, and instead confines himself largely to the Scriptures. The author of *De triumpho Christi* includes only the heroes and heroines of faith to be found in the pages of the Old Testament in his description of the inhabitants of hell to whom Christ preaches when he descends to the underworld after his death. By contrast, Jacopo Sannazaro's *De partu virginis* (1526), which tells of the incarnation and the birth of Christ in 3 books of hexameters, combines pagan and Christian divine beings in an admixture which sometimes approaches the bizarre. When Sannazaro describes Christ walking on the water of the Sea of Galilee, for instance, the poet tells his readers that the Savior was surrounded by Nereids and that his feet were kissed reverently by Neptune.[58] *De partu virginis* is one of the most charming of all the Renaissance biblical epics, but it did not prove nearly so influential in the coming decades as Vida's *Christiad*, whose author conformed more closely to the precedent set by Macarius Mutius and introduced no frankly pagan deities into his Christian epic.

iv. *Sedulius and Milton*

Epic treatments of the life of Christ continued to be very popular well into the 17th century. To name a few: 1. Johannes Klockus' *Christiados priscae et novae libri XII* (1601); 2. Giles Fletcher's *Christs Victorie and Triumph in Heaven and Earth, over and after Death* (1610), "the best known English biblical poem of the period;"[59] 3. Diego de Hojeda's *La Christiada* (1611), in 12 cantos totalling 15,792 hendecasyllabic lines, considered by one critic to be "the finest mystical epic in Spanish;"[60] 4. Jean

---

[57] I use the 1499 *incunabulum* published in Venice by Franciscus Lucensis, the Cantor of St. Mark's, and Antonius Francisci. I have made the following emendations: *trifaucem* instead of *trafaucem* and *Erebi* instead of *erebri*.

[58] See the discussion of Sannazaro in Thomas Greene, *The Descent from Heaven: A Study in Epic Continuity* (New Haven and London, 1963), pp. 144-70. According to William J. Kennedy, *Jacopo Sannazaro and the Uses of Pastoral* (Hanover, 1983), p. 184, Sannazaro mentions Sedulius "with enthusiasm" in a letter of 1521 written to Antonio Seripando.

[59] Lewalski, *Milton's Brief Epic*, p. 91.

[60] *OCSL*, p. 278. On the works which may have influenced Hojeda, see M. Meyer, *The Sources of Hojeda's La Christiada*, Michigan Publications in Language and Literature 26 (Ann Arbor, 1953).

d'Escorbiac's *La Christiade* (1613), like the *Paschale carmen* written in five books; 5. Estiene de Sanguinet's *La dodécade de l'Evangile* (1614); 6. Natalis Donadeus, *De bello Christi*, of the same year and also in 12 books; 7. Joannes Mellius de Sousa, *De reparatione humana* (1615), in eight books of hexameters; 8. Marcantonio Laporelli's *La Christiade, poemo heroico* (1618), in 24 books of terza rima; 9. François Du Port, *De Messiae pugna, victoria, triumpho* (1621); 10. Martin Opitz's *Evangelienepyllion* (1628); 11. Nicolas Frénicle's *Jésus crucifié* (1636), in five books, "the best known of the French Biblical poems," according to Lewalski; 12. Alexander Ross' *Virgilii evangelisantis Christiados* (1638), a Virgilian cento in 13 books; 14. Robert Clarke's *Christiados, sive de passione Domini et Salvatoris nostri Jesu Christi* (1670), in 17 books.[61]

Most of the biblical epics of the 16th and 17th centuries, however popular they may once have been, now languish in relative obscurity. At present the only biblical epics which can be said to enjoy any kind of popularity at all in the English-speaking world are John Milton's *Paradise Lost* and (to a lesser extent) *Paradise Regained*. How likely is it that their author would have known of his fifth-century precursor? The question has been asked before and has received various answers. T.W. Baldwin speaks confidently of the "powerful shaping influence these Christian poets [mentioned by John Colet in the statutes of St. Paul's] had been upon Milton."[62] Donald Clark, on the other hand, concludes on the basis of his study of the curriculum of St. Paul's that there is little reason to believe that Milton spent any time at all in school "peddling over Sedulius and other such small practitioners of later or middle-aged Latinity."[63] Milton did attend St. Paul's School in London (he probably entered the school in 1615), where Dean Colet had required 16th-century schoolboys to read Sedulius. Even though it is impossible to ascertain for certain whether or not Milton read the *Paschale carmen* at St. Paul's a century later, we do know that Sedulius was still being used at St. Saviour's in not far distant Southwark in the 1560s and that Milton did read some of the other Christian authors recommended by John Colet, such as Lactantius, Prudentius, and possibly Proba.[64] So it is not unreasonable to

---

[61] For these and other examples, see Lewalski, *Milton's Brief Epic*, pp. 87-93 and Kirconnell, *Awake the Courteous Echo*, pp. 315 ff.

[62] Baldwin, *Small Latine and Lesse Greeke* I, pp. 128-9.

[63] Donald L. Clark, *John Milton at St. Paul's School* (New York, 1948), p. 126. Clark is quoting with approval from David Masson, *The Life of John Milton*, new and rev. ed. (London, 1881) I, p. 84.

[64] On Milton's knowledge of Lactantius, see K.E. Hartwell, *Lactantius and Milton* (Cambridge, Mass., 1929). On a possible borrowing from Proba in Milton's *Paradise Lost*, see A.F. Leach, "Milton as Schoolboy and Schoolmaster," *Proceedings of the British Academy* (1907-8), 308.

suppose that he also read the *Paschale carmen*. Sedulius must have been
something of a household name even in the early 17th century. The
Paschale carmen would still have been in circulation during Milton's
lifetime, and it is difficult to believe that such a voracious reader as
Milton would not at some point have come into contact with Sedulius'
biblical epic. At the very least, Milton must have known of the fifth-
century poet second-hand. In the preface to Giles Fletcher's *Christs Victorie and Triumph in Heaven and Earth over and after Death*, a work which
Milton apparently knew well, the author mentions approvingly the name
of Sedulius "who sang the historie of Christ with as much devotion in
himself, as admiration to others."[65]

It is possible to discover general resemblances and specific verbal
echoes in Milton's poetry which suggest that he may have read the
Paschale carmen. It is very likely, for instance, that Milton's choice of a
four-book format for *Paradise Regained* was based upon tradition.[66] The
biblical epics of Juvencus and Sedulius were handed down through the
Middle Ages and often appeared in their first printed editions in four
books.[67] Many of the general thematic motifs which run through the
Paschale carmen appear also in *Paradise Regained*, such as the word of God
as food and the superiority of Christian poetry like David's to that of
classical authors like Homer.[68] More specific examples of Sedulian echoing or borrowing may be sought in Milton's phraseology. In their
descriptions of the boy Jesus in the temple, for example, both Sedulius
and Milton make a point of emphasizing the reversal of the usual
teacher-student relationship. Sedulius (2. 137-8) calls Christ "the real
teacher" *(iure magister)* sitting in the midst of and teaching the teachers
of the law *(magistros legis)*. Milton, too, describes Jesus as "teaching not
taught" *(Paradise Regained* 4. 220). Both poets also emphasize the usually
ravenous nature of the birds that brought food to Elijah by the brook of
Cherith. Sedulius marvels:

> . . . alesque rapinis
> deditus atque avido saturans cava guttura rostro
> tradidit inlaesam ieiunis morsibus escam. (1. 171-3)

Milton observes:

> . . . the Ravens with their horny beaks
> Food to Elijah bringing Even and Morn,

---

[65] On Milton's knowledge of Fletcher, see Lewalski, *Milton's Brief Epic*, p. 79.
[66] See Lewalski, *Milton's Brief Epic*, p. 102.
[67] See above Chapter 5, n. 4.
[68] On food-word imagery in *Paradise Regained*, see Lee Sheridan Cox's treatment of the
subject in *English Literary History* 28 (1961), 225-43.

Though ravenous, taught to abstain from what they brought.
(2. 267-9)[69]

Like Sedulius, Milton uses serpentine imagery (*Paradise Regained* 1. 120)
to describe Satan as he approaches Christ in the wilderness (cf. *Paschale
carmen* 2. 186). Sedulius' description of Satan as "cunningly trained in
setting forth deceptive feasts" (*fallaces dapes*) might also have been the
basis for the tempter's banquet of dainties which disappears magically in
the second book of *Paradise Regained*. In the biblical account of the temptations, there is no indication that Satan himself had food to offer Christ,
nor is there any mention of viands more extravagant than simple bread.[70]

It should be pointed out that none of this, of course, constitutes con-
clusive proof that Milton was directly influenced by the *Paschale carmen*.
There were other, more recent precedents, for instance, for writing a
short epic of four books on a biblical subect. Alexander Ramsay's *Poemata
sacra*, Giovanni Battista Marino's *Strage de gli innocenti* (1610), and Fletcher's *Christs Victorie and Triumph* were all written in four books. No matter how instrumental the role that Juvencus and Sedulius played in
establishing such conventions in the first place, their influence on an
author so far removed as Milton might very well have been indirect. Furthermore, there were other sources from which Milton could have drawn
some of the language and ideas which *Paradise Regained* has in common
with the *Paschale carmen*. For example, the irony of a twelve-year old
teaching the teachers did not occur only to Sedulius. Erasmus wrote a
prayer, which continued to be used in St. Paul's School into the twentieth
century, which begins: "We pray unto thee, Jesus Christ, who as a boy
twelve years old, seated in the temple, taught the teachers themselves. .
. ."[71]

Milton may have known the *Paschale carmen*, but he never mentions the
fifth-century poet by name and does not quote from his work. In *The
Commonplace Book* Milton cites Prudentius' *Peristephanon*, but otherwise he
betrays little active interest in the Christian poets of Late Antiquity.
Milton's silence may be significant. In a youthful and abortive effort to

---

[69] I use the edition of Merrit Y. Hughes, *John Milton: Complete Poems and Major Prose*
(New York, 1957).

[70] Lewalski's suggestion (*Milton's Brief Epic*, p. 128) that Milton's description of
Christ's victory over Satan in terms of Heracles' defeat of Antaeus may owe its origins
to *Paschale carmen* 2. 198-200 is dubious. It is not clear that Sedulius actually has Antaeus
in mind when he describes the devil in conflict with Christ as: *ter sese adtollens animo perstare
superbo / terque volutus humo fragili confidere bello*. Sedulius is more likely referring to Genesis
3. 14, where the serpent who tempted Eve is consigned to a life of crawling on its belly
and to a diet of dust. Even though it rises up here to attack Christ, it is more comfortable,
the poet suggests, on the ground which nourishes it.

[71] Quoted in Clark, *John Milton at St. Paul's School*, p. 45.

write a poem on Christ's passion in 1630, he praised the *Christiad* of Vida ("Loud o'er the rest *Cremona*'s trump doth sound"). If the 22-year old Milton did know of Sedulius and other Christian poets of Late Antiquity who told of Christ's "Godlike acts and his temptations fierce, and former sufferings," he clearly preferred more recent attempts in the genre. Vida's epic was constructed along more classically oriented lines than Juvencus' or Sedulius' lives of Christ. Using, as it does, sophisticated narrative techniques like flashback and inventing episodes not found in the Gospels, Vida's epic must have been more to the taste of young John Milton than the exegetically oriented and less imaginative products of the fourth, fifth, and sixth centuries. The *Paschale carmen* may indeed have had a direct influence on Milton's biblical poetry, but it was perhaps more negative than positive. If Milton learned anything from Sedulius, it was probably how *not* to write a biblical epic.

Whether directly or indirectly, positively or negatively, we can be sure that Sedulius did exert some degree of influence on his poetic descendants of the 16th and 17th centuries. These "new" biblical epics must have been measured by some of their readers, if not by the authors themselves, against a "horizon of expectations"[72] that had been established in great part by such Christian classics as the *Paschale carmen*.[73] Especially in the first part of the 16th century, Sedulius and other canonical masters of the biblical epic enjoyed something of the same status as Horace for lyric poetry, Seneca for tragedy, and Virgil for the epic in general. To be sure, Sedulius' "authority" had diminished considerably by the time Milton was writing his poetry, but his presence, however faded, may still be felt in the biblical epic products of the 17th century.

The second half of the 17th century witnessed a dramatic decline in the production of biblical epics. The tradition had been under criticism for some time. Already in the 16th century Torquato Tasso had rejected biblical subject matter for the epic because it left too little scope for poetic invention. He himself had chosen a non-biblical subject for his highly influential Christian epic, *Gerusalemme liberata*. By the middle of the 17th

---

[72] For this expression see Hans Robert Jauss, *Toward an Aesthetic of Reception*, trans. Timothy Bahti (Minneapolis, 1982), pp. 22-4.

[73] Milton certainly was accused of being too imaginative in his treatment of sacred story. Charles Leslie, for example, criticized "the adventrous flight of Poets who have dress'd Angels in Armour, and put Swords and Guns into their Hands, to form romantick Battels in the Plains of Heaven, a scene of licentious fancy, but the Truth has been greatly hurt thereby. . . ," (From *The Theological Works* [1721] I, pp. 777-8, as quoted in *Milton: The Critical Heritage*, ed., John T. Shawcross [London, 1970] I, p. 117.) Undoubtedly Leslie would have found the relative restraint of Sedulius' imagination more to his liking.

century neo-classical principles were determining epic theory and practice both in France and England, and more and more Christian epic poets were following Tasso's example in rejecting biblical subjects, drawing instead on "Christian profane history."[74] In 1654, for instance, Georges de Scudéry produced a Christian poem on the life of Alaric. In 1658 Pierre Le Moyne wrote an epic on the life of Saint Louis. Abraham Cowley defended the biblical epic against contemporary critics in a preface to his *Davideis* (1656), but he was swimming against the tide.[75] By the 18th century the biblical epic had virtually disappeared from the literary scene. Friedrich Gottlieb Klopstock's *Der Messias* (1748-73), although still acknowledged as a masterpiece of German literature, represented a last gasp rather than a revival for the *Christiad* tradition.

The tide in the fortunes of Sedulius and other biblical poets of Late Antiquity turned decisively in the 17th century. The number of editions dropped off dramatically, and there is little evidence that they continued to be read in the schools. By the early part of the 18th century Johann Georg Walch (1693-1775) was complaining of the neglect of the Christian poets of Late Antiquity in general. Even their names, he laments, are no longer recognized by the average schoolboy: *indignum sane est, Christianos poetas adeo negligi, ut ne nomen quidem juventuti scholasticae sit cognitum.*[76] The *Paschale carmen* did find an occasional devotee like Oluf Borch (1629-1690), who was enthusiastic in his praise of Sedulius[77] or I.J. Pyra, who mentions Sedulius approvingly in *Der Tempel der wahren Dichtkunst* of 1737,[78] but despite isolated efforts to revive Sedulius' fortunes, the general trend was not to be reversed.

v. *Conclusions*

Even though the biblical epic and, indeed, the verse epic itself are no longer popular literary forms, the tradition of adapting biblical narratives

---

[74] See Gilbert Highet, *The Classical Tradition* (New York and London, 1949), pp. 261 ff., for a good overview of the so-called "Battle of the Books" waged in the 17th and 18th centuries. The superiority of poetry with Christian or biblical subjects to secular poetry was one of the issues under debate.

[75] Lewalski, *Milton's Brief Epic*, p. 99.

[76] From his *Historia critica latinae linguae* (Leipzig, 1716) as quoted by Arevalo in *PL* 19, 510.

[77] See the quotation by Arevalo in *PL* 19, 510:
Dictio eius facilis, ingeniosa, numerosa, perspicua, sic satis munda, si excipias prosodica quaedam delicta, et in primis Christianae pietatis commendatrix.

[78] See the quotation in Herzog, *Bibelepik*, pp. xii-xiv. Herzog's observations on the decline of the biblical epic tradition (p. xviii) are worth repeating here:
Der klassizistische Horizont hat die spätantike-barocke Tradition ersetzt. Die spätantike Epik schwindet aus dem Bewusstsein der Epiker wie der Gebildeten überhaupt; sie wird dann im späten 19. Jh. in der Nachschlagbarkeit der Handbücher und Editionen endgültig mumifiziert.

to other literary idioms is alive and flourishing. Historical novels based on biblical events have been popular throughout this century. One of the great narrative achievements in German literature, Thomas Mann's tetralogy, *Joseph und seine Brüder* (1933-43), draws its subject matter from the last chapters of Genesis. Taylor Caldwell's *Great Lion of God* (New York, 1970), a life of St. Paul, and more recently, Joseph Heller's light-hearted *God Knows* (New York, 1984), which relates the life of David, king of Israel, are based on biblical episodes.[79] The Bible has also been successfully set to film. Cecil B. De Mille's *The Ten Commandments* (1956) takes the viewer from the opening chapters of Exodus to the crossing of the Jordan. John Huston's *The Bible* episodically covers the first 22 chapters of Genesis from creation to the near-sacrifice of Isaac. *Samson and Delilah* (1949) retells the story line of Judges 13-16. According to one count, approximately fifty films have been produced which are based on the Old Testament.[80] The New Testament has also been extensively mined for cinematic subject material. *The Greatest Story Ever Told* (1965) is a film rendering of the life of Christ with special emphasis on the passion. Pier Paolo Pasolini's *Il vangelo secondo Matteo* (1964) follows the Gospel of Matthew quite closely and, unlike many biblical films, has met with critical acclaim.[81] *Jesus Christ Super-Star* and *Godspell* (1973), controversial musicals and films based on the Gospels, were quite popular in the early 1970s. In 1977 Franco Zeffirelli directed a cast of stars in *Jesus of Nazareth*, a six and one-half hour television production which Judith Crist called "the best film of its kind."[82] More recently a made-for-television movie, *Peter and Paul*, has retold the story of the heroes of Arator's *De actibus apostolorum*. These twentieth-century attempts to recast biblical stories in various media have encountered and tried to solve many of the same difficulties faced by the authors of biblical epics: the incompatibility of content and form, the problem of invention, the mixture of "sacred" and "profane." Like their late antique counterparts,

---

[79] For an exhaustive bibliography (approximately 600 pages) on literary works based on the life of Jesus "from the earliest Christian writings through 1984," the reader is advised to consult Alice J. Birney, *The Literary Lives of Jesus: An International Bibliography* (forthcoming from Garland Press).

[80] Jon Solomon, *The Ancient World in Cinema* (New Brunswick and New York, 1978), p. 107.

[81] One critic, for instance, as quoted in Solomon, *The Ancient World in Cinema*, p. 116, observes:
> It [*Il vangelo secondo Matteo*] is Pasolini's accurate, believable, and theologically powerful cinematic interpretation of Matthew. If only Pasolini had smeared a bit of honey on the lip of this cup of bitter absinthe, he could have had one of the most descriptive, absorbing, and widely acclaimed films of its era.

[82] Richard H. Campbell, Michael R. Pitts, *The Bible on Film: A Checklist, 1897-1980* (Metuchen, N.J. and London, 1981), p. 179.

these modern efforts have also met with varying degrees of critical acclaim. Jon Solomon explains:

> Part of the difficulty stems from the general public's knowledge of the Bible and its marvelous stories; if filmmakers digress too far from the biblical narrative, they inevitably produce what seems to all to be an insincere and far-fetched plot. On the contrary, if the filmmakers restrict themselves completely to the Old Testament narrative they will almost inevitably produce a dry and unhistrionic enactment.[83]

Even though his artistic descendants continue, with varying success, to set biblical subjects to popular literary and cinematic forms, Sedulius' *Paschale carmen* itself is largely forgotten. The once popular fifth-century rendering of the life of Christ disappeared (for all practical purposes) from the literary consciousness of the western world with the decline of the biblical epic in the 17th century. When it resurfaced in the late 19th and 20th, it was only as the subject for a chapter in a literary history or an occasional doctoral dissertation. Nor are there many today who would lament the *Paschale carmen*'s present neglect or maintain seriously that Sedulius deserves the same kind of popular attention and critical respect as Virgil. Suggestions (such as Sister A. Stanislaus') that Sedulius be read "in the fourth-year Latin classes, as well as in college," to my knowledge, have never been taken up.[84]

The present study is not meant to suggest that the *Paschale carmen* be restored to the privileged status it formerly enjoyed as a Christian classic. If there is a distinction to be made between "verse" and "poetry" (the difference being that "poetry is not merely a cultural artifact" which it is necessary to reconstruct "by painstaking semantic archaeology" in order to enjoy), then it would indeed be difficult to argue that the *Paschale carmen* still speaks clearly and directly as "poetry," as "a tool of mediation," across the ages.[85]

One reason why Sedulius' epic seems remote today, one suspects, is the austerity of its vision of Christ. The fifth-century poet portrays the hero of his poem as a solitary and sometimes aloof Savior, confident of his divine vocation, the majestic lord of creation. The analogues in the world of late antique art are the stern, almost intimidating mosaic representations of Christ (for example, on the triumphal arch of the church of S. Apollinare in Classe in Ravenna). In more modern Christian art and theology, by contrast, it has been popular to emphasize the

---

[83] Solomon, *The Ancient World in Cinema*, p. 107.

[84] A. Stanislaus, "The Scriptures in Hexameter," *CW* 32 (1938), 99-100.

[85] Karl Morrison, in his review of Peter Godman, *Poetry of the Carolingian Renaissance*, in *Speculum* 61 (1986), p. 930, makes this distinction between "poetry" and "verse" in reference to the literary products of the Carolingian poets.

more human figure of the helpless Christ in swaddling clothes in Bethlehem or in agony in the garden of Gethsemane. The hero of the *Paschale carmen* has none of the tenderness and little of the vulnerability which characterizes the Christ of the poetry of Bernard of Clairvaux (1090-1150) and Richard Crashaw (1613?-1649) or the artistic representations of Rembrandt (1606-69) and Georges Rouault (1871-1958).

Sedulius himself, in addition, could hardly be described as a towering poetic genius. The *Paschale carmen* points the way to *The Divine Comedy* and *Paradise Lost*, but as a poet Sedulius cannot begin to match the breadth of vision, the imaginative verve, or the creative fire of a Dante or a Milton. It should be noted, however, in all fairness, that literary works are only given value by their readership—an artistic product has no real life without some audience at some time who appreciates it—and it is indisputable that the *Paschale carmen* was highly valued by a surprisingly long line of European readers. It also seems clear, at least to this reader, that even if the *Paschale carmen* is not on an artistic level with Virgil's *Aeneid*, it is a more artistically and thoughtfully constructed work—a "better" poem to put it baldly—than many of its critics have suggested.

But the question of absolute or relative literary value aside, what the present study of the *Paschale carmen* has shown is that Sedulius' biblical epic is (at the very least) an important and fascinating cultural artifact, which deserves more attentive reading than it has usually been given. In some ways, the *Paschale carmen* reveals to the historian of Late Antiquity as much about the theological and cultural perspectives of its age as, say, the more exhaustively studied *De trinitate* or *De doctrina christiana* of Augustine.[86] In its juxtaposition of classical and Christian elements, Sedulius' poem "imitates," if you will (rather than ignoring or simply analyzing), the chief cultural tension of Late Antiquity. For the student of the Middle Ages, the formative influence of Sedulius' *Paschale carmen* (as standard schoolroom fare in the Middle Ages and the early modern period) on the language and thinking of generations of impressionable schoolboys also warrants profounder consideration. And for the literary historian, the *Paschale carmen* and other biblical epics of Late Antiquity

---

[86] Historians of the early church have traditionally concentrated on doctrinal works of importance for the history of theology, like Augustine's *De trinitate*, to the neglect of works such as the biblical epic which might provide a more representative picture of the popular piety and culture of an age. In all probability, the *Paschale carmen* enjoyed a wider readership and a greater popular influence than Augustine's difficult and lengthy treatise on the Trinity. The neglect is due, at least in part, to the assumption which J.P. Koehler identifies in his *Lehrbuch der Kirchengeschichte* (Milwaukee, 1917), p. 2: "dass der eigentliche Hauptinhalt der Kirchengeschichte die Gestaltung der Lehre sei." Koehler observes that "die Dogmatik ist nur *eine* Form des Lebens" and in his own study offers a corrective approach to the writing of church history.

deserve more than mere mention for the role they played in the evolution of the epic in general and the emergence of the biblical epic tradition in particular. Sedulius and other Christian poets of Late Antiquity have traditionally been neglected, in part, no doubt, because of the usual departmentalization of higher learning into fields such as the Classics, Medieval Studies, the History of Ideas, Church History, etc. The *Paschale carmen* and other biblical epics of Late Antiquity have tended to fall between the scholarly cracks, as it were, ignored by classicists, medievalists, and church historians alike. For anyone, however, who is interested in understanding and appreciating not only the "golden ages" of the past but "the entire continuum of literary and cultural history" in the ancient and medieval world, the biblical epics of Late Antiquity amply reward reappraisal.[87] One of them, Sedulius' *Paschale carmen*, is an invaluable Latin witness to the theological concerns and the literary ideals of Christian Late Antiquity and a work of fundamental importance for a significant European poetic tradition.

---

[87] Fannie J. LeMoine, "Classics, the Academy, and the Community," *Federation Reports: The Journal of the State Humanities Councils* (1984), 23.

BIBLIOGRAPHY

i. *Editions and Translations of the Paschale carmen*

Corsaro, Francesco. *Sedulio poeta*. Pubblicazioni dell'istituto universitario di magistero di Catania, serie letteraria, no. 2. Catania, 1956. (Italian translation.)

Huemer, Johannes. *Sedulii opera omnia*. *CSEL* 10, 14-146. (Critical edition.)

Kuhnmuench, Otto. *Early Christian Latin Poets*. Chicago, 1929, pp. 254-72. (Text and English translation of selected passages.)

Scheps, Nicholas. *Sedulius' Paschale carmen, Boek I en II: Ingeleid, Vertaald en Toegelicht*. Delft, 1938. (Text, translation, and commentary.)

Sigerson, George. *The Easter Song: Being the First Epic of Christendom by Sedulius, the First Scholar-Saint of Erinn*. Dublin, 1922. (English translation of selected passages.)

Spitzmüller, H. *Poésie latine chrétienne du Moyen Age*. Paris, 1971, pp. 117-8. (French translation of selected passages.)

Swanson, R.A. "Easter Poem," *CJ* 52 (1957), 289-97. (English translation of Preface and Book 1.)

ii. *Editions of Other Latin Biblical Poetry of Late Antiquity*

Arator, *De actibus apostolorum* (ed. A.P. McKinlay). *CSEL* 72. Vienna, 1951.

Avitus, *Poemata* (ed. R. Peiper). *MGH AA* 6. 2, 203-94. Berlin, 1883.

Claudius Marius Victor, *Alethia* (ed. P.F. Hovingh). *CC* 128, 117 ff. Turnhout, 1960.

"Cyprianus Gallus," *Metrum super Heptateuchum* (ed. R. Peiper). *CSEL* 23. 1. Vienna, 1891.

De evangelio (ed. R. Peiper). *CSEL* 23, 270-4. Vienna, 1881.

De Iesu Christe Deo et homine (ed. Georg Fabricius). *Poetarum veterum ecclesiasticorum opera christiana*. Basel, 1562, pp. 761-4.

Dracontius, *Carmina* (ed. F. Vollmer). *MGH AA* 14, 23-113. Berlin, 1905.

"Hilary," *Metrum in Genesin* (ed. R. Peiper). *CSEL* 23, 231-9. Vienna, 1891.

Juvencus, *Evangeliorum libri quattuor* (ed. J. Huemer). *CSEL* 24. Vienna, 1891.

Miracula Christi (ed. Theodor Birt). *MGH AA* 10, 412-13. Berlin, 1892.

Proba, *Carmen sacrum* (ed. K. Schenkl). *CSEL* 16, 569-609. Vienna, 1887.

Prudentius, *Carmina* (ed. M.P. Cunningham). *CC* 126. Turnhout, 1966.

Rusticius Helpidius, *Tristicha* and *Carmen de Iesu Christi beneficiis* (ed. F. Corsaro). Catania, 1956.

iii. *Literary, Philological, and Textual Studies Devoted to Sedulius*

Bastiaensen, A. "L'antienne *Genuit puerpera regem*, adaption liturgique d'un passage du *Paschale carmen* de Sedulius," *RB* 83 (1973), 388-97.

Bitter, E. "Die Virgilinterpretation der früh-christlichen Dichter Paulinus von Nola und Sedulius." Diss. Tübingen, 1948.

Boissier, G. "Le *Carmen paschale* et l'*Opus paschale*," *RPh* 6 (1882), 28-36.

——"Sedulius," *Journal des savants* (1881), 553-66.

Caesar, C. "Die Antwerpener Hs. des Sedulius," *RhM* 56 (1901), 247-71.

Candel, J. *De clausulis a Sedulio in eis libris qui inscribuntur Paschale opus adhibitis*. Tolosa, 1904.

Corsaro, Francesco. *La lingua di Sedulio*. Raccolta di studi di lett. crist. antica 11. Catania, 1949.

——*L'opera poetica di Sedulio*. Raccolta di studi di lett. crist. antica 9. Catania, 1948.

——*La poesia di Sedulio*. Raccolta di studi di lett. crist. antica 1. Catania, 1945.

——*Sedulio poeta*. Pubblicazioni dell'istituto universitario di magistero di Catania, serie letteraria, no. 2. Catania, 1956.

Donnini, M. "Alcune osservazioni sul programmo poetico di Sedulio," *RSC* 26 (1978), 426-36.

Fischer, Hertha. "Sedulius qua ratione auctores antiquos adhibuerit." Diss. Vienna, 1936.

Frank, G. "*Vossianus* Q 86 and *Reginensis 333*," *AJP* 44 (1923), 67-70.

Gladysz, B. "De extremis quibus Seduliana carmina ornantur verborum syllabis inter se consonantibus," *Eos Suppl.* 18 (1931).

——*Dogmatyczne Teksty w Poetyckich Utworach Seduliusa*. Posnan, 1930.

——"Rym w Poezji Seduliusa," *Kwartalnik Klasyczny* 1930, 77-84.

Grillo, A. "La presenza di Virgilio in Sedulio poeta parafrastico," *Présence de Virgile* (Paris, 1978), pp. 185-94.

Huemer, Johannes. *De Sedulii poetae vita et scriptis commentatio*. Vienna, 1878.

——"Zur Bestimmung der Abfassungszeit und Herausgabe des *Carmen paschale* des Sedulius," *ZOG* 27 (1876), 500-5.

Jungandreas, W. "Die Runen des *Codex Seminarii Trevirensis* R. III. 61," *Trierer Zeitschrift* 30 (1967), 161-9.

Ker, N.R. "British Museum, Burney 246, 285, 295, 341, 344, 357," *BMQ* 12 (1938), 134-5.

Klissenbauer, Ed. *Quaestiones de Seduli Paschali carmine*. Vienna, 1939.

Leimbach, K. *Über den christlichen Dichter Caelius Sedulius und dessen Carmen paschale*. Goslar, 1879.

Lewine, C. "The Miniatures of the Antwerp Sedulius Manuscript. The Early Christian Models and their Transformations." Diss. Columbia University, 1970.

Looshorn, J. "Cölius Sedulius und seine Werke," *ZKT* 4 (1880), 74-89.

Lülfing, H. "Ein Brief Siegmund Hellmans an Emil Jacobs zur Seduliusüberlieferung," *Philologus* 115 (1971), 179-82.

Manton, G.R. "The Cambridge Manuscript of Sedulius' *Carmen paschale*," *JTS* 40 (1939), 365-70.

Mayr, Theodor. *Studien zu dem Paschale carmen des christlichen Dichters Sedulius*. Augsburg, 1916.

McDonald, A.D. "The Iconographic Tradition of Sedulius," *Speculum* 8 (1933), 150-6.

Meritt, H. "Old English Sedulius Glosses," *AJP* 57 (1936), 140-50.

Opelt, Ilona. "Die Szenerie bei Sedulius," *JbAC* 19 (1976), 109-19.

Pieri, G.M. "Sulle fonti evangeliche di Sedulio," *Atti e memorie dell'accad. tosc. di sc. e lett. La Columbaria* 39, n.s. 20 (1969), 125-234.

Rand, E.K. "Note on the *Vossianus* Q 86 and *Reginenses* 333 and 1616," *AJP* 44 (1923), 11-12.

Tibiletti, C. "Note al testo del *Paschale carmen* di Sedulio," *Forma futuri. Studi in onore di Michele Pellegrino*. Turin, 1975, pp. 778-85.

iv. *Studies Which Include Considerations of the Paschale carmen*

Amatucci, Aurelio. *Storia della letteratura latina cristiana*. 2nd ed. Turin, 1955, pp. 335-9.

Bardenhewer, Otto. *Geschichte der altkirchlichen Literatur*. Freiburg im Breisgau, 1924, IV, pp. 642-7.

Baumgartner, A. *Die lateinische und griechische Literatur der christlichen Völker*. (*Geschichte der Weltliteratur* IV). Freiburg im Breisgau, 1900, pp. 195 ff.

Colombo, Sisto. *La poesia cristiana antica*. Rome, 1910, I, pp. 156-62.

Costanza, Salvatore. "Da Giovenco a Sedulio: I proemi degli *Evangeliorum libri* e del *Carmen paschale*," *Civiltà classica e cristiana* 6 (1985), 253-86.

Duckett, E.S. *Latin Writers of the Fifth Century*. New York, 1930, pp. 77-81.

Ebert, A. *Allgemeine Geschichte der Literatur des Mittelalters im Abendlande.* 2nd ed. Leipzig, 1889, I, pp. 358 ff.

Ermini, Filippo. *Storia della letteratura latina medievale dalle origini alla fine del secolo VII.* Spoleto, 1960, pp. 273-9.

Fontaine, Jacques. *Naissance de la poésie dans l'occident chrétien: Equisse d'une histoire de la poésie latine chrétienne du IIIe au VIe siècle.* Paris, 1981, pp. 248-52.

Gudeman, A. *Geschichte der altchristlichen lateinischen Literatur vom 2-6 Jahrhundert.* Berlin, 1925, pp. 109-11.

Herzog, Reinhart. *Die Bibelepik der lateinischen Spätantike: Formgeschichte einer erbaulichen Gattung I.* Theorie und Geschichte der Literatur und der schönen Künste 37. Munich, 1975.

Kartschoke, Dieter. *Bibeldichtung: Studien zur Geschichte der epischen Bibelparaphrase von Juvencus bis Otfrid von Weissenburg.* Munich, 1975.

Krüger, Gustav. *Die Bibeldichtung zu Ausgang des Altertums.* Giessen, 1919, pp. 9-12.

Labriolle, Pierre de. *History and Literature of Christianity.* Trans. Herbert Wilson. New York, 1924, pp. 474-6.

Manitius, Max. *Geschichte der christlich-lateinischen Poesie bis zur Mitte des 8. Jahrhunderts.* Stuttgart, 1891, pp. 303-12.

Moricca, U. *Storia della letteratura latina cristiana.* Turin, 1932, III, pp. 46-58.

Raby, F.J.E. *A History of Christian-Latin Poetry from the Beginnings to the Close of the Middle Ages.* Oxford, 1927, pp. 108-10.

Roberts, Michael. *Biblical Epic and Rhetorical Paraphrase in Late Antiquity.* Liverpool, 1985.

Schanz, M. *Geschichte der römischen Literatur bis zum Gesetzgebungswerk des Kaiser Justinians.* Munich, 1920, IV. 2, pp. 368-74.

Simonetti, M. *La letteratura cristiana antica greca e latina.* Milan, 1969, pp. 343-4.

Weyman, C. *Beiträge zur Geschichte der christlich-lateinischen Poesie.* Munich, 1926, pp. 121-37.

Witke, Charles. *Numen litterarum: The Old and the New in Latin Poetry from Constantine to Gregory the Great.* Mittellateinische Studien und Texte 5. Leiden, 1971, pp. 206-18.

Wright, F.A. and Sinclair, T.A. *A History of Later Latin Literature.* New York, 1931, pp. 73-4.

Wright, Neil. "The *Hisperica famina* and Caelius Sedulius," *Cambridge Medieval Celtic Studies* 4 (1982), 61-76.

v. *Other Secondary Works Cited*

Altaner, B. "Eustathius, der lateinische Übersetzer der Hexaëmeron-Homilien Basilius des Grossen," *ZNTW* 39 (1940), 161-70.

Alter, Robert. *The Art of Biblical Narrative.* New York, 1981.

Baldwin, T.W. *William Shakspere's Small Latine and Lesse Greeke.* Urbana, 1944.

Bardy, Gustave. "L'église et l'enseignement au IVe siècle," *RSR* 14 (1934), 542-9.

Beeson, C.H. *Isidorstudien.* Quellen und Untersuchungen zur lateinischen Philologie des Mittelalters 4. Munich, 1913.

Benko, Stephen. "Virgil's Fourth Eclogue in Christian Interpretation," *ANRW* 31. 1. Berlin and New York, 1981, pp. 646-705.

Birney, Alice. *The Literary Lives of Jesus: An International Bibliography.* Garland Press, forthcoming.

Bolton, W.F. *A History of Anglo-Latin Literature, 597-1066.* Princeton, 1967.

Brandes, W. "Studien zur christlich-lateinischen Poesie," *WS* 12 (1890), 303.

Brenk, Beat. *Die frühchristlichen Mosaiken in S. Maria Maggiore zu Rom.* Wiesbaden, 1975.

Bright, David. "Theory and Practice in the Vergilian Cento," *ICS* 9. 1 (1984), 79-90.

Brown, Peter. *The World of Late Antiquity, A.D. 150-750.* New York, 1971.

Bull, R.J. "A Note on Theodotus' Description of Shechem," *HTR* 60 (1967), 221-7.

Campbell, Richard and Pitts, Michael. *The Bible on Film: A Checklist, 1897-1980.* Metuchen, N.J. and London, 1981.

Chadwick, Owen. *John Cassian*. 2nd ed. Cambridge, 1968.

Charlet, Jean-Louis. "Prudence lecteur de Paulin de Nole: A propos du 23e quatrain du *Dittochaeon*," *REA* 21 (1975), 55-62.

Clark, Donald. *John Milton at St. Paul's School*. New York, 1948.

Clark, E. and Hatch, D. "Jesus as Hero in the Vergilian *Cento* of Faltonia Betitia Proba," *Vergilius* 27 (1981), 31-9.

——*The Golden Bough, the Oaken Cross: The Vergilian Cento of Faltonia Betitia Proba*. Chico, Calif., 1981.

Coleiro, E. *An Introduction to Vergil's Bucolics with a Critical Edition of the Text*. Amsterdam, 1979.

Collins, J.J. "The Epic of Theodotus and the Hellenism of the Hasmoneans," *HTR* 73 (1980), 91-104.

Comparetti, D.P.A. *Vergil in the Middle Ages*. Trans. E.F.M. Benecke. New York, 1929.

Connelly, Joseph. *Hymns of the Roman Liturgy*. New York, 1957.

Contreni, John. *Codex Laudunensis 468: A Ninth-Century Guide to Virgil, Sedulius, and the Liberal Arts*. Armarium codicum insignium 3. Turnhout, 1984.

Cooper, C.G. *An Introduction to the Latin Hexameter*. Melbourne, 1952.

Curtius, Ernst Robert. *European Literature and the Latin Middle Ages*. Trans. Willard Trask. New York, 1953.

Di Cesare, Mario. *Vida's Christiad and Vergilian Epic*. New York, 1964.

Dobschütz, E. von. "Das Decretum Gelasianum," *Texte und Untersuchungen* 38. 4 (1912), 281 ff.

Doignon, Jean. *Hilaire de Poitiers avant l'exil: Recherches sur la naissance, l'enseignement, et l'épreuve d'une foi épiscopale en Gaule au milieu du IVe siècle*. Paris, 1971.

Downey, G. "The Emperor Julian and the Schools," *CJ* 53 (1957), 97-103.

Driver, G.R. and Hodgson, L., eds. *The Bazaar of Heracleides*. Oxford, 1925.

Duckworth, George. *Foreshadowing and Suspense in the Epics of Homer, Apollonius, and Vergil*. Princeton, 1933.

——*Vergil and Classical Hexameter Poetry: A Study in Metrical Variety*. Ann Arbor, 1969.

Ehlers, Wilhelm. "Bibelszenen in epischer Gestalt: Ein Beitrag zu Alcimus Avitus," *VC* 39 (1985), 353-69.

Ermini, Filippo. *Il centone di Proba e la poesia centonaria latina*. Rome, 1909.

Ernst, U. *Der Liber Evangeliorum Otfrids von Weissenburg: Literarästhetik und Verstechnik im Lichte der Tradition*. Cologne and Vienna, 1975.

Ernst, U. and Neuser, Peter-Erich. *Die Genese der europäischen Endreimdichtung*. Wege der Forschung 444. Darmstadt, 1977.

Evenepoel, Willy. *Zakelijke en Literaire Onderzoekingen Betreffende het Liber Cathemerinon van Aurelius Prudentius Clemens*. Verhand. Acad. voor Wetensch., Lett. & Schone Kunsten van België, Kl. der Lett. 41, No. 91. Brussels, 1979.

Frey, Leonard. "The Rhetoric of Latin Christian Epic Poetry," *Annuale mediaeval* 2 (1961), 15-30.

Fuhrmann, M. "Die lateinische Literatur der Spätantike. Ein literarhistorischer Beitrag zum Kontinuätsproblem," *A&A* 13 (1967), 56 ff.

Gamber, S. *Le livre de 'Genèse' dans la poésie latine au Ve siècle*. Paris, 1899.

Gebser, A.R. *De Caii Vettii Aquilini Iuvenci presbyteri hispani vita et scriptis*. Jena, 1827.

Godman, Peter, ed. *Alcuin: The Bishops, Kings, and Saints of York*. Oxford, 1982.

——"The Anglo-Latin *opus geminatum* from Aldhelm to Alcuin," *Medium aevum* 50 (1981), 215-29.

——*The Poetry of the Carolingian Renaissance*. Norman, Oklahoma, 1985.

Golega, Joseph. *Studien über die Evangeliendichtung des Nonnos von Panopolis. Ein Beitrag zur Geschichte der Bibeldichtung im Altertum*. Breslauer Studien zu historische Theologie 15. Breslau, 1930.

Grabar, André. *Christian Iconography: A Study of its Origins*. Trans. Terry Grabar. Princeton, 1968.

——*Early Christian Art from the Rise of Christianity to the Death of Theodosius*. Trans. Stuart Gilbert, James Emmons. New York, 1968.

Greene, Thomas. *The Descent from Heaven: A Study in Epic Continuity.* New Haven and London, 1963.

Gutman, Y. "Philo, the Epic Poet," *Scripta hierosolymitana* 1 (1954), 36-63.

Hagendahl, Harald. *Latin Fathers and the Classics: A Study on the Apologists, Jerome and other Christian Writers.* Studia graeca et latina gothoburgensia 6. Göteborg, 1958.

Hannson, Nils. *Textkritisches zu Juvencus.* Lund, 1950.

Hartwell, K.E. *Lactantius and Milton.* Cambridge, Mass., 1929.

Herzog, Reinhart. "Exegese-Erbauung-*Delectatio*: Beiträge zu einer christlichen Poetik der Spätantike," in Walter Haug, ed., *Formen und Funktionen der Allegorie: Symposion Wolfenbüttel 1978*, Germanistiche Symposien-Berichtsbände 3. Stuttgart, 1979, pp. 52-69.

——"La meditazione poetica: Una forma retorico-teologica tra tarda antichità e barocco," in *La poesia tardoantica: Tra retorica, teologia e politica*, Atti del V corso della scuola superiore d. archeologia e civiltà medievali (Messina, 1984), 75-102.

Highet, Gilbert. *The Classical Tradition.* New York and London, 1949.

Homeyer, Helene. "Der Dichter zwischen zwei Welten: Beobachtungen zur Theorie und Praxis des Dichtens im frühen Mittelalter," *A&A* 16 (1970), 141-51.

Hudson-Williams, A. "Virgil and the Christian Latin Poets," *PVS* 6 (1966-7), 11-21.

Jahn, Otto. "Über die Subscriptionen in den Handschriften römischer Classiker," *BSG* 3 (1851), 335 ff.

Janson, Tore. *Latin Prose Prefaces: Studies in Literary Conventions.* Acta Universitatis Stockholmiensis. Studia latina stockholmiensia 13. Stockholm, 1964.

Jauss, Hans Robert. *Toward an Aesthetic of Reception.* Trans. Timothy Bahti. Minneapolis, 1982.

Karpp, Heinrich. *Die frühchristlichen und mittelalterlichen Mosaiken in Santa Maria Maggiore zu Rom.* Baden-Baden, 1966.

Kelly, J.N.D. *Early Christian Doctrines.* 2nd ed. New York, 1960.

Kempf, Th. *Christus der Hirt: Ursprung und Deutung einer altchristlichen Symbolgestalt.* Rome, 1942.

Kennedy, William J. *Jacopo Sannazaro and the Uses of Pastoral.* Hanover and London, 1983.

Keydell, Rudolph. "Nonnos." *RE* 17, 917-20.

Kirkconnell, Watson. *Awake the Courteous Echo.* Toronto and London, 1973.

Knight, W.F. Jackson. *Accentual Symmetry in Vergil.* 3rd ed. Oxford, 1950.

Koehler, J.P. *Lehrbuch der Kirchengeschichte.* Milwaukee, 1917.

Kollwitz, J. "Christusbild," *RAC* 3, 1-24.

Koster, Severin. *Antike Epostheorien.* Palingenesia 5. Wiesbaden, 1970.

Ladner, Gerhardt. "The Impact of Christianity," in *The Transformation of the Roman World*, ed. Lynn White. Berkeley, 1966, pp. 59-91.

Laistner, M.L.W. "The Christian Attitude to Pagan Literature," *History* 20 (1935), 49-54.

——"Pagan Schools and Christian Teachers," *Liber floridus: Mittellateinische Studien* (St. Ottilien, 1950), pp. 47-61.

——*Thought and Letters in Western Europe, A.D. 500-900.* Rev. ed. Ithaca, 1957.

Lapidge, M. and Herren, M. *Aldhelm: The Prose Works.* Ipswich and Totowa, 1979.

Lausberg, Heinrich. *Handbuch der literarischen Rhetorik: Eine Grundlegung der Literaturwissenschaft.* Munich, 1960.

Leach, A.F. "Milton as Schoolboy and Schoolmaster," *Proceedings of the British Academy*, 1907-8, 295-318.

Legner, Anton. *Der gute Hirt.* Düsseldorf, 1959.

LeMoine, Fannie J. "Classics, the Academy, and the Community," *Federation Reports: The Journal of the State Humanities Council*, May 1984, 22-7.

Lewalski, Barbara. *Milton's Brief Epic: The Genre, Meaning, and Art of Paradise Regained.* Providence, 1966.

Lewis, J.P. *A Study of the Interpretation of Noah and the Flood in Jewish and Christian Literature.* Leiden, 1968.

Lieberg, Godo. "Seefahrt und Werk: Untersuchungen zu einer Metapher der antiken, besonders der lateinischen Literatur, von Pindar bis Horaz," *Giornale italiano di filologia* 21 (1969), 209-40.

Lindsay, Jack. *Song of a Falling World: Culture during the Break-up of the Empire (A.D. 350-600)*. London, 1948.

Ludwich, A. *Aristarchs homerische Textkritik nach den Fragmenten des Didymos*. Leipzig, 1884.

——"Eudokia die Gattin des Kaisers Theodosius II als Dichterin," *RhM* 37 (1882), 206-25.

Lynch, William. *Christ and Apollo*. New York, 1960.

Manitius, Max. *Geschichte der lateinische Literatur des Mittelalters* in *Handbuch der Altertumswissenschaft* 9. Munich, 1911-31.

——"Zu Dracontius' *Carmina minora*," *RhM* 46 (1891), 493-4.

——"Zu Juvencus und Prudentius," *RhM* 45 (1890), 485 ff.

——"Zu späten lateinischen Dichtern," *RhM* 45 (1890), 153-7.

Mansi, J.D. *Sacrorum conciliorum nova et amplissima collectio*. Paris and Leipzig, 1901-27.

Marold, Karl. "Otfrids Beziehungen zu den biblischen Dichtungen des Iuvencus, Sedulius, Arator," *Germania* 32 (1887), 385-411.

——"Über das Evangelienbuch des Iuvencus in seiner Verhältniss zum Bibeltext," *Zeitschrift für die wissenschaftliche Theologie* 33 (1890), 329-41.

Marrou, Henri. *St. Augustin et la fin de la culture antique*. 2nd ed. Paris, 1949.

Marti, Heinrich. *Übersetzer der Augustin-Zeit: Interpretation von Selbstzeugnissen*. Studia et testimonia antiqua 14. Munich, 1974.

Maspero, Jean. *Histoire des patriarches d'Alexandrie*. Paris, 1923.

McClure, Judith. "The Biblical Epic and its Audience in Late Antiquity," *Papers of the Liverpool Latin Seminar* 3 (Liverpool, 1981), 305-21.

McKenna, M.M. "The 'Two Ways' in Jewish and Christian Writings of the Greco-Roman Period. A Study of the Form of Repentance Parenesis." Diss. University of Pennsylvania, 1981.

McKinlay, A.P. *Arator: The Codices*. Cambridge, Mass., 1942.

McNamee, M.B. *Honor and the Epic Hero*. New York, 1960.

Meyer, M. *The Sources of Hojeda's La Christiada*. Michigan Publications in Language and Literature 26. Ann Arbor, 1953.

Murru, F. "Analisi semiologica e strutturale della *Praefatio* agli *Evangeliorum libri* di Giovenco," *WS* 14 (1980), 133-51.

Nestler, H. *Studien über die Messiade des Iuvencus*. Passau, 1910.

Nodes, Daniel. "Avitus of Vienne's *Spiritual History* and the Semi-Pelagian Controversy. The Doctrinal Implications of Books I-III," *VC* 38 (1984), 185-95.

Norberg, Dag. *La poésie latine rythmique du haut Moyen Age*. Studia latina holmiensia 2. Stockholm, 1954.

O'Donnell, J.J. *Cassiodorus*. Berkeley, 1979.

Ogilvy, J.D.A. *Books Known to Anglo-Latin Writers from Aldhelm to Alcuin (670-804)*. Studies and Documents 2. Cambridge, Mass., 1936.

Opelt, Ilona. "Die Szenerie bei Iuvencus," *VC* 29 (1975), 191-207.

Otis, Brooks. *Ovid as an Epic Poet*. Cambridge, 1966.

Pease, A.S. "The Attitude of Jerome towards Pagan Literature," *TAPA* 50 (1919), 150-67.

Pillinger, Renate. *Die Tituli historiarum oder das sogenannte Dittochaeon des Prudentius*. Versuch eines philologisch-archaeologischen Kommentars. Denkschr. der Österr. Akad. der wiss. Phil.-Hist. Kl. 142. Vienna, 1980.

Poinsotte, J.M. *Juvencus et Israël. La représentation des Juifs dans le premier poème latin chrétien*. Paris, 1979.

Quadlbauer, F. "Zur *Invocatio* des Iuvencus," *Grazer Beiträge* 2 (1974), 185-212.

Quacquarelli, A. *Il leone e il drago nella simbolica dell'età patristica*. Quad. di vet. Chr. 11. Bari, 1975.

Quasten, J. "Das Bild des guten Hirten in den altchristlichen Baptisterien und in den Taufliturgien des Ostens und Westens," *Pisciculi: Studien zur Religion und Kultur des Altertums*. Münster, 1939, pp. 220 ff.

Ramsey, Boniface. "A Note on the Disappearance of the Good Shepherd from Early Christian Art," *HTR* 76 (1986), 375-8.

Rank, Ronald. "The *Apotheosis* of Prudentius: A Structural Analysis," *CF* 20 (1966), 18-31.

Reedijk, C. *The Poems of Desiderius Erasmus.* Leiden, 1956.

Reynolds, L.D. and Wilson, N.G. *Scribes and Scholars: A Guide to the Transmission of Greek and Latin Literature.* 2nd edition. Oxford, 1974.

Riggi, C. "Lo scontro della letteratura cristiana antica e della cultura greco-romana," *Salesianum* 39 (1977), 431-53.

Roncoroni, Angelo. "Sul *De passione Domini* Pseudolattanzio," *VC* 20 (1975), 208-21.

Rose, H.J. *A Handbook of Latin Literature from the Earliest Times to the Death of St. Augustine.* London, 1936.

Rowland, R.J. "Foreshadowing in Vergil, *Aeneid* VIII, 714-28," *Latomus* 27 (1968), 832-42.

Schanzer, Danuta. "The Anonymous *Carmen contra paganos* and the Date and Identity of the Centonist Proba," *REA* 32 (1986), 232-48.

Schlieben, Reinhard. *Christliche Theologie und Philologie in der Spätantike: Die schulwissenschaftlichen Methoden der Psalmenexegese Cassiodors.* Arbeiten zur Kirchengeschichte 46. Berlin, 1974.

Schrader, R.J. "Arator: Revaluation," *CF* 31 (1977), 64-77.

Schreckenberg, H. "Juden und Judentum in der altkirchlichen lateinischen Poesie," *Theokratia* 3 (1973-75), 81-124.

Schumacher, M. "*Imitatio*—A Creative or an Annihilating Force?" *CF* 20 (1966), 47-56.

Schwabe, L. *De Musaeo Nonni imitatore liber.* Tübingen, 1876.

Sellars, R.V. *The Council of Chalcedon: A Historical and Doctrinal Survey.* London, 1953.

Shawcross, John T., ed. *Milton: The Critical Heritage.* London, 1970.

Skutsch, Otto. "Symmetry and Sense in the *Eclogues*," *HSCP* 73 (1969), 153-69.

Smalley, Beryl. *The Gospels in the Schools c. 1100-c. 1280.* London and Ronceverte, 1985.

Solomon, Jon. *The Ancient World in Cinema.* New Brunswick and New York, 1978.

Springer, C.P.E. "Aratus and the Cups of Menalcas: A Note on *Eclogue* 3. 42," *CJ* 79 (1983-84), 131-4.

——"Sedulius' *A solis ortus cardine*: The Hymn and its Tradition," *Ephemerides liturgicae* 101 (1987), 69-75.

——"The Last Line of the *Aeneid*," *CJ* 82 (1987), 310-313.

Stanislaus, Anne. "The Scriptures in Hexameter," *CW* 32 (1938), 99-100.

Stendahl, Krister. *The School of St. Matthew and its Use of the Old Testament.* Philadelphia, 1968.

Stevenson, J. *Creeds, Councils, and Controversies: Documents Illustrative of the History of the Church, A.D. 337-461.* New York, 1966.

Swete, H.B. *Theodori ep. Mops. in epistolas b. Pauli commentarii.* Cambridge, 1882.

Szövérffy, Joseph. *Die Annalen der lateinischen Hymnendichtung.* Berlin, 1964.

Thilo, G., Hagen H., eds. *Servii grammatici in Vergilii carmina commentarii.* Leipzig, 1887.

Thraede, Klaus. "Epos," *RAC* 5, 983-1042.

——"Untersuchungen zum Ursprung und zur Geschichte der christlichen Poesie," *JbAC* 4-6 (1961-3), 108-27, 125-57, 101-11.

Van der Nat, P.G. *Divinus vere poeta. Enige beschouwingen over ontstaan en karakter der christelijke latijnse poëzie.* Leiden, 1963.

——"Die *Praefatio* der Evangelienparaphrase des Iuvencus," *Romanitas et Christianitas.* Amsterdam, 1973, pp. 249-57.

Vega, A.C. "Juvenco y Prudencio," *La ciudad de Dios* 157 (1945), 209 ff.

Vessey, David. *Statius and the Thebaid.* Cambridge, 1973.

Vine, Aubrey R. *The Nestorian Churches.* London, 1937.

Wehrli, M. "*Sacra poesis:* Bibelepik als europäische Tradition," *Festschrift für Friedrich Maurer.* Stuttgart, 1963, pp. 262-83.

West, David and Woodman, Tony, eds. *Creative Imitation and Latin Literature.* Cambridge, 1979.

Weitzmann, Kurt, ed. *Age of Spirituality*. Princeton, 1980.

Widmann, H. *De Gaio Vettio Aquilino Iuvenco carminis evangelici poeta et Vergilii imitatore*. Breslau, 1905.

Wiles, M.F. "Theodore of Mopsuestia as Representative of the Antiochene School," *The Cambridge History of the Bible*. Cambridge, 1970, pp. 489 ff.

Wilkinson, L.P. *Golden Latin Artistry*. Cambridge, 1963.

Williams, Gordon. *Change and Decline: Roman Literature in the Early Empire*. Sather Classical Lectures 45. Berkeley, 1978.

Williams, Schafer. *Codices Pseudo-Isidoriani: A Paleographico-historical Study*. Monumenta iuris canonici. Series C: Subsidia, v. 3. New York, 1971.

Wilpert, Joseph. *Die Malereien der Katakomben Roms*. Freiburg im Breisgau, 1903.

——*I sarcofagi cristiani antichi*. Rome, 1929-36.

Winstedt, E.O. "Mavortius and Prudentius," *CQ* 1 (1907), 10-12.

——"Mavortius' Copy of Prudentius," *CR* 18 (1904), 112-5.

Wyss, B. "Gregor von Nazianz. Ein griechisch-christlicher Dichter des 4. Jahrhunderts," *Museum helveticum* 6 (1949), 177-210.

Zetzel, J.E.G. "The Subscriptions in the Manuscripts of Livy and Fronto and the Meaning of *Emendatio*," *CP* 75 (1980), 38-59.

INDEX OF PASSAGES

Includes references to and quotations of specific passages from ancient and medieval texts.

GENERAL INDEX

The following index contains personal names, names of anonymous literary works, and general subjects.